THE

URBAN

PROCESS

THE
URBAN
PROCESS

CITIES IN INDUSTRIAL SOCIETIES

Leonard Reissman

THE FREE PRESS, *New York*
COLLIER-MACMILLAN LIMITED, *London*

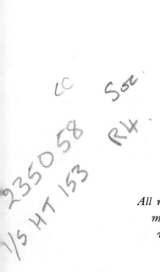

Second printing May, 1966

Library of Congress Catalog Card Number: 64-20301

Collier-Macmillan Canada, Ltd., Toronto, Ontario

FOR

MY FATHER

AND MOTHER

PREFACE

URBAN SOCIOLOGY has suffered a curious fate at the hands of its practitioners. The city, which is inherently cosmopolitan, has been treated with an exceptional provincialism. American sociologists until quite recently have shown a notable disregard for cities outside of the United States. Similar sentiments are held by English, French, and, more recently, Indian sociologists toward the cities in their countries. Here and there, of course, attempts to cross beyond national boundaries have been made, usually to great advantage, as in the work of Balandier on Africa, Davis on India, and that of comparative theorists such as Hoselitz, Moore, Lerner, and Eisenstadt. Such study, however, has been more the exception than the rule in urban sociology. Along with the provincial outlook there is another peculiar feature in urban studies. The city, which is doubtless the most complex social aggregate man has ever created, has been treated with unjustified simplicity in theoretical conceptions. Sociologists have shown a penchant for viewing the city through the maze of statistics as if, by some cabalistic ritual they performed, the sociology of the city would be revealed.

There are, no doubt, good scientific reasons for both reactions, arising from the necessity to abstract and simplify. The techniques of sociology cannot presently encompass the full and complex richness of urban society, so it was necessary to concentrate upon those things that could be treated with the research tools at hand. Furthermore, confronted by the pressing problems of cities in his own territory, the American, British, or French sociologist had little reason to leave home. Fifty years or so of pursuing this more cautious and limited goal, however, has been quite enough time to prove that provincialism and scientific timidity cannot achieve the aim of understanding the structure and the dynamics of urban society.

My motives in adding yet another book on the subject of urban sociology were two: First, I was not convinced that everything worth saying about urban society has been said, even though the literature on the subject is formidable. Secondly, I was convinced, and still am, that the spread of urbanization to the non-Western world, accompanied by a number of refreshing, comparative urban studies, provided the most important source of information in decades for a serious urban sociology. Concerning the first point, there is little that needs to be said here, and most of my detailed criticisms are set down in the chapters that follow. I am not being deliberately unkind to my professional colleagues when I say that much of the sociological literature on the city can be read almost without any notion that the city is a phenomenon that has revolutionized the societies in which we live. Too many books on the subject can be classified either as cautious, even ingenious, statistical summaries that get no further than the necessarily confined statistics let them, or as studies that use the city as the unavoidable context for the study of some other phenomenon, such as the family, religion, personality, power structures, or juvenile delinquency. Certainly it is legitimate to study the above subjects without concentrating upon the city, but how valid can the conclusions be without including the urban environment as an integral part of the force that shapes and molds them? Statistics are a vital part of the scientific enterprise but they should not be so heavily burdened with the demand that they generate scientific hypotheses, especially since we must rely on statistics to test the validity of the hypotheses.

My second motive is also clarified in the chapters that follow, especially the last, where a typology of urbanization is described. One cannot help but read in the current reports on cities in non-Western nations a resemblance to the history of Western societies and their urban developments. Urban sociology has been given its first opportunity for large-scale international comparisons to help pull it away from its earlier provincialism. Even the statistics on urban population, which have been so narrowly employed in the study of American cities, gain a new and dramatic meaning when cast against the statistics of other countries. If the period up until the last war was marked by the provincialism of urban-rural comparisons within one country, then the present era must be distinguished by the broad, world comparisons that are forced upon us.

I do not mean that suddenly all earlier urban studies have become obsolete. There is as much need as ever to keep informed about the urban trends in, say, the United States. Census documents and similar reports still must be analyzed for whatever information they can yield about where we are moving. European sociologists must perform that service, because they have not been as interested in the subject as the Americans and they need to build a body of knowledge about their own cities. They, as we, are faced with an array of problems arising out of the urban milieu that requires expert attention: metropolitan sprawl, urban renewal, extended transportation and service facilities, suburbanization, racial and ethnic relations, social institutional shifts, and the maintenance and spread of acceptable standards of living. The suburban commuter caught in his automobile or in his train has little patience for discussions; he demands action. The slum dweller, shackled to a standard of life that seems barely to have progressed beyond nineteenth century standards, should not have to wait for our utopian dreams to be realized. These and hundreds of other urban problems demand the best talent that can be mustered to solve them, and if not to solve them, at the least to ameliorate them in a manner that is consistent with our conceptions of dignity, right, and responsibility.

Unfortunately, there has been a marked proclivity among urban specialists, sociologists included, to believe that urban problems exist in a vacuum. The kind of vacuum depends upon the training of the specialist. If he is a traffic engineer, he comes to see the metropolis in his terms and shows an appalling unconcern for other, equally relevant dimensions. If he is a town planner, a similar blindness seems to set in. The urban sociologists and political scientists are not immune to this charge, either. Thus the energy that goes into studying a particular city usually produces no lasting solutions. The traffic jams are still with us, the beautifully planned developments turn out somewhat less than beautiful, and the suggestions for metropolitan reform seldom are accepted or translated into action.

There are no easy solutions and I do not mean to suggest that there are. But if the relatively short history of the industrial city has shown us anything, it has been that cities get concerned about their problems only after the problems become chronic. It has always been after the event that attention is turned to solution or amelioration. By then, the next set of problems is already being generated. We have not come very far from the situation of Colonial Boston, where stringent fire and police regulations were established only after parts of the city burned to the ground and after its citizens were being regularly robbed. American and European authorities continue to permit ribbon developments to spread into the countryside, despite decades of experience with the problems inherent in such uncontrolled sprawl. Let us not be naïve: the same experience has also taught us that social responsibility is not easy to establish when economic self-interest is involved or when existing power constellations see their positions threatened.

Before the reader is misled, let me emphasize that this is not a recipe book for urban and metropolitan solutions; several recent books purport to do something like that. In fact, this book is not about problems or solutions at all, except in one sense: We must first understand the dynamics of urban society if we are ever to foresee the problems that such society will produce. This applies as much to the older and more complex problems of Western metropolitan societies as it does to the nascent or emergent problems of non-Western, developing, urban societies. Nor should the reader expect to find descriptions of cities as he knows them, for the very sound reason that such descriptions are available elsewhere, and description is not the *raison d'être* for this book.

The purpose of this book is to analyze critically the information about urban society for a theory of urban society. I had in mind a framework for constructing a theory that would depend upon past ideas and upon information that was available on developed and developing urban societies. No final theory is detailed in the closing chapter. However, what is described is an important basis for the next steps in constructing a theory of urbanization and, by extension, of urban society. Even as it now stands, I believe, it represents a meaningful advance over existing urban theories. The reader must, naturally, be the judge of the success of that effort, although the final judgment must await empirical testing. It cannot depend only upon the outcome of a contest between my bias and the reader's. I trust, however, that my purpose is clear enough throughout the pages of this book so that I will avoid criticism for not doing what it was not my intention to do.

No scholarly book is written in isolation. How does one acknowledge, though, the intellectual stimulation, the willingness to listen, or the many actions by one's colleagues that subtly and directly contribute to one's work? To my colleagues at Tulane University I am indebted for all of those things, and I must especially thank Kalman H. Silvert for awakening me to the importance of nationalism, and Thomas Ktsanes for instinctively knowing what makes sense and then intellectually convincing me of it. To those I met at the London School of Economics and Political Science, especially David V. Glass, Julius Gould, and Donald G. MacRae, I am further indebted for suggestions and tolerance in hearing me out. Special acknowledgment is also due to Aline Pick Kessler for her careful, wise, and sensitive editorial assistance. The Tulane Council on Research made it possible for me to spend an academic year in London, thereby giving me time and opportunity to make use of the excellent materials available at the School. A senior post-doctoral fellowship from the National Science Foundation and a fellowship at the Center For Advanced Study in the Behavioral Sciences similarly gave me the opportunity to devote the time needed to complete the manuscript. The responsibility for the ideas expressed here, of course, is mine.

LEONARD REISSMAN

CONTENTS

THE

URBAN

PROCESS

i

THE URBAN
ACHIEVEMENT

THE CITY probably is man's greatest achievement. Perhaps very few people caught today in urban slums or urban traffic would agree, but if the whole stretch of history is considered, then the statement is credible.

No one knows, of course, just when human beings left the land for the denser and more restricted urban residence, but one expert holds that the city is at least five thousand years old. According to Gordon Childe, an "urban revolution" occurred in Mesopotamia in the third millennium B.C., creating some three cities with populations estimated from 12,000 for the smallest to 24,000 for the largest.[1] Nor is there any certainty why human beings took that step or felt impelled to take it, but again, some historians see the city as an advanced achievement of social evolution: once man had progressed beyond a purely pastoral and agricultural existence and was able to better control his environment, he was ready to build cities. It meant an ability to fashion a physical and social environment that was more complex than any man had had before. This interpretation is probably based more on clever hindsight than on substantial historical fact. Yet, one point is clear: man needed to develop his society considerably beyond the primitive struggle for existence before the city could be feasible. The city modulates man's dependence on nature at the same time that it accentuates his dependence on the social requirements for his existence.

Make no mistake about the genius of the urban achievement. Consider first the sheer technical knowledge and skill required to keep a relatively large number of people alive under urban conditions. The provision of food, shelter, sanitation, and health at a level adequate to keep people alive and productive under urban conditions. Consider next, even more important, the social organization required to keep those people safe, orderly, and willing to stay. The city could not flourish by the code of every man for himself, so the problems of economic distribution, of division of labor, and of government had to be settled and all sorts of rules had to be created. What is more, there had to be a reasonably high level of consensus about these arrangements. Not that the city depends on democratic agreement, nor that it arose by social contract, but at the very least the city must rely on the acceptance of minimal rules. The plan worked, for even ancient peoples had time to build temples, to fashion philosophies, and to create art, proving that man finally had advanced a good way beyond the persistent biological struggle to stay alive.

No one would dispute that the urban achievement, monumental as it has been, has also been constantly imperfect. Many problems have accompanied the urban dweller from the beginning. The problems seem to have grown at a rate that matches the rate of urban growth itself. Try as he repeatedly has, man has never solved them all at any time in his long urban history. Misery, frustration, and inconvenience have been his partners in the city, and whenever he has partially solved one set of problems, the future has destroyed his meager success by bringing others. He has envisioned an urban utopia but has never seen it. He spends almost unbelievable sums of money to rectify his past mistakes nurtured in avarice, but money is never enough. He dreams of beauty but awakens to nightmares compounded of failure, anxiety, and desperation. Never has he achieved a fully satisfactory solution for urban living, and the best he has been able to do in five thousand years has been but a reasonable approximation. Still, he continues to build and develop cities.

Severe as the problems have been, they are compensated for by the achievements that cities—and cities alone—have reached in the development of culture. Science, art, and literature, as well as personal freedom, broad personal horizons, and imagination have been the products of urban development. Nor were these advances simply the inevitable results of men's evolution that would have developed in time under any conditions. Rather, these consequences depended on the encouraging environment of the city, and without it the advances in the human situation likely would have never occurred. "City air makes one free" was the medieval legalism, still true today in the social realm. In the city man found the priceless component that loosened his imagination and gave him the time to apply it to the human situation. The city, in every historical period, has fostered the latest triumphs of man over his environment and of man's understanding of himself. "In all ages and areas, from ancient Egypt to modern America, the highest development of human mentality, initiative and achievement has been in urban communities." [2] The history of mankind is the proof.

The city is hard to study or to understand. This is to be expected in view of the many human activities it contains. Urban existence depends upon an intricate web of factors and forces: physical realities (e.g. space, buildings, population) are intimately tied to social reality (e.g. consensus, communication, institutions, and rules). The city today is of greater complexity than ever before if only because of its size and population density, to say nothing of the increased variety of services it now offers. But there is a more important reason for this urban complexity. Urbanism now dominates Western civilization, and cities have assumed a commanding position in other areas of the world as well. The study of the city perforce has become the study of contemporary society. The centers of decision and the triggers for social change are located in cities, and it is urban not rural societies that control the world's destiny. We can no longer study the city's rise as an isolated event against the backdrop of a world dominated by peasant and primitive traditions; that view ceased to be relevant more than two hundred years ago, with the advent of industrialism. On the contrary, we are totally in and of the city. We are engulfed by the very phenomenon we seek to study and to understand.

The rest of this book takes up the characteristics of cities and the forces that shape cities, but let us consider a few of the dominant features that mark the contemporary city and give it its distinctive tone.

One of the most obvious urban features, after size and congestion, is variety. The city is a place of contrasts, an environment of extremes. The countryside is remarkably uniform in its appearance, especially today where the mark of large-scale agriculture is the vast acreage planted in one crop. Similarly, the modern suburb has an architectural uniformity, which is the mark of large-scale real estate development. When a large expanse of land can be developed as a single package, whether in crops or in houses, the economics of development demand a standard product.

The city, on the contrary, has been built piecemeal, growing by the accretion of people and the buildings they required. Each historical era is frozen for some period of time in the architecture of buildings and monuments, streets and tracks. Magnificence shares urban space with ugliness, orderliness with chaos, rationality with mysticism, and the old with the new.

The full spectrum of urban architecture today shows the most evident contrasts. Slums, parenthesized by outdoor toilets and the daily accumulation of the refuse of living, are backed up by new apartment towers that are the *dernier cri* of residential design. An eight-lane freeway is suspended over a narrow cobblestone street that has somehow been forgotten in urban development or isn't worth the money to remove. The spires of a massive cathedral loom over the abstract shape of a modern church and the crude transformation of a store-front church. Restaurants, funeral parlors, banks, pawnshops, and bars are adjoined. The pigeons, those ubiquitous urbanites, rest on the weathered shoulder of a patriot astride his granite horse and coo to other pigeons seeking a bit of level footing on the polished abstraction of a newer statue. A library or a museum mutes the noises of the city; a ballpark or a playground adds uncounted decibels to it. There are the street and the park, the plaza and the vacant lot, the skyscraper and the hulks of buildings partially demolished by man or nature.

Everywhere the eye rests are the products of man's generosity and social consciousness: hospitals, museums, parks, schools, universities, and the edifices of government. Yet in this Jekyll and Hyde world, the city shows too the effects of man's rapacity and calculating self-interest: slums, shoddiness, grime, and an ever-present sense of fraud and deceit.

The city's theme of variety is also to be seen among its people. They differ in every way that people can: in appearance, dress, and actions. Again in contrast with the farm or suburb, urban people work at a variety of jobs and wear the distinctive marks of their work. A variety of work uniforms may be seen daily, distinguishing doctors and milkmen, doormen and generals, waitresses, clerks, students, businessmen, artists, policemen, and innumerable others. What one farmer wears, all farmers wear. What one suburban housewife wears during the day, her neighbors also wear. In the city, on the other hand, the occupational uniform is the modern badge of office to identify a job, to confer privileges and designate responsibilities. These uniforms of work are so commonly understood that without much deliberate thought we act on our recognition of them.

The wearers of these uniforms represent every type and every nuance of the human character, normal and abnormal: genius, ignorance, creativeness, conformity, power, weakness, talent, pretension, sanity, and idiocy. The city is large enough to contain all of these human variations and is sufficiently diversified so that there is room for all types. Urban populations are socially heterogeneous and so diverse that every human wish, whim, and impulse can be satisfied. The most esoteric hobbies are organized into clubs: collectors of match folders or of teacups, owners of Edsel cars and so-called antique automobiles. Bizarre religion-like cults are organized for those who believe the end of the world is scheduled for a week from Tuesday next, for those who believe the millennium is imminent, and for those who are prepared to believe anything. Apparently, most of the things that urbanites do, whether for work, for play, or for escape, must be organized. For example, an issue of the *New Statesman* announces the following events in London for a typical week: a meeting of the Buddhist Society, lectures on spiritualism, a lecture at the Pushkin Club, a lecture in Greek on Byron, a discussion of architecture, a meeting on the problems of illegitimacy, and a lecture at the Schopenhauer Society, "Schopenhauer and Music," not to mention several art exhibitions, concerts, and other entertainments. Most other large cities duplicate this astounding variety of activities; the above selective list should not be considered as exceptional. Everything is permitted, even madness, provided only that it does not harm or inconvenience others.

William Munro has put it concisely: "The city has more wealth than the country, more skill, more erudition within its bounds, more initiative, more philanthropy, more science, more divorces, more aliens, more births and deaths, more accidents, more rich, more poor, more wise men and more fools. It is characteristic of city life that all sorts of people meet and mingle without in the least understanding one another." [3]

The city is a rational environment even though its inhabitants sometimes manifest actions irrational by any standard. The quality of rationality has been a constant urban feature since antiquity, although it has been elevated to its highest expression as a general principle in the industrial city. The use of land, for example, has been determined largely by the dominant needs and ethos of the city in each period. In the medieval city, the wall and the curving streets apparently were designed for the defense of the city against barbarian invaders. It was therefore easier to foil or to delay the invaders. The wide, straight avenues of the post-medieval era were designed for pomp and parade, to dazzle the citizenry by the massed, marching army returning home after victory, and presumably to advertise the need for more taxes. In the industrial city, the use of land is primarily determined by urban economics, which is to say, by the anticipation of profit. The skyscraper was a rational and direct response to high land values in the search for profits. Air was free and it was plainly profitable to build *up*, for each square foot added above ground counterbalanced the price paid for each square foot on the ground. The translation into reality of this simple principle awaited only the advances in engineering knowledge. There are obvious limits to this formula: type of subsurface, building costs, and the proportionate space required to maintain the building that is not rentable, such as elevators, corridors, heating, and so on. The tenement was created for the same reason: to house more people on the same plot of land and thereby to increase the landlord's profits. The urban slums stay no matter how much they may offend us because they remain profitable. They return a good profit from a minimal investment. What is more, the land they occupy may increase in value as the city grows and the demand for land increases.

The gridiron street pattern of most industrial cities, especially in America, is a result of shortsighted economy and of rationality untempered by aesthetics. Here the rational principle is evident, allowing land to be surveyed quickly and accurately, then easily assessed and subdivided. An urban sqare, in this manner, can be as standardized as a dollar and just as easily converted into multiples. Interestingly enough, the suburban developer's penchant for crescent street patterns and cul-de-sacs is a calculated one, designed primarily to entice home buyers with the vision that they have exchanged the city for the near-country. Rationality exercised for economic gain continues to hold, for where the crescent is too expensive a plan, the suburb emerges in the familiar pattern of ruler-straight lines.

The rational spirit flows not only into street patterns and land use. It dominates the very behavior and outlook of the urbanite, as well. His activities are measured by the clock: there is a time for everything and everything is done in its time. Time *is* money. Working, eating, playing, traveling, or sleeping for the urbanite are determined by the hour and minute. The minute specification is necessary if the activities of millions are to mesh. Trains and buses are dispatched to carry the timed peaks of passenger traffic, offices and shops are opened for business at designated times, and literally thousands of other urban services must watch the hour and, like participants in a grand ballet, must move on cue.

This domination of the rational spirit has been a mark of

the city throughout its history. During the centuries-long hold of Catholicism over the civilized world—the medieval period of the universal church—the cities were dominated by reason and their inhabitants rationalized the Bible and the church edicts. The medieval university, an urban institution, nurtured an approach to religion and religious thought that followed the lines of logic. The city, unlike the country, never turned completely and finally toward a religious mysticism stimulated by unreasoning faith.

Yet, the city is not entirely an environment of reason. It also can stimulate an irrational reaction. Some individuals react against the measured rationality and the calculating spirit of the city. Some take on a double life: on their jobs, during the day, they are reasonable citizens, but at night they emerge quite different. Bizarre cultists, charismatic messiahs, and demagogues seem to wait around the fringes of urban society for those whom the city has baffled, frustrated, or defeated. Their arrivals and departures coincide with the cycles of prosperity and misery. For other persons, the reaction takes the form of personal destruction in alcoholism, drug addiction, psychosis, or ultimately, suicide. Depressions, wars, or any other threat to individual security create situations that can trigger large segments of the urban population into stampeding toward anyone who gives them a message of hope. In this environment that has been outstanding for science, for logic, and for intellect can be nurtured the mystical, the irrational, and the most unreasoned social forces. In the city the rationalist and the mystic can both be heard, the charlatan and the scientist can both achieve their goals.

Since it allows such great variety, why the city has been labeled by some as an unnatural or artificial environment is hard to understand. It should be argued rather that the city is quite natural, precisely because it does elicit so widely from human potential. That the city is man made does not make it an artificial product, except by the most narrow definition of what is natural, a definition by which man could be cast only in a passive role where nature dictates and man must obey. Such a view, however, denies man his uniqueness and creativity. He is not an animal but a human being with culture, language, imagination, skill, and creativeness. These thoroughly human qualities have produced the city and fashioned it into what it is.

I realize that these points touch upon major philosophical issues concerning the nature of man that are not directly at issue. I would emphasize only that the city must be considered as a human invention; one very much like society itself, that man has evolved to organize his existence. That the invention is imperfect, that it created problems neither anticipated nor wanted, is certainly correct. Imperfection, however, is not artificiality. Rather, it is the measure of man's ignorance about himself and about his environment.

Until recently the argument against what was seen as urban artificiality was supported by rural nostalgia. The crashing pace of urbanization, which has wiped out many rural areas, has now stilled much of the rural argument. The city, it was argued, was not meant to be man's natural environment. By faith and spurious logic it was contended by some that the farmer, the peasant, the primitive—anyone but the urbanite—was closer to nature's intentions, as if anyone could know what those intentions were. Man's life was seen as more properly guided by the natural rhythm of the seasons, not by the mechanical rhythm of the urban clock. These notions are on the level of fairy tales of water sprites and wood nymphs. In point of fact, it is hard to see what is so natural or idyllic about an environment that cuts down man's life expectancy, that forces him to fight like an animal for a minimal existence, and that is intellectually and morally stultifying. For better or worse, the world is on its way to becoming massively urban, and the quaint peasant societies and primitive cultures still hidden in the backwaters and un-touched for centuries are now, for the most part, doomed. The nations of the West have long since been transformed and those on other continents are soon to be. Walden Pond is a chimera, a bit of nostalgia that represents for some an imaginary retreat from the city and the world pressures of the moment. We have come to the stage where Walden is only to be reached by a super-highway, through the television-antenna forest, and di-rected all the way by road signs. Urbanism is inundating all areas of the world and its force is a testament to the nature of man himself and to the potency of the product that he has created.

The city is still an imperfect product physically and socially. Yet, we should not let our sensitive awareness of urban problems totally discolor our approach to urban society. Throughout the centuries of urban history there have been recurrent crises, and probably never more than in the last hundred years, as we have realized that something could be done about those problems, that they were neither natural nor inevitable. But there is little chance for a perfect solution; the economics of avarice, the politics of ignorance, make the perfect city only a utopia. There is no paucity of solutions, but instead a conservatism of values and interests, that does not let us try them. We are still unwilling to change our habits or jeopardize our interests to solve some of these problems.

The crises that have occurred and recurred touch every facet of urban existence. The cities of ancient Greece and the Roman Empire, for example, were marked by decades of struggle between the aristocracy and the lower social orders. Something of that sharp animosity can be sensed in Fustel de Coulanges' description of the ancient cities.

In every city the rich and the poor were two enemies, living by the side of each other, the one coveting wealth, and the other seeing their wealth coveted. No relation, no service, no labor united them. The poor could acquire wealth only by despoiling the rich. The rich could defend their property only by extreme skill or by force. They regarded each other with the eyes of hate. There was a double conspiracy in every city; the poor conspired from cupidity, the rich from fear. Aristotle says the rich took the following oath among themselves: "I swear always to remain the enemy of the people, and to do them all the injury in my power." [4]

The walled cities of medieval Europe answered the need for protection but created other problems. The walls limited expansion without affecting population growth except by increasing mortality. Congestion increased the severity of plague, magnified the deficiences of health and sanitation and the damage of fire. Perhaps the medieval city was remarkable for the functionality of its architecture, for the harmony of its plan, and the psychic security it engendered, as some historians and town planners today aver. Some of this speculation is surely a reaction more to the evils of the present than to the delights of the past. It overlooks the obvious misery, deprivation, and danger that were also characteristic of medieval cities and towns. The accounts of the period, say, of London in the thirteenth century or of the Italian cities in the fifteenth century, do not portray a uniformly glamorous place in which to live, especially for the majority in the lower social orders.

Colonial cities in the United States encountered a series of problems that even by the early seventeenth century had become typical urban problems in Europe. The urban cycle was always the same: Population growth transformed the village into a city and thereby introduced it to a set of problems that people recognized only after they became obvious. Then, as now, the ideal plans and their realization were seldom allowed to interfere with each other.

Carl Bridenbaugh has described the problems faced by American colonial cities and the belated steps they took to handle them.[5] The need for fire prevention, without which an entire town could be destroyed, prompted a number of ordinances. But it was only after a great fire in 1679 destroyed an estimated one hundred and fifty buildings that the General Court of Massachusetts ordered that all new dwellings be constructed of "stone or bricks, & covered with slate or tyle." The penalty for failure to comply with the court's order was a fine twice the value of the building. Bridenbaugh wryly noted, however, that "the measure was not well adapted to a locality which afforded no building stone and where brick construction was still expensive. The inability of the poor to comply with its terms led to its frequent suspension and modification, and frame houses continued to be erected in the town for many years."[6] The practice survives today under the illogical name, "nonconforming usage."

Crime had become a major problem in colonial cities before the end of the seventeenth century. The records for Boston showed a steady increase during the years for such crimes as "assault, arson, breaking and entering, embezzlement, fighting and brawling, manslaughter, theft, and the reception of stolen goods." [7] The solution offered was the formation of night watches or military watches to protect the security of citizens during the night hours. Apparently, these arrangements were not always effective, for colonial cities decided at different times either that they could not afford the watches or that they were really unnecessary. Citizens from time to time were forcibly enlisted to serve their turn and thereby give evidence of their civic spirit. Nor were these the only problems. Water, public health, welfare, and public and private morality presented other difficulties.

Many of the problems of modern cities are but variations of problems that seem always to have been present in cities. Water, for example, is an intensive problem today in the cities of the American Southwest and Far West as well as in England. Crime and delinquency are still very much part of the contemporary urban picture. Added to these centuries-old troubles are newer variations on old themes: transportation, taxation, and housing. Today, downtown shopowners are worried about suburban shopping centers; home owners are concerned about losing money because of a shift in the population; city administrators are squeezed between increasing expenses and decreasing revenues; parents are shocked by changes in the school population, and stampede into other locations; civil defense officials are confronted with the impossibility of protecting urban populations. The list of those who are affected by urban problems could be expanded to include everyone who lives in or near a city.

The point is this: the city has always meant problems, crises, and sometimes, partial solutions. It has never been a perfect environment. It seems likely that such imperfection is an inevitable feature of urban complexity. Very often, what we overlook in the city by concentrating on its peculiar problems is the considerable sense of solidarity and accomplishment to be gained by working to solve, or at least to ameliorate, the problems that confront it. Bridenbaugh very nicely makes this point in his discussion of American colonial history and, it seems to me, what he has to say can apply equally well to our own time.

By 1690 inhabitants of every colonial village had had to face certain problems of urban living which required solution not by individual but by community effort. In the country a man might construct his own home, build his fire, erect his privy, and dispose of his rubbish without thought for the well-being of his neighbors, but in town these things became objects of community concern and gradually of civic ordinance. In the country a man might be little affected by the poverty or wrong-doing of others, but the towns soon discovered their civic responsibility in the combatting and control of these social evils.[8]

Cities are communities only because they command allegiance, social consensus, and belief, and even, at times, a civic spirit. Recognizing this fact makes invalid the argument that cities have destroyed the "sense of community" except in a very narrow definition of "community." What those who hold to that argument are saying, more accurately, is that a special kind of community has disappeared: the small, the intimate, and the traditional. This again is an expression of rural nostalgia. After all, the city is as "human" a community as any society can be. The desire to return to more intimate social relations, to what has been called the "human scale," is as understandable as it is impossible to achieve. Let us keep urban analysis as free as possible from a blind emotionalism that tries mainly to turn back the clock. First, there should be a clear understanding of what the city *is*, then, of what might possibly be changed to reach some reasonable set of goals. The reiteration of such loaded terms as "human scale" or "the sense of community" really does not help us understand urbanization and its consequences. It is time that we were done with them, except as fictions, if the goal of understanding the city and urban society is to be achieved.

The city, quite obviously, is here to stay as long as man himself. Perhaps an urban utopia free of all but the most picayune annoyances can be attained, but certainly not before man has attained a better understanding of himself, his motives, and his society.

The panoply of the city itself is accompanied by a variety of interests of those who take the city as their subject. Every art form is represented by painters, poets, composers, novelists, sculptors, and essayists. Then there are the professionals and those who specialize in the applied arts: doctors, public health officers, engineers, lawyers, architects, landscape architects, and city planners. Each of the social sciences has a specialty devoted to urban study. Add the other specialists from the church, the military, government, labor, and industry and the range of interests is indeed impressive.

It is clearly necessary that any book concerned with the city must specify limits. My primary concern is with the sociology of the city. Among other things, this will involve us in a critical survey of earlier sociological ideas about the city; theories and near-theories that later knowledge has shown to be inadequate. The survey necessarily must include more than strictly sociological theories alone, especially those by town and city planners. The purpose of this survey is twofold: to acquaint the reader with the range of ideas that have centered about the city and to suggest the elements of a more adequate urban theory.

It is my bias, shared by other sociologists, I would presume, that a sociology of the city is prerequisite for any understanding of the city and how it functions. For example, the problems of urban transportation and attempts to solve them are more reflections of social organization and human motivation than of traffic engineering. So, too, slums, urban renewal, and crime are problems of social organization, much less than they are consequences of bad planning. Unless they affect the social dynamics involved, solutions can be only temporary. Evidence to prove this generalization can be found in every city today.

However, the solution of urban problems is not the central concern of this book; the analysis of urban society is.

The sociological study of the city focuses on people, social institutions, space, and their interrelationships. Demographic studies of the urban population are included as are studies of urban psychology. Indicative of the latter are the descriptive monographs initiated by Park in the 1920s on the hobo, the taxi-dance hall hostess and patron, the slum dweller, the tenant in furnished rooms, the Negro, the Jew, and the Italian. Urban personality and its environment come within the range of the sociologist's interest.

Social institutions and their functioning in the city provide the primary orientation for the urban sociologist. Study of such institutions in the city as family, church, government, and school reveals clues that help us make sense of urban society. Increasingly, the sociologist has had to consider the urban impact upon those and other institutions, for the transformation of Western nations into city-dominated societies is an inescapable fact. How has urbanization affected the structure of the family, the church, or government? How do these institutions in turn, style and shape the urban environment? What can be taken as the specifically urban characteristics of such institutions and what do these characteristics then tell us about the character of society, generally, even in nonurban places? These are some of the questions to which the urban sociologist wishes to find answers.

The sociologist is also interested in urban space and its social effects. The location, per se, of industry in a city is not a sociologically significant fact. When the location of a factory in a given neighborhood, however, transforms it and the kind of population that lives near it, then we are, in effect, dealing with *social* space. Planning roads is the job of engineers and traffic experts, but the effects of highways upon suburban growth is of sociological interest. The design of cities is the city and town planner's job but the realization and the social consequences of the design are in the sociologist's domain. It is not important to set lines rigidly separating one specialty from another, but it is important to recognize that each urban specialist enters a study of the city with a specific orientation and a clear and distinct set of goals.

For the sociologist, the city is both an opportunity and an enigma. In the first instance the city is a social laboratory. It was this conception that so intrigued Park, Burgess, MacKenzie, and their students in the early 1920s. The city, because of its size and heterogeneity, confronts the sociologist with a profusion of social forms nowhere else duplicated. In one place are to be found both the complex implications of social organization and the numerous evidences of social disorganization. For example, if it is presumed that the family has certain minimal functions to perform in society, then the study of the urban family can reveal the myriad ways in which these functions can be performed, as well as the points where those same functions break down.

The city is also an enigma. Size and variety provide opportunities for sociological analysis but become obstacles to method. In a small town or in a village it is possible to view the whole social picture almost at once, but in studying the city we must settle for narrower views. There is clearly no alternative but to accept this severe limitation that has plagued urban study, and adapt our methods as best we can.

The particular focus I wish to adopt, and one that is basic throughout this book, is on the industrial city alone. This limitation of historical emphasis is sure to displease all those specialists who prefer to keep the entire five thousand years or so of urban history intact. I see no alternative but to divide the city's history somewhere and consider only one section of it. After all, it is only an assumption that "the city" is a continuous historical development. The ancient city, the medieval city, and the industrial city are, in fact, quite different social phenomena. Let me defer explanation of the reasons for this view in order first to set down some of the primary features of the industrial city.

The industrial city is more than just a place that contains factories. It is the city of our time, the response to the industrial revolution, the residence of industrialized society. This means that we are interested in the whole spectrum of cities in industrial societies though particular cities may have as their main economic function not industry, but government administration, education, shipping, or tourism. No date can be set for the birth of the industrial city in the West, where it first began, because so complex an event does not emerge full-blown; it must be the consequence of numerous prior events. For purposes of convenience let us consider the industrial city to be about two and one half centuries old, appearing in the early eighteenth century and following in point of time the postmedieval city, or what Mumford has called the "baroque city." [9]

The primary push for the emergence of the industrial city was, quite obviously, the growth of industry.[10] Industrialization, for most social scientists, connotes the whole set of political, social, demographic, and economic consequences that follow from its technological changes. In the economic sphere it meant, among other things, the creation of an open market, the rational pursuit of profit, the development of corporate forms, and the expansion of bureaucracies. Industrialization also meant a greater use of inanimate sources of energy, hence an increase in man's productivity and a release from much of the time needed for sheer survival.

The shift in the center of economic gravity from the land to the market and the factory transformed the social structure of medieval society and assured the victory of the city over the country. Rigid social divisions became more fluid. The older land-based aristocracy and the guild-based monopolies were destroyed as was the principle of exclusiveness upon which they depended. Not only did industrialization create a greater division of labor and thereby more social divisions than before, but it prevented a monopolization of the economic machinery for many decades to come.

A social revolution of this magnitude could not proceed without an ideology to support it; an explanation, in effect, that legitimized these enormous changes as natural, desirable, and necessary. Democracy replaced the older forms of oligarchy and monarchy, both of which were ill-adapted to the demands of industrialism. Above all, the rising bourgeoisie required a measure of personal freedom that had previously been reserved for the few. Constitutional guarantees were also needed to replace the "rule by whim" by which a monarch or an elite had ruled before, for it became impossible to calculate rational economic actions without dependable legal guarantees to serve as guides.

The political ideology of nationalism also appeared in this period as part of the economic and political configuration of the industrial revolution. Like democracy and constitutionalism, nationalism was a necessary condition, apparently, for the success of the new industrial order. Loyalty to the nation replaced the former narrower loyalties. Village loyalties were too narrow a basis to support an effective integration of the whole society, and even under early industrialism, let alone later stages, the nation is the smallest economic and social unit that can be effective. Loyalty to a king or a feudal lord also had to be replaced, because industrialism seemed to require a more abstract ideal, such as the nation, or the common good.

Coupled with nationalism was an ideology that supported colonial expansion as a means by which the rest of the world could be viewed as part of the nation. Empire and nation were parts of the same entity, in the minds of the colonizers. Imperialism expressed an economic need to secure whatever materials were lacking in the nation and to use the colonies as part of the nation's assets.

These several ideologies, democracy, nationalism, and imperialism, provided the necessary rationale to support the social changes initiated by the middle classes emerging into power. The ideologies justified the changes and commanded loyalty for them. That these newer ideologies were accepted, there is no doubt. They command the same dedication, the same sense of belief, and the same strength of natural laws as the ideologies they had replaced. No medieval oath of fealty was more binding than the beliefs created and nurtured by industrialism.

All of these massive changes resulted in the emergence of the industrial city from the older cities of the medieval period. Cities developed and people came to live in them at a rate that has not yet begun to wane. The reasons for urban growth under the impetus of industrialization are many and complex. Among these were the push from the land through enclosure movements, or heavy taxation to provide an urban labor force, and the economic pull of the city itself for individuals as well as for industrial and commercial enterprises.

All of these separate elements, I would like to re-emphasize, were parts of the same industrial complex. The new requirements in one sphere of life affected other spheres, and it is relatively unimportant at this point to establish any priority. The industrial city, in other words, formed the wave of the most thoroughgoing social revolution we have ever known. Further, each of the aspects of industrialization that has been mentioned contributed, in one way or another, to the character and form of the industrial city. The rationality as well as the individualism so characteristic of the industrial ethos produced much of the city as it is seen today: the order without planning, the controlled chaos.

The rationality and individualism of industrial cities certainly had their roots in an urban history that antedated the rise of industrialization. The sense of order can be traced back to the cities of antiquity, as can the philosophy of individual freedom. Yet, their consequences were confirmed in a unique form in the industrial city, and this is our primary concern.

Some will object that the emphasis upon the industrial city destroys the sense of historical continuity in urban study. Two rejoinders can be made. First, the city in each of the major periods of human history has been a highly specialized phenomenon, particularly adapted to each historical epoch. Although cities in different periods resemble each other in some ways (e.g., size), the social bases of urban organization have differed. The religious basis of the medieval city, for example, is not at all like the scientific and technological basis of the industrial city, nor are the two types of cities or their social philosophies the same. In the first, the church was the architectural and moral center of the city, while in the second, the factory has become the dominant symbol. We ought not to be misled by our own semantics: the word "city" has been transformed throughout our history, as has the phenomenon that it denotes.

A second rejoinder is simply that the history of urbanism is not my first interest here. This is not to deny that the city, or indeed almost any major social occurrence, has historical roots that antedate and explain its appearance. But, it is one thing to trace a history of urban development from, say, the Sumerian Period to the present; it is quite another to take that history as a point of departure and to concentrate only upon the most recent period. My purpose is not to trace the historical similarities but rather to explain the character of the industrial city and its contemporary form. This is best accomplished by cutting down the historical range.

Foreshortening the focus to the industrial city alone has the advantage of permitting greater attention to the characteristics of the city as we know it. Instead of a comparative, historical, urban sociology, I have concentrated on an analytic sociology of the industrial city. This specification necessarily limits the universality of the conclusions. Clearly, no conclusion can be drawn about the cities of antiquity or of the medieval period; nor, perhaps can the conclusions we reach be applied to nonurban societies, except by way of contrast. Only the utility of the conclusions for understanding industrial urban society will prove whether the particular focus taken here is valuable.

ii

A TYPOLOGY
OF URBAN STUDIES

URBAN SPECIALISTS today, including city planners, engineers, and social scientists alike, seem to be driven by some inner compulsion to perform detailed rituals, by which, however, they are only dimly hopeful that they can find salvation. Consider the traffic engineer juggling variations of one-way street patterns to alleviate traffic jams which threaten to choke the city. Consider the planner zoning this block or that to halt or isolate the gigantic social forces at work in the city. Or consider the social scientist examining each new census of the city for some statistical pattern, only to find that the pattern he discerns never seems to remain the same. Urban studies in the past few decades have been overwhelmed by a frantic search for facts, from which it is hoped a systematic explanation of urban society can be drawn. The census, for example, has been used more frequently by urban sociologists as a primary source to generate hypotheses than as a necessary adjunct for thoughtful generalizations. The result of all this activity is that we are far richer in statistics than in theory. We know more facts than we have been able to assimilate. We have spent more time sharpening knives than using them.

Obviously, to know facts is important and necessary. It should go without saying that any theory of urban society depends upon them. But we seem to be at a stage where we suffer from an embarrassment of facts: we have more unsystematized data than we can use, and each new census or statistical report swamps us anew. For example, a good deal is known about how people get to work, whether by automobile or public transportation, but relatively very little is known about the motivations for these actions. There are figures on the number and location of churches and bars, but much less information on why people go to either one. We can make rather exact statements about the number of television sets owned by an urban population, but we cannot say anything quite as definite about how they are used. There are excellent statistics on housing, but there is insufficient knowledge about the people who live in houses. In short, we do not always have the facts that would be most useful for analysis of urban society.

A major reason for the inadequacy of theory is undoubtedly due to the complexity of the city. The city simply outruns the technical equipment that the sociologist has, and its full dimensions as a social environment have not been grasped. The full range of urban events cuts across a number of sciences: demography, sociology, economics, political science, psychology, architecture, and engineering, not to mention the life sciences that might also be included. This in itself confounds the proper study of the city, since no one can be an expert in everything.

Another possible reason for the lack of good urban theory seems to be the reactions that the city apparently evokes in those who study it. The early urban ecologists, for example, impress one as having been fascinated, almost hypnotized, by the intricate variety they found in Chicago. Small wonder, in a city that contained almost every nationality and religion, a range from poverty to wealth, and a developed industrial empire as well.

Rural sociologists and others have been much less ardent

or enthusiastic, preferring to see the city as an evil and artificial environment rather than as a place of mystery and challenge. For those critics, the city was an unnatural creation that destroyed man. What they saw was real enough: overcrowding, immorality, artificiality, apathy, and all the rest of a long and dreary inventory of problems. But what they would substitute was unrealistic: a rural idyll or an urban utopia. Neither was a solution, but so eager were these critics to make their point that they lost the sense of objectivity. Largely as a result of their super-critical descriptions, we continue to criticize the city more often than we praise it, to magnify its faults more often than we stress its advantages. In any case, such discussions have hardly slowed the pace of urban growth.

As for more formal urban theory, there have been two kinds. These are more fully described in later chapters but it can be said here that both have been rather limited in their utility. Both types fall short of supplying a coherent and systematic conception of urban society and of urbanization.

The older and more popular type, "comparative urban theory," has emphasized differences between urban and nonurban societies. In most cases such theories were concerned with urbanization; that is, with the social transformation of nonurban into urban society. Included in this category are the theories of Tönnies, Weber, Maine, Durkheim, Becker, and Redfield. What they all shared was the view that the city and its rural counterpart represented the extremes of a continuum of social organization. Between the two extremes, then, all societies, as determined by one or more criteria, could be placed. The extremes have been variously labeled: folk-urban, sacred-secular, *Gemeinschaft-Gesellschaft*, status-contract, and so on. Some of the variables according to which destinations were made have included size, social homogeneity, secularism, ethos, and extent of labor specialization.

The other type of theory was peculiarly American. Known as "human ecology," or "urban ecology," it was associated most with Park and his colleagues and students at the University of Chicago, beginning in 1915. The theory generally was developed by applying the principles of plant and animal ecology to urban society and its institutions. It aimed at specifying a set of basic patterns and principles by which people and their institutions were distributed in the city. At the height of its popularity in American sociology, ecology was elegant and exciting. It produced a number of monographs that in some ways are still the best descriptions we have of urban life. Twenty years of critical evaluation, however, have not dealt kindly with ecology and it has perforce retrenched, becoming less elegant. Yet, the true critical test of ecology was that of time and circumstances. The theory simply failed to weather and be applicable to the changes that cities have experienced; much that Park and his associates had described was a picture of Chicago at a certain phase in its history and was not universally applicable to urban life. Ecology turned out to be more time-bound and culture-bound than the ecologists or anyone else thought, a most damaging argument in an era of world-wide urban expansion.

It is necessary to set an intellectual history of urban theory before considering the elements that should go into such a theory. This means that the major ideas about the city have to be identified and evaluated. The inventory should accomplish the double purpose of acquainting the reader with what has been written and, more importantly, of setting the perspective of an urban sociology.

To do this in a systematic way I have constructed a typology or classification of urban studies. The typology is not a theory but it does organize a rather large and varied literature. This is the only claim that is made for its use here.

The typology is created by two dimensions: one is the kind of problem studied; the second is the kind of data used.

Problems can be either applied or theoretical. An applied problem is practical; that is to say, it is one that considers a situation in terms of the action needed to improve it. Study and action are intimately connected. Traffic, housing, the decline of the business district, and urban renewal are the sorts of practical or applied problems intended here. In each instance, there is more or less concern in the urban community about the situation which, if not immediately soluble, might perhaps be alleviated. The problem generates its own pressures for solution. Theoretical problems, on the other hand, only have meaning

within a scientific, not an applied, context. Theoretical problems need not be related to a concrete situation nor accordingly
to their solutions. Problems of theory are raised by theoretical
inconsistencies rather than physical inconveniences. The theorist
is concerned with explanation rather than with solutions to
practical problems. How to classify cities, for example, is a theoretical problem and its solution would in no way directly alter
the urban environment.

Regarding the second dimension of the typology, the
methods and data used to solve any problem can be either quantitative or qualitative. The distinction is obvious. Quantitative data
require objective numerical measurement: the number of people
traveling between parts of the city, the number of cars that
pass a given signal point, the size of the labor force, or the size
of the population.

Qualitative data are based on information that is less amenable to measurement and concretization. The ideas on which
they depend usually remain too abstract or unspecified to be
confined within the hard limits required for measurement. This
does not mean that they are any the less valuable, only that they
are a different order of information. The analysis of systematic
qualitative information depends upon logic, internal consistency,
and, if possible, comparison. For example, the increased secularization brought about by the industrial city is essentially a qualitative datum that can be defended by inference from the decline
of religious values or the shrinking of extended family and
kinship ties. Hopefully, such qualitative statements might be
translated into measurable quantities; for instance, how people
answer questions on religion in an attitude questionnaire, or
questions that ask them to name their relatives. Church attend-
ance could be tabulated, or a census taken of all those living
in a common household, as ways of measuring secularizing influences. It would be a mistake, however, to always demand
quantitative proof. There is still a good deal of room in urban
analysis for qualitative study assessed on its own grounds.

Quantitative measurement is preferred by social scientists
wherever possible. Yet it is apparent that many valuable ideas
cannot yet be transformed into quantities. Partly this is because
there are no data of the sort required and partly, because the

ideas need greater specification. The consequences of Frank Lloyd Wright's philosophy of planning, for example, cannot be so measured. Why should anyone feel impelled to try? It can be reasonably assessed in its own logical terms.

The four possible categories of the typology are shown in Figure 1.

Figure 1—A Typology of Urban Specialists

	TYPE OF PROBLEM	
TYPE OF DATA	Applied or Practical	Theoretical
Quantitative	Practitioner	Empiricist
Qualitative	Visionary	Theorist

Each type of specialist is described simultaneously by the type of problem he studies and by the type of data or information he uses. Let me say at once that not all urban specialists are included in this classification. Urban historians are the most obvious exception, principally because they do not consider either of the two kinds of problems identified here. This does not mean that historical description is irrelevant, but that it is not directly concerned with an urban sociology. Urban geographers, too, are not specifically considered, again, because their interests are not directly relevant. But any classification is limited, and as a tool for description this typology functions reasonably well.

The empiricist and the theoretician are primarily sociologists, and will therefore occupy us most. They share an interest in theoretical problems rather than in applied or practical ones. They differ principally in the way they approach a sociology of the city and secondarily, in the choice of method which defines the kind of theory each envisions. The empiricist prefers quantitative measures as the basis for any conclusions he would offer. He therefore emphasizes indices of population size, of the occupational structure, or of economic functions. The theorist, on the other hand, is attracted more to a general set of categories, and measurement becomes secondary. The subjects of his interest tend to be broadly defined (e.g., the family, urban personality, or the rise of rationality) and indexed with difficulty, if at all. The major exception to this characterization is the urban ecologist, especially in the Park tradition. Even though measurement was important for ecological theory, he is classified here as a theoretician, for reasons which will be made clear. More recent ecologists, however, might be considered as empiricists, with a few exceptions, because measurement has become increasingly important in their work. This mixture of theory and empirical research found in human ecology tends to make it a bridge between the empiricist and theoretician. These finer distinctions, however, are described in later chapters.

Practitioners and visionaries are different types from those just described. Practitioners are immersed in the daily world of the city, intimate with its problems, and professionally dedicated to waging a continuous series of short-term wars with urban problems. Visionaries usually begin with a recognition of such practical problems but they then move on to find rather broad solutions, even to total reconstruction of urban society. The practitioner's job forces him into patchwork solutions, forever tied to the immediate situation and what can reasonably be accomplished. The visionary's solutions, however, suggest an eagerness to wipe the slate clean and begin afresh. He is a man impelled by a vision, which is his philosophy of planning. Included here are the town planners and the architects turned social philosophers: Howard, Wright, Saarinen, Le Corbusier, Mumford, the Goodmans, Neutra, Gropius, and Gallion. Their solutions, aimed at revitalizing and reforming the industrial city, depend on massive changes not only in architectural styles but also in social and political institutions.

§ The Practitioner

The practitioner is a person usually employed by government at any of its several levels of jurisdiction. He is either a full-time employee of government or a consultant to it. From the standpoint of urban theory, his contribution comes from the facts he can provide on the city, but he is not primarily a theorist. To be sure, he follows certain general principles in his work, as for example, does the traffic engineer, but this is more an application of professional knowledge to a given problem than a deliberate attempt to devise theory. Practitioners often are ambivalent, sincere men caught between the immediate demands of a job and their personal convictions about what needs to be done. City planners, for example, must balance the idealism of their professional training against the realism of politics that defines their work. The long view must constantly be altered by the political demands of the moment, yet it must not be forgotten. It is impossible to plan radically under the daily pressures of local officials, realtors, businessmen, and neighborhood improvement associations, all of whom have a stake in keeping things as they are. If planners are to keep their jobs, they must be aware of the real economic and political forces at work. Yet, they hold on to the image of what they would like to see happen, according to some ideal plan. These opposing forces require that the city planner possess special skills to control them; indeed, a good deal of his time is consumed in just that battle.

From a realistic view, the practitioner's job is even more impossible than that, because there is so little chance of actually overcoming the problems he is paid to handle. In every phase of his work there can only be the temporary solution meant to alleviate the surface symptoms, never a solution to the underlying problem. That is why we are likely to be forever talking about metropolitan and urban problems. Often too, the solution that is accepted acerbates other problem areas, if, indeed, it does not in the long run worsen the very problem it was designed to solve. Lewis Mumford, for example, has correctly observed that laying down longer and faster highways does little to relieve traffic congestion, but aggravates the congestion by attracting more cars to use the highways. It has been certainly true for American cities that highway improvement increases the traffic it carries almost at once; highways become overtaxed and inadequate almost from the moment they are opened to traffic. Rush-hour traffic on the Los Angeles freeways leaves no doubt about that.

The decisive feature of the practitioner's position is an almost complete lack of power to affect urban trends in any significant way. Confronted most of the time by the con-

sequences of previously unplanned actions, he is further restricted to a narrow range of possible steps he can take to solve
the problems they have raised. It is not that he lacks judgment
or knowledge; he lacks the means to do almost anything of
positive and lasting consequence. As a government employee
he is often prohibited from developing long-range plans designed to attack problems at their core. Government officials,
dependent upon the voter, are forced to show immediate and
concrete results if they are to be returned to power, and this
pressure molds the policy for the practitioner to follow. Pres-
sured by party organizations, by business associations, and by
an aroused and discontented public, the practitioner is forced
to act, and to act for the moment.

Because the concerns of the practitioner are only tangential
to the major theme of this book, I do not wish to devote a great
deal of space to this type. However, because, like any urbanite,
I share the frustrations faced by the practitioner and because
these aspects of the general urban problem receive the greatest
publicity, I wish to describe some of the main problems faced
by the practitioner and to indicate briefly their character.

Transportation

Every urbanite is exercised about some phase of urban transportation: highways and expressways are overcrowded, commuter trains are decrepit and unreliable, city traffic is sluggish,
parking space is insufficient, public transportation is inadequate,
there are too many trucks, buses, and taxis on the streets, and
so on. Transportation is the one problem area upon which
governments have spent the most time and money. Yet, as
everyone probably knows, this is not a self-contained problem
but the consequence of a number of converging urban trends.
One of the most concise summaries of the trends has been
written by C. McKim Norton of the Regional Plan Association.[1]
"What are the significant current development trends of urban
areas in relation to metropolitan transportation?" asks Mr. Norton. First, he identifies the suburban spread. As each census
since 1940 has documented, American suburbs are growing at

a faster rate than the central cities that they ring. The movement to the suburbs stands to become the greatest population migration that America has ever seen. Nor are Americans alone in this; the conurbations of England, the *banlieue* around Paris, the spread of Tokyo-Yokohama, and the suburban explosion around Rome are evidences that suburbanization is by no means an American monopoly. Suburbanization necessarily has put more cars on the roads surrounding the city and has brought more traffic into the city than any other single development since the invention of the internal combustion engine. More people throughout the world now travel further each day than ever before.

A second trend Norton identifies is the location of new industrial plants in a suburban belt skirting the periphery of the city. Additional traffic is forced on the highways not only to bring the workers to their jobs but also to carry goods. In the steady publicity for decentralizing industry to get it out of the central city, the consequences of adding to traffic congestion elsewhere is seldom recognized. Yet, it is in this way that future urban problems are created by solving an existing urban problem. Third, the movement of suburban populations creates and stimulates the movement of services: department stores, groceries, gas stations and professional and personal services go out to be near the demand. All of these services, in their turn, depend on motor transportation for their supplies and their customers. Finally, "many types of commercial and professional enterprise which once were considered typical central city activities" have located in suburban areas. Research laboratories, insurance offices, regional offices of national corporations, and commercial research institutions are some of the examples mentioned by Norton.

All of this traffic in and around the city is building up to the biggest traffic jams that an unfettered imagination can visualize. Yet urbanites in increasingly greater numbers continue to choose the private automobile over the public transport facility. City officials and practitioners, of course, would prefer that the reverse were true. The more people who would ride buses, trains, and subways, the fewer cars there would be competing for scarce space on the streets, or for parking areas. Norton has presented a startling illustration of what this can mean:

This point may be most simply illustrated by southern Manhattan, which presents the problem in its most extreme form. Three and a half million persons enter this area on a typical business day. If half of this number came by car, with an average of two persons per car, it would require ten square miles of parking space and at least a doubling of bridge, tunnel, and arterial highway and street capacity. If *everyone* came in by car, parking garages five stories high, covering all the blocks of Manhattan south of 52nd Street would be required.[2]

In spite of the greater cost in money, time, and convenience, the suburbanite prefers his own car for travel into the city. As a consequence, public transport is faced with a steady decrease in passenger revenues and an increase in costs of operation. The only alternative has been to raise fares, which in turn forces another segment of persons away from using public transportation and toward using their own automobiles. In classical economic fashion, the price increase has forced a change in preference. The cycle continues as public transport is ever again faced with the need to raise fares because of the resulting drop in revenues.

The practitioner, as a city planner or as a traffic engineer, is restricted in what he can do even to ameliorate metropolitan traffic, let alone solve the problems it produces. Within the city, where land is developed, the cost of widening streets is very high. The outlay needed to acquire right-of-way under the law of public domain is frequently more than most cities can afford, even with substantial state and federal aid. Even so, many cities have been forced into such costly acquisition because streets that were built before the turn of the century—as most of them were in those sections of the U.S. now forced to carry most of the load—simply are not broad enough to carry today's load of vehicles. Aside from this there are temporary solutions that are often instituted: one-way street patterns, prohibited turns, or synchronized traffic lights.

Cities in Europe are even more restricted in what they can do because street patterns are older than in the U.S. and more impervious to change. The narrow streets, the plazas, and the overhanging houses from the medieval period set most of the boundaries within which planners must work. Law, ownership, and historical sentiments combine to freeze most European cities into their present patterns, to be thawed only by such catastrophes as the mass bombing of the last war.

Drastic steps are usually necessary and some cities have moved toward increasing the mileage of limited access highways. By this means, more traffic can be moved more quickly over longer distances; the suburban commuter, especially, has an easier drive to work and home if things go according to plan. Unfortunately, they do not always do so. Better highways increase the size and spread of suburban populations; bigger automobiles take up more road space; accidents pile up lines of traffic in a matter of minutes during peak hours. The drive to work and home is not as quickly accomplished as was planned.

In another move, some cities have begun to block vehicular traffic into the central business district, converting it into a pedestrian mall. This move is generally intended to save the center of the city both economically and aesthetically, making it more accessible and more attractive to shoppers. There is undoubtedly some logic behind the plan; architecturally, at any rate, the effects can be seen, as in Philadelphia. The traffic problem, however, is not solved as much as it is deferred to a larger area. Furthermore, it is not at all clear that these plans are leading to a renaissance of the central city.

At considerable public expense, cities have been moving to increase the amount of parking space available in the central business district. Some have accomplished this by underground parking facilities. In other cities, private owners have torn down blighted buildings and converted the space into parking lots. Each move in this direction tends to make the automobile a bit more attractive, thereby swinging away another portion of disgruntled commuters and shoppers from public transit. These measures, instead of ameliorating the situation, often tend to increase the severity of the problem itself.

This working at cross purposes, hemmed in by features of the urban environment that cannot be changed or modified, is characteristic of the practitioner's dilemma. He must try to provide solutions to problems on a number of fronts simultaneously even though those solutions never get to the core of the problem and often cancel each other out. Furthermore, urban trends have a way of progressing unseen by the planners until it is too late and they are upon us. For example, it seems as though suburban families are moving back into the city as their children grow up and marry, quite likely setting the next population movement into motion. Without having successfully solved the problems that now exist, the practitioner must be prepared to meet the problems of the future that are, even now, already in the making.

Clearly, such a course of partial, provisional, and incompatible solutions is futile. I suspect that we rush into these temporary solutions, knowing in advance that they are inadequate, partly because we believe some action is better than no action and partly because we refuse to recognize the complexity of the situation. No effective solution of the urban traffic problem, or any other urban problem, is likely to be achieved until we admit that we are dealing with a society that is structured and changing, as is any society; until we recognize that urban changes are facets of broader ongoing changes that can and must be understood.

Government

Suburbanization has complicated not only traffic but also a whole range of problems by the creation of metropolitan areas. In many cases those areas do not follow existing political and administrative boundaries but straddle them. Suburbs, which are socially and economically wedded to the cities they surround, frequently lie in a county or a state other than the central city itself. For the practitioner, this adds confusion to an already overwhelming set of problems. He finds solutions harder to effect simply because several levels of government are now involved. The formal lines of government that divide the metropolitan area often create the greatest barrier to effective action even for those problems that are obviously common to all. We must then first clarify the administrative and legal channels through which action is taken, before considering the action itself.

This condition is not limited to the United States. As a result of the recommendations of the Royal Commission on Local Government in Greater London,[3] the British Parliament has passed a bill calling for the reorganization of the Greater London area. The bill will reshuffle existing administrative authorities and reallocate such services as education, town planning, housing, and social services among the newly defined governmental units. All of this was not without tremendous political significance, of course, and the reorganization plan met much resistance. This was further proof, as if any were needed, that power is not willingly nor easily surrendered or modified.

The matter can be illustrated by considering the case of traffic once again. It is evident that highways begin in areas outside of the city, in another county or in another state. Yet, it is the city which instigates the traffic and attracts it. To follow strictly the existing governmental jurisdictions in planning highways within the metropolitan area is unworkable because it is plainly irrational. Each governmental unit affected could not be allowed to exercise autonomy in its decision without reference to the other units involved in traffic planning. Not, that is, if utter chaos is to be avoided. Clearly, there is the need for cooperative planning or the creation of some new unit that more closely matches the functional structure of the metropolitan region.

The pressing need has stimulated a number of administrative devices and changes to answer the problem of governmental jurisdictions.[4] Victor Jones has compiled a succinct summary of the methods that have been tried or proposed. One set of such devices involves few or no changes in the existing governmental pattern and includes such measures as these: increasing the jurisdiction of the central city for some purposes outside of its conventional boundaries; cooperative metropolitan planning that includes all the governmental units involved; the extension of state and federal administration; and the creation of special districts or authorities. Another set of proposals would fundamentally alter the existing governmental jurisdictions: annexing adjoining territories and consolidating them within the central city; consolidating cities and counties; establishing a metropolitan area government; and creating a "metropolitan city-state." Each proposal holds some advantages but usually many more disadvantages. The greatest barrier to any fundamental change, Jones concluded was that "units of local governments are tough organizations with many political and legal protections against annihilation or absorption by another government." [5]

In the meantime, special authorities created to handle specific problems have become increasingly popular, even as the proliferation of such multiple jurisdictions is bound to confound the basic problem even more.

Another problem of government, not immediately related to jurisdiction, is the damaging economic situation to which most cities are being progressively pushed. Since the suburban move is made predominately by those in the middle and upper income groups, the city loses a vital source of its revenues through property taxes and shares of sales or other use taxes. The population that remains in the city comes predominantly from the lowest income group and requires the greatest amount of service from the city as, for example, police, fire, and welfare services. Yet this group contributes and has contributed the lowest proportion of any group to the cost of such services. The financial position of most cities has thereby become quite unstable, and has no hope of immediate improvement, especially from state legislatures that are heavily rural in their representation. Legislative reapportionment in the United States may offer some relief for cities by giving them a more effective voice in state legislatures, but this change is by no means certain or immediate.

And the fact that the city is called upon, as part of our current civic philosophy, to provide more and more services and facilities, makes the problem even more difficult. Roads, airports, railway terminals, street lighting, water, sewage, garbage collection, public transit, and the like are services that must continue to be provided no matter how few people remain and regardless of their ability to pay. Where adjoining suburbs have voted for annexation, of course, the city has regained some of its lost revenues. However, many suburban communities prefer to incorporate or remain under a county jurisdiction. Part of this decision is undertaken in the belief that property taxes will be lower, but they do not always remain so as more services come to be required in the suburbs. Someone has to pay such costs.

The answer to the problem obviously requires some restructuring of the older definitions of jurisdiction. Yet, this involves policy decisions that are beyond the limits of the practitioner's job. He is forced to work within existing limits, for the most part. There are too many political pressures for keeping things as they are, from the city, from the state, and especially from officials in newer suburban areas who have found their power increasing with the increase in population. Formerly small and ineffective county governments have expanded rapidly in personnel, jurisdiction, and functions, for the county has usually been the only existing unit of administration in the newer suburban developments.

Housing

Housing can be mentioned as a final example to illustrate the nature of the practitioner's concern. Slum clearance, urban renewal, and redevelopment continue to be outstanding urban problems. Proper renewal of deteriorated urban centers, it is argued, and perhaps validly, is one way of regaining population and decreasing the metropolitan spread. If cities can be made more attractive and competitive with suburban developments, the suburban migration might be halted. By building good housing within a realistic and competitive price range and by renewing the blighted urban areas, the city may regain its former residents. Urban renewal is expensive and for many cities is out of economic reach even with federal support. Yet it needs to be done not only to regain population but for social reasons as well. Slums are bad from any point of view. However, getting agreement for an adequate urban renewal program and effecting a program are not easy tasks.

Suburban housing patterns are now creating the problems of the future. The developer is usually free to build as he wishes, guided only by his desire for profit. The history of inadequate planning and a laissez-faire philosophy are being duplicated again in the suburbs, and we seem to have learned little from the past. The developer builds as densely as he wishes, limited only by what he believes can be sold. Usually, there are no zoning restrictions upon him; consequently we see the curious situation in which one of the major battles of urban development, zoning, won too late for the industrial city, now being lost without a struggle in the suburbs. Often aided by local officials who see their chance for power tied to population increase, the suburban housing developer is given carte blanche.

Another problem created by suburban housing is that few requirements are placed upon the developer to allow for public schools, parks, or other public facilities. Apparently, we have not progressed far enough in our philosophy of civic responsibility to insist collectively that a realtor pay attention to more than his own immediate profit. He is still considered as an entrepreneur, free to conduct his business within only the broad legal limits of economic activity. The fact that by his actions of bringing 1000 or more families, say, together within a housing development he thereby creates new needs and new demands at the community level that would otherwise not arise, somehow does not come to be interpreted as part of his responsibility until it is too late. Governments soon find that they have permitted suburban development to take place at a higher cost than they were prepared to pay. Home owners soon discover that such costs must be borne by them. Someone has to pay for the new schools and the new roads. Buying land for those needed facilities costs more once the land has been improved and its value has risen.

The practitioner is aware of these consequences of unplanned development and the problems which they raise. Suburbs grow and expand, shopping centers proliferate, more and more people move, and the metropolis spreads out unplanned and unrestricted. The results are as quick to appear as they are inevitable: traffic congestion, inadequate public facilities, and inadequate planning standards. The practitioner must enter into this maelstrom to find reasonable solutions. His hands are too often tied, however, because there are few legal avenues open by which he might reverse the trend. He is forced to dance to a tune not of his choosing. He is prevented at almost every step from free action by existing political restrictions, by pressure groups, by the jealousy of newly won authority, and above all by a prevailing urban philosophy of laissez faire. Yet, throughout it he must somehow come up with some suggested action to relieve the more odious and unpleasant aspects of the situation. Under these circumstances there seems to be little more for him to do than juggle street patterns, expand highway facilities, buy more land at inflated prices, and provide more services—all with decreased revenue. The practitioner, who understands the total situation, must endure endless frustration.

The tragedy is everyone's. The problems faced by cities today were conceived in the past, and the problems of tomorrow are being created today and taking the same forms as those of the past. What has been learned from the past is applied to the present too slowly and too late.

iii

THE VISIONARY:
PLANNER FOR
URBAN UTOPIA

TO THE visionary the city is a problem environment, one that has developed without plan and one more sensitive to the narrow economic demands of the moment than to the lasting moral and social needs of individuals. He sees in the industrial city what the practitioner has seen: congestion, slums, blight, inefficiency, and all the other consequences of civic irresponsibility. Although both types are impressed by the same urban realities, they differ markedly in the interpretations they give to them. For the practitioner, congestion, blight and the rest of the shoddy inventory are the problems; for the visionary they are but the symptoms. The basic problem is the ethos and organization of industrial society itself. This difference separates the visionary from the practitioner. Because of it they are oriented differently in their study of and solutions for urban problems. The practitioner, as earlier described, is committed by his job to piecemeal solutions that can be enforced quickly, such as

widening streets, zoning, partial urban renewal, or streamlining
some phase of governmental organization. The visionary is a vehe-
ment opponent of these temporary measures. Rather, he insists
that radical surgery is the only way to save the patient. The
point is sharply made by Mumford who establishes the visionary's perspective in this respect. "Much recent housing and city
planning has been handicapped because those who have undertaken the work have had no clear notion of the social functions
of the city. . . . And they did not, apparently, suspect that there
might be gross deficiencies, misdirected efforts, mistaken ex-
penditures, here that would not be set straight by merely building sanitary tenements or widening narrow streets." [1]

The visionary concentrates, then, on practical problems but is
concerned with long term qualitative considerations and social
needs, and approaches these problems through a social ideology
and an aesthetic philosophy. In brief, an urban problem for the
visionary includes anything that violates his high standards of
morality and aesthetics. His solution is usually nothing short
of a massive reconstruction of metropolitan society. Standards
of such a high order, after all, should not be compromised.
The practitioner is committed to a job; the visionary is dedicated
to an ideal.

The visionary's ideals are contained in The Plan: a blueprint,
more or less detailed, for building into reality those forms, those
values, and those qualities which he believes the city must contain. Sometimes, he even takes the trouble to indicate how we
can reach that goal. In its fullest form, the blueprint includes not
only plans for buildings, homes, and the general physical format
of the city, but also definitions of what urban social institutions
are to be included, and even the new psychology of the urbanite
that is to emerge from all this. This is no picayune puttering
with street plans or building facades or zoning regulations. It
is a manifesto for an urban revolution.

The ideological roots that sustain the visionary go back to
the middle of the nineteenth century and the protest, predominantly by socially conscious intellectuals, against the evils of
industrialism. The protest centered on the effects of industrialism
rather than on industrialism per se. It was more in opposition to

the social system than to the machine. The benefits of industrial technology for human progress were more or less conceded. The argument, however, was with the social system that subordinated man to the machine and to the profit motive. The answer lay not in wrecking the machine but in controlling its social and ecological consequences. These indictments probably reached their highest pitch in the writings of Marx, in Engels' description of English factory life, and in Booth's classic studies of life and labor in London. These writings described with care the human consequences of industrialism: the effects of poverty, child labor, the erosion of the human spirit, and the senseless lives of the mass of people caught up by the factory and the city. It was in this period that dehumanization or alienation were understood in their crudest sense: depriving the individual of the barest essentials of humanity. By our own time of affluence, they are much more subtly and sophisticatedly defined.

What added fire to the intellectual's protests, aside from the real misery they saw, were the intolerable social discrepancies created by industrial society and above all else, the differences between rich and poor. For the intellectuals the discrepancy was a betrayal of a promise. About one hundred years before, with the onset of the industrial revolution, society had been dedicated to a new social philosophy that emphasized human dignity, the rule of law, the triumph of reason, and freedom. These new values were to replace the aristocratic rigidity, religious dogmatism, and monarchical absolutism condoned by the medieval philosophy of society. What the intellectuals had not seen was that the new ideology was meant to apply only to a small segment of society, not to all of it. By the middle of the last century, the intellectuals apparently were shocked into reality and they saw a social nightmare instead of the promised dream. Mandeville's *Fable of the Bees,* an allegory that argued that society as a whole benefited even as individuals suffered from the laissez-faire economic activity of its citizens, became a fairy story not even accurate for activity in the hive. The rule of law became a codified disregard of social responsibility. The new ideology became based more on the unassailable primacy of the natural order, of which the social order was conceived to be a part, than on the ability of man to shape his social order. In short, the gap between the promise of industrialism and its reality, especially in the city, became too wide to be ignored.

The disenchantment with industrial society emerged in one of three ways, depending upon the value placed on industrialism and the social change thought to be needed. (1) Reaction against it all by which industrialism was entirely, if naively, discredited. The machine, the factory, and the city were considered to be beyond salvation in that they could not add anything worthwhile to society. In a reaction against industrialism the tightly comforting security of medievalism was sought through its image of a rediscovered rural utopia. This philosophy has continued, in one form or another, up to the present, where it has become centered around the small community as the alternative to the metropolis. (2) Reform of some features of industrial society to keep such advantages as labor-saving machinery, release from monotonous tasks, and the comforts that machines could fashion. The reformers championed what Mannheim has called a "spatial wish," the projection of utopia into space.[2] By controlling industrialism for the benefit of all in a new social environment, the reformer argued, man could once again progress. Applied to the city, this view became the basis for the "Garden City" and its variations. (3) Revolt was yet a third alternative. The revolutionary accepted industrialism as a necessary historical phase; history neither could be set back to some earlier epoch nor could it be stopped. Industrial society could not be preserved as it was, nor could it be remodeled, even in part. Instead, a massive reconstitution was required, by which all existing institutions, values, and social mechanisms would be replaced by a new social order forging into reality the unfulfilled promises of industrialism. Mannheim, once again, has called these wish fulfillments "chiliasms," projections of dreams into time, the social utopias.

The visionary at one time or another has been identified with all three of these disenchanted responses to industrialism. Ebenezer Howard set forth one such spatial utopia in some detail. Later visionaries, such as Frank Lloyd Wright, perceived that tampering with the urban pattern necessarily involved changing economic mechanisms, political administration, and

social philosophy. And throughout much of the writing by
visionaries, the simple desire to return to a rural civilization is
obvious again and again.

§ Planning as a Social Movement

The above description of the visionary, of his reactions to the
industrial city, and of the manner he chose to enforce his values,
all imply the elements of a social movement. A "social movement" is used here in its sociological meaning, to identify a con-
certed response by a group in support of a set of values. It need
not involve organization, although the town planning movement did have organization. It does not require that the participants know they are part of a movement, although such was
the case here. Social movements, in other words, are not always
conscious, explicit, or fully organized. It is possible, within the
meaning intended here, for individuals separately to promulgate
an idea or a cause, either without steps to attain the end or without consciousness of having company in their endeavor.

I have used this conception of a social movement to avoid
the implication that the visionaries were tightly organized behind
a single set of beliefs. Quite the contrary, for the visionaries were
too individualistic to be led, too authoritarian to be politicians
in a democracy, and, in some cases, too egomaniacal to com-
promise their beliefs in order to move further toward their
ultimate goals.

To add perspective to the analysis of the visionary's plans,
therefore, let me cast him explicitly into that framework, into
the role of leader of a social movement.

Planning, as understood by the visionary, should be kept
clear from what is usually understood by that term today. For
the visionary, planning expresses an ideology of urban reform
and revolt. It goes beyond the piecemeal planning of the practitioner, for one thing. For another, it has a facade of rationality that is characteristic of most planning, but in the case of
the visionary there is less reason and more emotion behind
the facade.

Four criteria can be used to establish the visionaries and

their plans as part of a social movement. First, the plans contained a set of propositions that could unify belief, even though these propositions were differently enunciated by different people. Most visionaries agreed that the city had deteriorated, that the industrial city was inhumane, and that the need for change was great. Although they disagreed about how to effect urban changes, there was no argument about the need for change.

Second, the movement had a history. Its point of origin, as earlier noted, was in the general protest against the effects of industrialism. The continued growth of technology, of science, of a factory society and a machine culture, added more substance to the visionary's argument and new examples of how inhuman industrial cities could become. The expansion of the industrial city, coupled with a prevailing philosophy more attuned to economic demands than to social needs, assured the visionary planners of a cause and identified an enemy—land owners, industrialists, and the like. The perseverance of these problems helped give the movement relevance, over time, and time in which to develop a sense of tradition and continuity. Social movements sparked into being by a topical issue, no matter how vital, dissolve once the issue has disappeared or else try to stay alive by moving on to other causes. In the case of town planning, the movement was able to capitalize on existing protests against industrialism, and it had sufficient time to mobilize some of those sentiments in its own behalf.

Third, the movement created a following. The followers, then as now, have been intellectuals predominantly, because they were the first to recognize the discrepancies between what was promised and what was attained by industrialism. The visionaries never seemed to be wise in the ways of mass politics, or didn't want to be, so the movement never spread. Mass protest movements properly led stay close to the ground to pick up a following, but utopian movements fly too high to be pursued by the masses. In certain cases, the visionaries were snobs by temperament, more entranced by their own ideals than dedicated to recruiting a following. The planning movement did find followers, however, although intellectuals predominated among it. What is more, the movement gained sufficient political strength to put some of its plans into effect: Howard's two garden cities, Letchworth and Welwyn, the Greenbelt towns of the New Deal era in the United States, and the British New Towns Act in 1946. The fact that there were followers, then, did give the movement some political reality. The importance of city planning and town planning today is further proof that we are considering more than the wishful dreams of a handful of politically ineffectual intellectuals.

Finally, the town planning movement had an organizing myth which did much to make it cohesive. The function of the planning myth was to condense a complicated intellectual message into shorthand which could readily be translated into action. The myth pointed to the existing evils and devised an overall answer to erase them. The shorthand of the myth avoided any reference to practical difficulties that might complicate the simple question and answer. The myth thereby became an appealing part-truth, attractive for its simplicity, as are most myths.

The myth put forth by visionaries was based on urban characteristics that were certainly real. The evils within the industrial city at the turn of the century were plentiful and easily described. The reason for the degraded urban situation, the explanation went on, was that the city had been allowed to grow without plan, or at least without reference to human values. Economic competition had been elevated to the status of a natural law, rationality was measured primarily by profit, and self-interest was considered the primary instinct of man. Moral values and civic responsibility were twisted to serve economic values. Little wonder the industrial city developed as it did. However, argued the planners, man is rational. He can plan and thereby create a better, more harmonious, and more humane environment for himself. The economic forces and scientific knowledge that produced the industrial city could be mobilized to build anew the planned city.

The plan does not necessarily prescribe social revolution. Rather, existing social forces can simply be directed into other channels in order to realize the full potentials of an industrial society. Howard, for example, was careful to point out that his plan for the garden city was neither socialistic nor communistic.[3]

The plan, then, stated the conditions and the means for attaining a new environment. It seemed on the surface desirable, feasible, and necessary. The myth that it contained was a naïve view of human motivation and of political structure: that reason is enough to change society from what it is to what we would like it to be. Above all, the visionary made the tacit assumption that his values were shared by most other people. This assumption proved to be the fatal flaw of most such plans.

Perhaps the best way to understand the visionary's contribution to an urban sociology is to look at some examples. Three have been chosen, each one because it is representative of a particular type. (1) Ebenezer Howard, the father of city planning and creator of the "garden city," a term that Osborn[4] notes has become part of all modern languages: *Cité-Jardin, Gartenstadt, Cuidad-jardin, Tuinstad;* (2) Frank Lloyd Wright for the brash plan; (3) Lewis Mumford for an approach that is sociologically informed. Many others, such as Saarinen, Le Corbusier, Gropius, Neutra, Sitte, the Goodmans, and Gallion are not included. They are important in their own ways, but a detailed analysis would not have added greatly to the fulfillment of the main intent of this discussion, to present a range of sociologically relevant ideas. After all, the main purpose is not to assess the relative merits of lineal cities, ribbon developments, super-blocks and the *ville radieuse,* but to consider the nature of urban society.

§ Ebenezer Howard: The Garden City

Howard's book, *Tomorrow: A Peaceful Path to Real Reform,* was first published in 1898, and with slight revisions reappeared in 1902 under the title *Garden Cities of To-Morrow.* The book placed Howard among the intellectuals of the protest movement of the last century. Apparently his protest was independently arrived at, for Howard did not pore over books or steep himself in the literature, at least according to F. J. Osborn's evaluation of him.[5]

Though not a scholar, Howard did know something of the intellectuals' protest of his time. He was a reader not only of the daily press but also of Edward Bellamy's *Looking Back-ward* and Henry George's *Progress and Poverty*. In any case, Howard tasted the flavor of protest that filled the period.

In a singular example of the organizing myth at work, Howard began by identifying the problem in a way calculated to win agreement from different quarters. It was

a question in regards to which one can scarcely find any difference of opinion. It is well nigh universally agreed by men of all parties . . . that it is deeply to be deplored that the people should continue to stream into the already over-crowded cities, and should thus further deplete the country districts.[6]

He took a short step to the solution.

All, then, are agreed on the pressing nature of this problem, . . . and though it would doubtless be quite Utopian to expect a similar agree-ment as to the value of any remedy that may be proposed, it is at least of immense importance that . . . we have such a consensus of opinion at the outset. . . . Yes, the key to the problem how to restore the people to the land—that beautiful land of ours, with its canopy of sky, the air that blows upon it, the sun that warms it, the rain and dew that moisten it . . . will be seen to pour a flood of light on the problems of intemperance, of excessive toil, of restless anxiety, of grinding poverty. . . .[7]

Howard's complaint was not only against urban congestion, but against the values of the industrial system that produced the city. It is worth quoting his remarks here in some detail, for in them Howard clearly showed the basis of his protest.

These crowded cities have done their work; they were the best which a society largely based on *selfishness* and *rapacity* could construct, but they are in the nature of things entirely unadapted for a society in which the *social side* of our nature is demanding a larger share of recognition. . . . The large cities of today are scarcely better adapted for the expression of the fraternal spirit than would a work on as-tronomy which taught that the earth was the centre of the universe be capable of adaptation for use in our schools. Each generation should build to suit its own needs; and it is no more in the nature of things that men should continue to live in old areas because their ancestors lived in them, than it is that they should cherish the old beliefs which a wider faith and a more enlarged understanding have outgrown. . . . The simple issue to be faced, and faced resolutely, is: Can better results be obtained by starting on a bold plan on comparatively virgin soil than by attempting to adapt our old cities to our *newer* and *higher* needs? Thus fairly faced, the question can only be answered in one way; and when that simple fact is well grasped, the *social revolution* will speedily commence.[8] [Italics added.]

These bold statements can be considered the garden city manifesto, and like the manifesto of Marx and Engels it identifies the evil, pinpoints the causes, and suggests the solution.

The crowded, industrial cities house the evils of our civilization. These evils have developed because the qualities of selfishness and rapacity have been valued long beyond their usefulness to society. They are now clearly out of tune with the social demands of a more developed, industrial society. In society, as in science, man must abandon outmoded methods and create new ones to meet current demands. Man is not, in Howard's view, at the mercy of uncontrollable social and natural forces. If the seventeenth and eighteenth centuries increased man's ability to control nature, then the task of the nineteenth century was to mobilize man's ability to control society. It was to this belief that Howard was dedicated, and it was to this conviction that his appeal was aimed.

To simplify his argument, Howard devised a now classic image: three magnets labeled "town," "country," and "town-country" are grouped around a rectangle labeled "The People: Where Will They Go?" The town and country each contained advantages (the positive pole) and disadvantages (the negative pole). Only the third, the town-country, was free of disadvantages, taking the best from the other two. The town magnet has the attractions of high wages, employment opportunities, amusements, edifices, and well-lit streets. However, it repels because of high rents and prices, excessive hours of toil, distance from work, foul air, slums, and gin palaces. The country magnet has the attractions of nature, sunshine, woods, and low rents; it repels because of lack of sociability, low wages, lack of amusement, deserted villages, and the lack of public spirit. It is only a clerical task to list the advantages of both as part of the town-country magnet: nature, opportunity, low rents and low prices, high wages, pure air and water, no smoke, no slums, bright homes, freedom, and cooperation. There are no disadvantages to the town-country, or garden city, life.

This was nature's way, Howard maintained in his argument, and it drew upon science, reason, and natural law. In the images and structure of his arguments and the facile way he led the argument to a determined conclusion, Howard exhibited the utopian mentality. He was sincere, convinced, and dedicated. His main objectives, W. A. Eden has observed, went well "with the ordinary aspiration of the class to which Howard belonged, the somewhat earnest, chapel going or chapel emancipated lower middle class which had lately acquired political power and was destined to inaugurate a revolution by returning the Liberal Party with its high majority at the General Election of 1906." [9]

Howard's plan was to purchase about 6,000 acres of open country and in the center, on 1,000 acres, to construct Garden City, for a population of 30,000. A green belt, i.e. countryside, was to surround the city with a natural wall much the same as the wall of the medieval city. The purpose of the barrier for the garden city, as for the medieval city, was to protect it against invasion and encroachment, not from the barbarians but from London's overflow population. At the same time, the green belt would also restrict urban growth from within. Much of his discussion of the plan concerned the financing of the venture: providing balance sheets which proved the plan to be economically sound and the Garden City to be a self-sufficient proposition. The sizes of building lots, street widths and locations, the location of public parks, factories, and agriculture were specified, although Howard emphasized that his description was meant to be suggestive, not final. A hypothetical budget was drawn up for roads, bridges, schools, a library and museum, parks and ornamentation, sewerage disposal, and for a sinking fund. From a reading of this description today, Howard emerges as a colonial clerk neatly setting down the row of figures on the balance sheet. Howard must have known intimately the Victorian mentality that he wanted to persuade, and probably shared it.

Howard's brief inventory of the obstacles to his plan was hardly complete, nor did he even spend much time arguing over the few he did choose to identify. Human nature, as it was then conceived, was a major obstacle. After all, people are selfish and not given to altruism. Howard's answer, such as it was, maintained that these qualities could not be allowed to make any difference. The garden city was economically feasible and socially necessary. If it failed, we were only inviting catastrophe, for cities would continue to grow unplanned and make us their victims. On the other hand, Howard held, once the Garden City was built and its feasibility proven, similar cities could be started and, as a result, a new day would dawn for England and eventually for mankind. Man would no longer be the victim of his industrial creation, but its master. He would discover that his real wealth lay in the land rather than in the marketplace or factory.

Most utopias remain dreams, and their authors die convinced that they held a secret to which the world unfortunately would not listen. Still other utopias, put to the tests of reality, failed because they were poorly conceived, with insufficient attention paid to the complex reality they sought to reform. So too did Howard taste the bitter fruit of reality. He lived to see two garden cities begun, and to see both flounder. He saw enough to show him, if not to convince him, that there were more obstacles to the realization of his plan than he had imagined. Still, there were some benefits, finally proven by the permanence of the experiments and by the financial value of the bonds of the garden cities, although many years after his death in 1928. The plan failed ostensibly for financial reasons, but more important, its failure could be traced to the revolutionary character of its ideas. For better or worse, Howard advocated an ideology of government ownership or control. To Victorians raised in the philosophy of laissez faire, the truth of which seemed self-evident, Howard was advocating no less than revolution. Neither his explicit denial of sympathy with communism and socialism, then active on the Continent, nor his bookkeeper's account sheet could disguise the revolutionary consequences of his ideas. Those who followed Howard were also to learn that their leader was talking of more than architectural reforms alone. Yet, Howard's intent was not to be revolutionary, but simply to pursue his assumptions to a realistic conclusion. Any plan or urban change such as he had in mind must challenge existing social mechanisms because those very mechanisms produced the evil he complained of.

Five years after the publication of Howard's book, a company was formed to build Letchworth, the first garden city.[10] The book became a best seller. A sizable amount of money was raised, although not enough. Of the authorized capital of £300,000, only £100,000 of shares were subscribed beyond the £40,000 pledged by the directors of the newly formed company. Heavy interest charges were incurred for the additional mortgages that were needed and a heavy financial burden was thus placed in the venture from the beginning. Money remained a problem, along with the inevitable dissension between the business and ideological leaders of the project. Nor were matters helped by the fact that Letchworth was a bad site, having few natural attractions. Public interest in the project quickly dissipated. After forty-three years, all of the accumulated dividends were finally repaid. "It was . . . indefatigable faith," wrote Rodwin, "which made Letchworth survive, despite all the difficulties, neglect, and derision."

With the cavalier attitude, obstinacy, and unquenchable optimism that are so characteristic of dedicated egomaniacs, Howard took an option on another piece of land in 1920, Letchworth's marked lack of success notwithstanding. Welwyn Garden City was located twenty miles northwest of London, on the same highway and railroad as Letchworth. Money, once again, was a problem, but this time the financing was more complicated by the economic depression of that period and the competition from the Letchworth venture. Tight money meant higher interest rates, and consequently the financial burden was heavier than it had been for Letchworth. The government advanced some funds, but these loans were sporadic, grudgingly given, and carried with them a right to participate in the management. Again, as in Letchworth, dissension was ever present between the lenders worried for their money and the planners worried for their ideals. After two major reorganizations, in 1931 and in 1934, a large part of the share capital was written off and restrictions on dividends were removed. Howard had died in 1928. Welwyn remained, although its development did not proceed fully according to plan.

Aside from lack of funds and dissension, the garden cities encountered less obvious but equally damaging obstacles. These were due to a naïveté about sociological factors, which, by the way, even later planners did not avoid. Rodwin has noted these in his evaluation of Howard.[11] First, Howard wanted to create a politically independent city. This requirement opened the door to a whole set of new problems concerning revenue and jurisdiction, besides further complicating the already complex administrative relationships between cities. By insisting on independence, Howard overlooked the nexus that existed, and continues to exist, between urban centers in an industrial nation.

Second, the direction of population movement did not fulfill Howard's prediction. Instead of people moving constantly into the large cities, as Howard had predicted for London, such migration leveled off and was redirected into the region around the large central city. *Urban* congestion, therefore, did not remain the key problem; *metropolitan* congestion was to complicate the problem even more. Third, the automobile and mass transportation significantly altered the urban journey from what it had been in Howard's time. He thought that people should walk to work, as one way of being close to nature. The automobile, as fact and as symbol, changed the urbanite's outlook; he would not remain a pedestrian. Urban traffic thereby became a major problem. Whether or not the garden city would have solved or would have exacerbated that problem is hard to say, even though it is a question contemporary planners take into account. Finally, Howard apparently gave little thought to human motivation; how to entice people to move into the garden city. His assumptions concerning human nature and human motivations were primitive and naïve. It is an ideological disease of visionaries, Howard included, that they assume their values to be the best for all. Do people in fact, want to live close to nature? Do they want to exchange concrete for meadows? The answer obviously must be that some do and some do not. It is the human variety that the utopian planner so frequently overlooks. He makes the unwarranted assumption either that people are alike or that they can be molded, shaped, and moved to conform to design, very much as buildings can. Rodwin concluded:

Unawareness of many of the pitfalls, coupled with the extraordinary loyalty to the idea of garden cities, ranks high among the factors which account for the survival of the two towns. Whatever judgment one may form of the experiment, the fact is that the leaders succeeded in their initial objective. [Only, it must be added, if that objective is very narrowly defined.]. . . . In the process of development, the towns also pioneered some significant planning innovations, including use and density zoning, a form of ward or neighborhood planning, employment of an agricultural greenbelt to control urban size, and unified urban land ownership for the purpose of capturing rising land values for the benefit of the residents.[12]

Welwyn and Letchworth were not the end of the garden city movement nor of its importance to the present discussion. During the Second World War, government officials in London foresaw the need for postwar housing and, to their credit, the necessity for directing some of the population out of London itself. Several Town and Country Planning Acts were passed and a Town and Country Planning Ministry created, all before 1945. In 1946, the New Towns Act was passed and "the building of cities for the first time in contemporary Western history became a concern of long-term national policy." [13] These developments are best shown in the story of Stevenage, one of the towns built under the national act, whose problems have been so excellently assessed by Harold Orlans.[14] Stevenage gives us a more recent perspective on the consequences of Howard's ideas and, at the same time, conveniently displays the principle limitations of sociological understanding of the visionaries.

Stevenage in 1945, immediately prior to its selection as a site under the New Towns Act, was in its development and location somewhere between a village and a town. It was within London's metropolitan influence, being a dormitory suburb for clerks and businessmen who commuted to London. However, it still valued its local traditions and agricultural activity. The project called for building a garden city in Stevenage to house a population of 30,000, and one proposal forecasted a population double that size within ten years. The partners in this venture were the Stevenage Urban Council and the Ministry of Town and Country Planning. Although a spirit of cooperation was present at the initial discussions about the project, it was not long before dissension, the ever-present threat in social planning, broke out between the partners. The local authorities resented the manner in which the Ministry pushed ahead with its plans without local consultation. The Ministry, apparently intent on making this project a national model, neglected its public relations in the local community.

Local residents organized themselves into the Residents' Protection Association to protest the Ministry's "tyranny of the acquisition of houses and lands, and the tyranny of control from Whitehall over homes." [15] The residents took legal action against the Ministry, and even though they lost the case, they did succeed in stopping any development during the time, so that only twenty-eight houses were built in the four and one-half years after the project started, instead of over 300 that were to have been completed, A key to the conflict, Orlans believed, was the ideological split between the rural conservatism of Stevanage residents and the public-welfare ideals of the Ministry. What the residents of Stevenage soon came to realize was that the garden city development meant the effective end to their tradition of local independence by the shift to greater public ownership and control. Relations had improved by 1950, after the court action, but the Residents' Protection Association remained for the "exploitation of opportunities to obstruct the progress of the New Town and to secure all possible concessions for property owners and ratepayers." Such was the stormy history of the garden city plan in Stevenage.

This brief history of the Stevenage project is meant to highlight certain sociological features, principally the kinds of objections that can develop when the visionary's urban ideals are concretized. I leave out the obvious economic and political problems that are raised and look at what are presumably picayune matters. Orlans' analysis is valuable because he has indicated not only the problems of the politicians but also those of the technicians.

One explicit aim of the Stevenage plan, as it is of most town plans, was to create a *balanced* community: "We want to revive that social structure which existed in the old English villages, where the rich lived next door to the not so rich, and everyone knew everybody." [16] The economic bases for this idea are perhaps reasonable, especially the attempt to achieve some

economic stability by having more than one industry or business
located in the town. As the above quotation shows, however,
behind the desire for balance is frequently the unconscious wish
for the norm, for what Orlans has called "the golden mean in
which all the parts of a community and all citizens would work
together harmoniously and without friction." [17]

Not all town planners, of course, agree on the desirability of
social balance. Even among those at Stevenage, a counter argument was advanced in support of a *homogeneous*, not a mixed
community, on the grounds that a deliberate mixture of social
classes would hamper the spirit of neighborliness. It is hard to
say which argument is more naïve. Both are based on private
values more than on social wisdom. There is only the narrowest
factual basis upon which to make a choice of population, and
this basis is the social consequences that would follow from
each alternative. The choice actually made, however, depends
heavily on the values the individual planner chooses to hold.
Howard, for example, wished to move the working man out of
an unhealthy city into the middle class atmosphere of the garden
city, where he might spend his time in the "healthy and fascinating pursuit of gardening." [18] Other planners envisioned a new
city with all social strata transformed by a mystical, architectural
osmosis into an equalitarian society. The troubles with this kind
of social engineering are manifold: Whose values are to guide
the plan; once enforced, who controls society and how does he
make it go in the proper direction?

One illuminating instance of the planner's naïveté concerning
Stevenage centered on the "Reilly Green," or common, which
took its name from a plan devised by Sir Charles Reilly. The
arguments supporting a common, around which small neighborhood units would be constructed, claimed that it would remedy
such defects as "loneliness, juvenile deliquency, parental cruelty,
poor health, declining birth-rate, late marriage, ignorance, prop-
erty-possessiveness, etc." [19] More judicious planners, undoubtedly, would not care to make so broad a claim. But the essence
of most plans is to restructure social life according to some
ideal, and to do it primarily through the manipulation of buildings and space and only secondarily, perhaps, through the manipulation of the people themselves. As one of the architects in

the national ministry reported: "We do not claim that a sensible physical arrangement of houses and other buildings normal to a good residential negihborhood will automatically produce a friendly and neighborly spirit. But we do claim that it will give considerable initial advantage to the development of a healthy social life." [20]

This statement illustrates a common misconception among town planners: that architectural forms can alter social forms. Some planners, like Frank Lloyd Wright, go even further, contending that architectural change is the *sine qua non* of social change. It is a narrow assumption, similar to the misconception that slums cause criminal behavior and delinquency. We know now that complex behavior and motives cannot be explained merely by simple physical facts. Tenements do not make criminals any more than mansions make law-abiding citizens. Social contacts in the family, school, and church, as well as other broader social phenomena, and many individual aspects of the personality shape the human product. The visionary, nevertheless, seems to insist on his belief that the individual who is put in a magic house, in a magic setting, and surrounded with what are essentially the trappings of middle class life, will emerge a stolid, socially acceptable human product in the middle class tradition. It is a highly doubtful assumption. Even granting its truth, one might ask: Why establish middle class traditions as the epitome of the good life?

Another aim of the visionaries is to reconstruct social life and this aim is frequently expressed in the "planned neighborhood." The planners of Stevenage were no exception. Arguments may develop over the optimum size of the neighborhood, whether the cul-de-sac is a way to achieve neighborhood social contacts or where to place the community center to maximize intended neighborhood relationships. There is little disagreement, however, about the desirability of creating a neighborhood to begin with. The neighborhood seems to be the *sine qua non* of every planner's dream. It is a primary element in his ideology, and in the neighborhood, he believes, is the basis of social control to effect wanted social changes. Planners believe, as Orlans concluded the New Town planners believed, "that sociability [the planned neighborhood] and community activity could be organized or, at least, encouraged by a congenial physical environment and genuine social reform which would counteract the consequences of industrialism, occupational specializations, and class segregation and conflict." [21] But, as Ruth Glass has correctly stated: "the return to the small self-contained urban [neighborhood] unit appears to be a forlorn hope. The existing trend is for a progressive division of labour and of interests. . . . This trend can be controlled but it cannot be cancelled." [22]

The visionary, like Howard, raised in a milieu of protest against the evils of industrialism, stands fair to be disappointed. His cause may be just, his vision bright, his side that of the angels. Morally and intellectually impelled to transmogrify industrial, urban man into a middle class, provincial, conforming, garden-city species, the visionary claims too much and knows too little. The Plan has him hypnotized into believing that this all is really feasible. But the dream cannot withstand reality, which he seems imperfectly to appreciate. He has, unfortunately, come to believe that massive social forces, with the impetus of centuries behind them, can be contained and redirected toward nirvana by an exquisitely designed community and a neatly planned neighborhood.

"Must utopia, realized, always disappoint?" Orlans asks, and answers:

To be persuasive and practical (to persuade different kinds of people and to be practiced in different times and places) a utopian idea must be relatively simple and generalized. But life is more complicated than any simple idea, and probably than *any* idea or image, one can have of it—"the inexpressible complexity of everything that lives" is how Tolstoy, for all his genius in expressing that complexity, put it. This is the rock upon which utopia, and reason itself, founders.[23]

§ Frank Lloyd Wright: Broadacre City

Wright was more than simply the American counterpart to Ebenezer Howard and his Broadacre City more than just the American version of Garden City.[24] Howard, as a true Victorian, after carefully adding up the economic costs and arguing for the feasibility of the garden city, had accepted much of the prevailing ideology. An overcrowded and congested London was bad business whereas a planned garden city was good business. Wright, on the contrary, never entered the market place to sell his plans. He much preferred to be the prophet on the mount shouting "Doom!" to the multitudes below. Wright felt the city and the industrial civilization that produced it must perish. They were the consequences of diseased values, and to achieve health, new values had to be established in a new environment. Wright was more consciously a social revolutionary than was Howard. He was prepared to recognize social mechanisms and willing to alter them. Howard's aim was to build a few garden cities to prove they were feasible, and by this publicity to have the revolt against the city initiated by society itself. Wright was more impatient. He wanted the wholesale decentralization of cities carried on simultaneously with the creation of Broadacre City. He had no patience with businesslike arguments to support his plan. Perhaps one could not blame him for his impatience and his loftiness, since he was so convinced that human civilization would be strangled by its industrial creation unless decisive and total action was taken. Any less drastic plan would have been hypocritical.

As the citizen stands, powerful modern resources, naturally his own by uses of modern machinery, are (owning to their very nature) turning against him, although the system he lives under is one he himself helped build. Such centralizations of men and capital as he must now serve are no longer wise or humane. Long ago—having done all it could for humanity—the centralization we call the big city became a centripetal force grown beyond our control; agitated by rent to continually additional, vicarious powers.[25]

The city, according to Wright, has perverted our values and has become the environment of false democracy, false individualism, and false capitalism. We have, by our inaction, allowed ourselves to be overwhelmed and dominated by falsity. "The citizen," Wright argued, "is now trained to see life as a cliché." He must be trained to see life as natural for "only then can the democratic spirit of man, individual, rise out of the ground. We are calling that civilization of man and ground . . .

democracy." [26] As for capitalism: "Out of American 'rugged individualism' captained by rugged captains of our rugged industrial enterprises we have gradually evolved a crude, vain power: plutocratic 'Capitalism.' Not true capitalism. I believe this is entirely foreign to our own original idea of Democracy." [27]

The cause of these perversions of our basic social values in the city is industrial civilization, where most of the visionaries locate the blame. Wright's contribution was to specify the causes more precisely. First, among these is *land rent*, and Henry George is resurrected as a guide to salvation. The rent for land has contributed to the "overgrowth of cities, resulting in poverty and unhappiness." Land values are artificial monsters that have taken over the destiny of the city, thereby removing us further from the natural state of mankind. Second, *money*, "a commodity for sale, so made as to come alive as something in itself— to go on continuously working in order to make all work useless. . . . The modern city is its stronghold and chief defender." [28] Here the Puritan and Jeffersonian in Wright emerges, berating man to get back to the land and to honest labor. Third, *profit*. "By the triumph of conscienceless but 'rugged individualism' the machine profits of human ingenuity or inspiration in getting the work of the world done are almost all funneled into pockets of fewer and more 'rugged' captains-of-industry. Only in a small measure . . . are these profits . . . where they belong; that is to say, with the man whose life is actually modified, given, or sacrificed to this new common agency for doing the work of the world. This agency we call 'the machine.' " [29] In these few words, Wright has fairly condensed the Marxian theory of surplus value. Fourth, *government* and *bureaucracy*. "In order to keep the peace and some show of equity between the lower passions so busily begotten in begetting, the complicated forms of super-money-increase-money-making and holding are legitimatized by government. Government, too, thus becomes monstrosity. Again enormous armies of white-collarites arise." [30] These are Wright's beliefs on the state of industrial civilization. The need for revolt is clear; the means are at hand.

Infinite possibilities exist to make of the city a place suitable for the free man in which freedom can thrive and the soul of man grow, a

City of cities that democracy would approve and so desperately needs. . . . Yes, and in that vision of decentralization and reintegration lies our natural twentieth century dawn. Of such is the nature of the democracy free men may honestly call the new freedom." [31]

How emphatically this point of view, so characteristic of the visionary, separates him from the mundane practicality of the practitioner. For Wright, the city in its present form cannot be saved, nor is it worth saving. A new environment must be envisioned and built. It must be one that is developed out of our technology, but one that excises the diseased growth that has infected our basic and still sound values. The plan is Broadacre City, realized by "organic architecture" or "the architecture of democracy."

Broadacre City was a more detailed utopia than Garden City. Wright had drawn not only the ground pattern (one acre to the individual) but also planned homes, buildings, farms, and automobiles. He also clearly specified the activities that would be permitted. Wright held definite views, to say the least, not only about architecture, but music, education, religion, and medicine as well. He was an authoritarian, some would say a messianic figure, as sure of the true and the good and the beautiful as were Christ and the early Christian prophets, along with Lao-tse and Mohammed, whom he sought to emulate.

Wright's plans for the physical setting and social order of Broadacre City were comprehensive. They contained small factories because the newer technology has made the centralized large factory obsolete, wasteful, and constricting. Office buildings housing the financial, professional, distributive and administrative services necessary for business, would be organized as a unit. Professional services would be decentralized and made readily accessible to the clients. Banks, as we know them, would be abolished and in their place there would be a "non-political, non-profit institution in charge of the medium of exchange." Money no longer would have the power it now has; therefore, the need for its "glamorization" would be removed. Markets and shopping centers would be designed as spacious pavilions to make shopping itself a pleasant and aesthetic experience. There would be apartments, motels, and community centers. Radio would carry great music to the people. "The chamber music

concert would *naturally* become a common feature at home."
[My italics.] Churches would be built, but the "old idea" of
religion would be replaced by a more liberal and nonsectarian
religion. There would be less concern with the hereafter, with
superstition, with prejudice, and with deference to authority.
With this new religion man, though still humble, would be made
more understanding of himself and more democratic towards
others.

Wright also had plans for education and the material to be
taught in the schools and university of Broadacre City. He
would replace the specialized, mass product of the universities of
his day with a student who would obtain a deeper understanding of nature's laws governing the human spirit. Education
would be a total and continuous process for the resident of
Broadacre. Aside from the schools, this would be accomplished
by "style centers," and "television and radio, owned by the
people [which would] broadcast cultural programs illustrating
pertinent phases of government, of city life, of art work, and
[would have] programs devoted to landscape study and planting or the practice of soil and timber conservation; and, as a matter of course, to *town planning* for better houses." [32]

This plan is not utopian, Wright argued, but rather a
description of elemental changes that he saw "existing or surely
coming." Either the vision is realized or society as we know it
is doomed.

This long discourse . . . is a sincere attempt to take apart and show . . .
the radical simplicities of fate to which our own machine skills have
now laid us wide open and [to] try to show how radical eliminations
are now essential to our spiritual health, and to the culture, if not
the countenance, of democratic civilization itself. These are all changes
valid by now if we are to have indigenous culture at all and are not
to remain a bastardized civilization with no culture of our own, going
all the way down the backstairs of time to the usual untimely end
civilizations have hitherto met.[33]

With Frank Lloyd Wright, the visionary's argument found
its most dramatic and radical expression, and its most completely detailed one. Wright magnified Howard's plan and
spelled out more specifically the visionary's discontent and re-

bellion against the industrial city. In Wright's words, the planned utopia became a loud protest against the evils of industrialism. His architectural philosophy was, at the same time, a radical social ideology. Wright recognized this and did not hesitate to make the connection clear. His principle contribution to the study of the city, if one does not care to accept his dream or his philosophy, was in the repeated insistence on the relationship between the city and the society that produced it. The contemporary city, for Wright, was a product of industrial civilization. One could not understand the first without the second, which included understanding all of its institutions: the political system, social stratification and the economic order, religion and education. Wright might be excused for his authoritarianism, for his failure to consider the motivations of individuals, for his brash structuring of existing social relationships into something he wanted. For he did grasp something of the underlying complexity that sustained the city as a social environment. That he refused to consider what others wanted, or what others thought, was- due to his conviction that he was absolutely right. Can the prophet, after all, have any doubts?

§ Lewis Mumford: The New Urban Order

Mumford added greater social realism to the visionaries' argument.[34] He was more aware than most of economic forces and social ideologies and their effect in shaping the city. For that reason, his analysis of the "new urban order" was sociologically informed. He showed little patience with the social engineers and architectural planners who have become so hypnotized by their own goals that they show little understanding of the existing environment from which they must begin.

I have selected Mumford for balance, to exemplify the more realistic dimensions of the visionary type. *The Culture of Cities*, both as urban history and as a sociological analysis of the contemporary city, is exceptional. Mumford, of course, is not alone in possessing realism, but, more than anyone else, he has combined his realism with an understanding of the city, and expressed it in a book that deserves its rank as a classic. Arthur B.

Gallion, for example, in *The Urban Pattern*,[35] has presented an urban history that is as informed and as sociologically realistic as Mumford's, yet in his analysis of the contemporary city Gallion seems to have forgotten the social variables he specified at the beginning, and he assumes the utopian mentality. In somewhat similar fashion, Percival and Paul Goodman, in *Communitas*,[36] have shown an exceptionally keen understanding of the forces of urban society, and they have incorporated that understanding into a standard by which to evaluate the plans of others. Their own plan for the future city tends, however, to fall short when measured against the same standard. This is due, I strongly suspect, to the fact that any plan for a future city must avoid many aspects of social, economic, and psychological relevance. It is impossible, it would seem, to to take all of these factors into account. The Goodmans try to guard against this by insisting upon the flexibility of their plan and upon its suggestiveness rather than its concreteness, as did Howard before them. Even so, it seems that The Plan must raise more problems than it solves.

It is not Mumford's history of urbanism that is my concern, but rather his analysis of what he has called the "social basis of the new urban order." Mumford began with an inventory of the architectural and sociological components that are available today for urban reconstruction. Modern architecture, he argued, has new materials to use and a wide engineering knowledge upon which to depend. Even more important, these new materials as the products of a "collective economy" are meant to be used by all persons; "one's economic position may entitle one to a greater or smaller quantity, but the quality is fixed." [37] "Collective largesse," not niggardliness, is the hallmark of our industrial civilization; what the Goodman's have aptly labeled a "technology of surplus." In short: the materials are available for urban reconstruction and in sufficient quantity and quality. Furthermore, architectural knowledge is also at hand to make use of these materials.

Modern hygiene has given us the knowledge not only to combat disease but to prevent it. The city of the future, unlike the city of the past or of the present, could now be built as a life-supporting environment. What has been learned from the past is that health is a collective responsibility: water and waste disposal, for example, have become the accepted responsibilities of urban governments. More important for the future, however, positive attitudes toward health and hygiene have become dominant, and the life-destructive environment of the city will not be readily tolerated. "The drift to the suburbs," Mumford contended as early as 1938, "which has been one of the most conspicuous features of the growth of cities during the past half century, was one response to the more constant concern with health and education that has characterized the life of the middle classes." [38] Perhaps so, but the wider emphasis upon health is certainly not misplaced.

The prolongation of youth is another value emphasized on the contemporary scene. In the earlier decades of industrialism, youth was cut short by child labor, and life itself was shortened by a studied avoidance of concerns with safety and the basic requirements of health. At present, however, the emphasis has changed; youth is prolonged through education, through sports, and through the medical gains that have prolonged life generally.

Another value that has undergone change has been the open-hearted acceptance of the new, as if for its own sake. It is a quality that Mumford called "the capacity for renewal," a positive willingness to look to the future rather than to the past for our direction. The monument has lost its significance for the contemporary city where men no longer glorify the past or allow themsleves to be chained to it. "Instead of being oriented, then, toward death and fixity, we are oriented to the cycle of life, with its never-ending process of birth and growth and renewal and death." [39]

The rejection of the monuments of the past has been coupled with the rejection of uniformity in man himself. From an interest in caste, we have turned to an interest in the individual personality. Even though occupation, regional background, or other major social categories may direct personalities toward conformity, the individual still retains a uniqueness and a character that has come to be idealized in the present. At the same time, Mumford argued, socialization has been an equally dominant demand; that is, an appreciation for the collectivity and for what it can add to the real meaning of individual liberty. The "dogmas of private property and individual liberty" of a century or more ago overlooked the highly central role that society must play in creating and guaranteeing such liberties.

The effect of these changes and conditions has been to give us the social philosophy, the technology, and the material means to alter our environment. What is more, the city can be altered to benefit more than just the few. The mode of existence that was once thought to be the natural privilege of only the aristocracy is now available to all as their right.

This, then, is the meaning of the change that has been slowly taking place in our civilizaion since the third quarter of the nineteenth century. The increase of collectivism, the rising of municipal and governmental housing, the expansion of co-operative consumers' and producers' associations, the destruction of slums and the building of superior types of community for the workers—all these are signs of the new biotechnic orientation.[40]

The change has been abetted by education, which has become as vital for the modern city as religion was for the medieval city. Through education, the masses can be transformed into intelligent individuals seeking to achieve common ends through cooperation and understanding. The transformation is, of course, still incomplete, primarily because we still treat education as a mass commodity rather than as a more individualized and private experience. The desired conditions for education become "small groups, small classes, small communities; in short, institutions adapted to the human scale."

Mumford has specifically noted that the social forces he has described as "bases of the new urban order" are not all operative. The gap between the present and the future as he foresees it is still there. This kind of recognition has made Mumford unique among the visionaries. When confronted with the fact of the contemporary city, he does not abandon the understanding he has shown in his earlier analysis of urban history. The same complex forces must be assessed in reading change into the future. Mumford has said himself that

social facts are primary, and the physical organization of a city, its industries and its markets, its lines of communication and traffic, must be subservient to its social needs. Whereas in the development of the city during the last century we expanded the physical plan recklessly and treated the essential social nucleus, the organs of government and education and social service, as mere afterthoughts, today we must treat the social nucleus as the essential element in every valid city plan.[41]

The plan for the future city, then, must take account of social relationships and must be cognizant of the functions meant to be served by the planned urban arrangements of the future. The point that most visionaries have consistently overlooked is that their own personal values, no matter how sincere, are simply not legitimate grounds upon which to insist that the city be recreated. Instead, as Mumford was at great pains to explain, the social needs and desires of the urban community must themselves be part of the equation and must provide the grounds for rebuilding. Neither can architectural design be used as the sole, or even primary basis for rebuilding the city. This argument is but a variation on past arguments—justly held in moral contempt—by which the factory and its demands were allowed to dictate the character of the urban environment. The emphasis by architects on, say, the functional home rather than upon the functional needs of a society—whatever they are—is misplaced and just as unfortunate as the tragic, misplaced emphasis in the last century on industrial, as opposed to social, development. Is Wright's design for urban living any more realistic, desirable, or democratic than what has emerged during the past century in a city catering to the demands of industry? Neither the nineteenth century's or Wright's solution has given fair voice to the people and their desires. The means taken to achieve a goal, as John Dewey has emphasized repeatedly, is itself part of that goal and will inevitably determine it. In the present context, then, the visionary's authoritarian insistence upon his plan cannot lead to democratic consequences. It is this kind of error that Mumford has avoided, in large measure, because he has been content to show the needs rather than to draw the plan itself.

§ Conclusions

The visionary has made several contributions to a sociology of the city. Behind the plans he has expounded, behind his sustained note of protest and his prophecies of urban doom—from metropolis to necropolis—there are to be found ideas that are integral to an understanding of the city. Social scientists, uncomfortable perhaps with the artistic language of the visionary and unwilling to understand the nature of his protest, have therefore omitted from consideration an important segment of information about the urban environment.

The visionary has succeeded even better than the social scientists in indicating the multiplicity of factors that, in effect, create the city as we know it. In some cases the visionary has done this explicitly. All three visionaries discussed here, for example, have shown a lively comprehension of the city's industrial roots. That these have not been sufficiently detailed is as much an indication of the limited understanding we all possess as of shortcomings peculiar to the visionary alone. In other instances, the visionary has shown the complexity of the urban environment implicitly, by the naïveté of his plans and by his failure in trying to realize them. Human motivations and human needs have most obviously been overlooked in many of the plans of the visionaries, or else have been seriously oversimplified. That people want to live in small communities and want to get back to nature is by no means an established fact, yet the visionary frequently assumes it to be so. A more proper balance can be provided by the sociologist in this respect from his knowledge of social values and social norms. However, even the sociologist frequently has been naïve in appreciating the urban complexity that he has chosen to study.

Beside the motivations of the individual there must be considered the structure of society itself. Political organizations and allegiances must inevitably become involved in any planned urban change, for the alteration sooner or later calls for a shift in the existing constellations of power. Similarly, the profit motive and the economic structure are implicated. Either the change must show a profit for those willing to support it or it must be convincingly shown that change is necessary for survival. Rarely do the visionary's plans satisfy the former condition, and as of now, they do not satisfy the latter condition, except for an elite group of disciples. What the visionary's failures give the social scientist should be an appreciation for the social mechanisms that he is trying to understand. Even though the scientist's immediate interest may not be in planned change, this evaluation of the visionary should contribute a measure of understanding of the factors involved. The studies of utopias are sociologically relevant not because of an interest in utopias, but because of an interest in the reasons why they fail. A morbid conclusion, perhaps, but true.

One final point: The study of the city carries with it, often implicitly, a social ideology and a social philosophy. The visionary has not run from protest but, on the contrary, has been eager to make his protest evident. Sociologists, on the other hand, disciplined in the need for objectivity, often let such values creep in the back door, as they stand at the front door proclaiming their objectivity. For years, although increasingly less so now, sociologists, nostalgic for a return to a rural way of life, studied the city critically and angrily. Even urban ecologists, as will be shown, made much of the objectivity of their methods. Yet their analysis often overlooked one of their own basic value assumptions: that the city was the result of economic rationality. Objectivity in science is necessary; about that there is little dispute. However, such objectivity is achieved not by hiding one's biases and refusing to look at them, but by recognizing them openly so that they do not clutter one's conclusions.

The industrial city, as the visionaries have shown, is an historical product of values that lie at the core of our civilization. It is inconceivable that any serious study of the city can avoid recognizing those values.

iv

THE EMPIRICISTS:
CLASSIFIERS
OF CITIES

THE CITY is a challenge, not only to practitioners and planners but also to social scientists. Even in the face of all its complex organization, size, and variety, urban society still needs to be understood. Given the dominance of urban society, it is all the more important that it be understood by social science. To the sociologist especially, the city as a social phenomenon has to be systematically understood by sociological theory and integrated with other facets of sociological inquiry. Indeed, there are few areas of sociology that are not touched by the facts of urban society.

The theoretical problems in the study of urban society are, in their own way, no easier to solve than the practical problems that occupy practitioners and visionaries. Although no human society is simple, the society of the industrial city is by all odds the most complex. Apart from the problems posed by size and heterogeneity, urban society is complicated to study because its elements are always changing; for the city belongs to the world community and is sensitive to the alterations in human affairs wherever they occur.

In our typology the empiricist is more interested in problems of theory than of practice and relies primarily on quantitative information to develop that theory. This reliance distinguishes him from the theorist, who insists that theoretical (i.e., qualitative) propositions—whether or not based on empirical data—come first. Measurement can make sense, the theorist contends, only when the theoretical framework has specified what is to be measured and why. Although this distinction is not always an absolute one of either-or, there is an unmistakable difference in emphasis between the two orientations.

Two types of empiricists can be identified. The first includes those who devise classifications of cities according to some index; the second, the ecologists to be discussed in the following chapter, who combine empirical techniques with attention to the theory that underlies the techniques.

§ The Rationale for Classification

Classification is one way of identifying patterns of similarity among events that would otherwise seem unrelated. It is probably the simplest technique, especially in social science, to reduce some subject matter to workable and practical limits. Classification, however simplified, is not arbitrary. It depends on theory to define the limits of interest, to relate that which is classified to other categories used in a science, and to make explicit the basis for classification. Not every classification, of course, is scientifically relevant, but every science depends upon some classification or other. On scientific grounds, then, there is strong support for a classification of cities as a means of study.

There is an even more obvious rationale for urban classification. Anyone who has been in at least two cities and has speculated on the differences between them, in effect, imagines an index to classify their differences and similarities. Size, for example, is a most obvious index; it impresses even the casual student of the city. Others prefer more abstract or impressionistic criteria, such as pace or "feel," whether the city is cosmopolitan or provincial, friendly or cold, raw or genteel, noisy or quiet. The selection of an index is limited only by one's imagination and ability to explain it.

Two kinds of indices that have been mentioned—size and impression—show in microcosm the dilemma faced by the social scientist who wants to classify cities. Size is a convenient index because it can be measured, yet it does not directly convey a sense of the quality and character of the city. Impressionistic criteria, on the contrary, catch the tone but are hard to define and to measure. The same difference exists between a poem by Sandburg or MacLeish about the city and a census report.

Artistic standards are open to disagreement, but the requirements for a good index are not.

1. *An index should be measurable.* This means not only that the units can be measured, but also that the index possesses other characteristics of a metric. For one thing, it should be objective in that its application is reliable and does not depend on the idiosyncratic judgments of the user. Anyone applying the index should get substantially the same results. The index should be standardized; that is, any unit of the index should be equal to any other in the way one degree on a thermometer is equal to any other, no matter where the measure appears on the scale. Finally, the index should be unambiguous, so that only the defined characteristic is measured, and is measured according to the definition given it by the index.

2. *It should be relatively fixed and constant.* This requirement is self-explanatory. There is little utility in an index that needs constant adjustment. For example, an index used in the last decade to classify cities should be as applicable today if it is to serve its function efficiently. Some classifications devised in the past have become outdated and therefore useless for comparisons. It should be evident that change is an inevitable condition of the

urban environment and any system of classification must contend
with it. Little is achieved, other than what the scientist learns
from error, by constructing an index that is outmoded by changing events.

3. *It should have functional relevance.* An index, to be
scientifically useful, whether it be a thermometer or a cost-
of-living index, must relate meaningfully to some area of
scientific concern. In the same way, an index that purports
to measure one or several urban characteristics should fit into
a theoretical framework. The variables that comprise the index
should be functionally related within urban society in a way
that makes sense. Otherwise, there would be little point in
making the measurement. There are probably many characteristics of cities that might be measured, but only those whose
relevance for a sociological theory of urban society can be
demonstrated are valuable. The number of people who live in
a city is a sociological characteristic that is potentially relevant,
but the annual rainfall is not. Further, to what and how the
index is relevant should be specified. All too frequently an index
is presented only with the hope that someone will find a use
for it.

4. *It should include as many important characteristics as are
needed.* Obvious or not, this point needs to be made: If too
many variables are included in an index it becomes more cumbersome than useful and does not increase its validity. There is,
ideally, a marginal number of variables which give an index its
maximum utility, and further additions do not increase its utility
to a commensurate degree. Call this last requirement the marginal
utility of an index. Variables that correlate highly with one another do not add any greater predictive power to an index and
should be eliminated. Where possible, then, the index should
depend upon a minimum number of variables that are not correlated with one another but that do in their combination account for the most relevant characteristics of urban society.

The purpose of this chapter is to describe some of the better
known indices for urban classification. Each one depends upon
different variables, yet the intent and the rationale behind them

is the same: to classify cities according to one or more characteristics, so as to comprehend better the dynamics of urban
society and to simplify the apparent complexity of cities.

§ Population Size

The simplest way to grasp the character of a city is by its
size, which also implies density: Just how many people live
there? Size is objective, capable of being measured, and sociologically relevant. The difference between a metropolis of millions and a town of thousands is sharp and sociologically
suggestive.

Size has sociological relevance and it is little wonder that it
has been used so often as the basis for an urban index. When
extremes are considered, size shows a satisfying functional relationship to social phenomena. For example, the greater variety
of activities available in the metropolis than in the town is in
part a function of the number of people who live in each.
Where there are a lot of people even the most esoteric interest
or activity can find enough supporters to become organized,
simply on the basis of probability.

Some defense has also been made for size as an index in more
subtle contexts. The rigid social control of the small town
through its intimate network of gossip and ridicule, it has been
argued, depends upon a personal familiarity that is only possible
in small groups. Beyond a certain number, however, this technique of social control is impossible. The metropolis, it is concluded, achieves its features of anonymity and impersonality by
its very size.

Such generalizations would seem to endow the differences of
size between cities with great promise as a sociological index.
But the final test of its usefulness depends more on its sensitivity to all differences, not just the differences between extremes. We need to know more about the function of size if it
is to be valid as an index for urban society.

One of the most detailed and systematic inventories of the

relationship between population size and urban characteristics
was that undertaken by Duncan and Reiss, using 1950 census
information.[1] A principal argument they advanced was that the
size of a city produced variations according to three sets of
factors: (1) selective migration, (2) family organization and
function, and (3) economic structure and function. To sub-
stantiate their argument they classified cities and other areas into
the following categories:

> Urbanized areas
>> 3,000,000 or more
>> 1,000,000 to 3,000,000
>> 250,000 to 1,000,000
>> Under 250,000
>
> Places outside urbanized areas
>> 25,000 or more
>> 10,000 to 25,000
>> 2,500 to 10,000
>> 1,000 to 2,500
>> Under 1,000 (incorporated)
>
> Other rural
>> Nonfarm
>> Farm

Next, they ordered a number of census variables into the eleven
size classes shown above. These variables generally were grouped
into one of the three sets. Variations, they then suggested, would
be considered as due to differences in size. Hence, concerning
selective migration, they found that large cities were more
attractive than small cities for long-distance migrants. As a result,
large cities were characterized by having disproportionately
more females and more young people, for these groups show
greater migration, and by having greater ethnic diversity than
places of smaller size. These characteristics were found to vary
consistently according to the size of the urban community.

The second complex of factors, family organization and functions, similarly was found to be related to size. Generally, the
larger the community, the smaller was the proportion of those

75 The Empiricists

married, the greater the proportion of women working, and the greater the number of specialized agencies competing with the family "in the performance of its traditional functions." Finally, as pertains to the economic structure, Duncan and Reiss found that here too size was relevant: The larger the community, the greater was the proportion of those in white-collar jobs, the higher the median income, the higher the median rent, and the greater the similarity between occupational distributions for males and females.

This brief summary of relationships that were found between the size of a place and some of its other characteristics should be enough to convey the way that size can be used as an index. There is little question that the Duncan and Reiss findings, as well as those of similar studies, point to some social and economic concomitants of urban size. Further, such characteristics as those specified by Duncan and Reiss corroborate one's impressions that, on the face of it, there would seem to be some reason for more exhaustive studies along these lines, in the anticipation that size could yield a valid and useful urban index. In fact, however, a close evaluation of size as an index points up several inherent limitations to its use. Duncan and Reiss's findings are more an indication of the best that can be expected than of the worst. Attractive as size may seem to the urban analyst because of its simplicity, he would do better to seek other measures.

The use of populaton size as an index has led to singularly limited, often obvious, findings about urban society. One reason perhaps for the reluctance to admit the unproductiveness of size as an index is because it seems so obvious and so real. Cities are big and their bigness is their most distinctive mark. No one argues that. The point is, however, that the differences between cities are more than differences of numbers. We already know that cities are big; the point is to make this fact tell us something more. If several decades of study on just this question are worth anything at all, it is in the realization that size has but very limited scientific utility.

For one thing, other factors confound the significance of population size as a sociological variable. A small town, say of 3,000 people, that is fifteen miles from a large metropolis is hardly to be considered as rural. In fact, that suburb is probably more urban, by any criterion, than a much larger city isolated in a farming region. But even this difference is less frequent today in highly urbanized countries, where the influences of the metropolitan centers are felt everywhere. Fewer small places are socially isolated, and the national effects of the market, national politics, and the values disseminated by the mass media render the differences in size or location less important. Thus, the Iowa farmer and the New Yorker are closer than they have ever been before. We find in countries like the U.S. or Great Britain that rural isolation, and with it rural attitudes, has disappeared for all practical purposes. The conclusion suggested by such changes is that a size index alone is inadequate to differentiate between the sociological characteristics of cities. It could perhaps be said that cities are conforming to a norm and, therefore, any index must be inadequate. It is more likely the case, however, that the differences have become too subtle to be identified simply by how big or small cities are.

Another fact that confounds the use of population size as an index is that social differences between cities, such as the distribution of power or race relations, need have no reference to size, yet they are highly relevant for our subject. The cultural history of a city, the unique events that have turned a city's development in one direction rather than in another, the ethnic pattern of its immigration—all of these developments have occurred without reference to size, but certainly comment upon the social character of cities.

Finally, there is an inherent methodological difficulty in the use of size as an index. The difficulty arises from the imperfect correlation between size and most of the characteristics it has been used to index. An increment of size does not always bring with it a corresponding increment in the other variables being compared. True, in general, as size increases so does a related characteristic, but very rarely with the regularity that size per-force does. For example, one characteristic associated with size is the percentage of white-collar workers. According to Duncan and Reiss the calculations based on the 1950 U.S. census showed the following relationships:

Table 1—Distribution of Clerical and Kindred Workers
in the United States by Size of City

Size of Place	Per Cent Clerical and Kindred Workers in Labor Force	Difference Between Per Cent and Entry Below It
Urbanized Areas		
3,000,000 or more	17.8	0
1,000,000 to 3,000,000	17.8	1.1
250,000 to 1,000,000	16.7	2.1
Under 250,000	14.6	1.0
Places outside urbanized areas		
25,000 or more	13.6	1.6
10,000 to 25,000	12.0	1.4
2,500 to 10,000	10.6	1.5
1,000 to 2,500	9.1	.9
Under 1,000 (incorporated)	8.2	

Reprinted with permission from Otis D. Duncan and Albert J. Reiss, Jr., *Social Characteristics of Urban and Rural Communities, 1950* (New York, John Wiley and Sons, 1956), p. 96, Table 33.

The percentages obviously increase reading up from the smallest town to the largest metropolis. As the last column indicates, however, the increase is irregular. The addition of about three-quarters of a million persons to a community is associated with a 2.1 per cent increase in the proportion of white-collar employees. Add another million people and the increase is just about one per cent, after which there is no increase at all in the proportion of white-collar workers.

The conclusion should be clear that size as an index of urban differences has only limited potential, and is more enlightening when comparing extremes—the metropolis and the small town—than the more numerous instances in between. An additional problem is the arbitrary assignment of the size intervals. Such arbitrary divisions are inevitable but they destroy the continuity of size as a meaningful variable. This means that one person can make the difference in whether a city is assigned to a category, say, below 250,000 or one above that figure.

§ Economic Function

The economic character of the city is almost as evident as its size. It has also been studied with almost the same frequency. The architecture of the city's economic activity is apparent in its factories, banks, office buildings, ball parks, restaurants and retail stores. The city, and especially the metropolis, is a specialized economic environment distinctively concentrated in the secondary and tertiary industries of manufacturing and service. This feature has been recognized, of course, as have been the consequences for the labor force, credit institutions, population movement, working hours, and the like. Some of the particulars of an urban economy have been well described in the *New York Metropolitan Survey;* it deals with an atypical city, but is an informative survey nevertheless.

No one would dispute the economic distinctiveness of the city as compared with the small town or hamlet any more than they might dispute the distinctiveness of size differences. However, as with size, there is no unanimity about how economic functions may be used as an index to differentiate between cities.

Again, as in the case of size, immediate impressions lend support to the plausibility of an economic index. Pittsburgh is different from Miami Beach, and both differ from Washington, D. C. A handy explanation is the dominating economic activity that establishes the particular flavor of each: steel, tourists, or government. Moreover, each type of industry makes its distinctive social demands from the community for the skills it needs, the education and training of personnel, and the types of community services that are emphasized. Washington, heavily populated with clerical and professional employees, offers services and activities attuned to the tastes of educated people with fixed incomes. Similarly, a resort city needs to provide those services that can attract tourists and that can induce them to spend their money. In other words, cities have to stay in whatever business gives them a special character.

Following from this reasoning, several studies have moved to construct economic indices to characterize cities and thereby to objectify these preliminary impressions. One interesting analysis by P. Sargant Florence has related economic functions to size, arguing that some activities can only be supported by cities of a certain minimal size.[2] For example, book publishing, the applied arts, and services to business establishments are to be found primarily in metropolitan areas, i.e., cities with over a million people. Wholesaling and newspaper publishing, however, can be found in cities between 200,000 and 1,000,000 population. Middle-sized cities—25,000 to 200,000—can support commercial printing, professional services, and construction activities. Economic efficiency is the guiding principle behind the location of these and other economic activities.

Attempts at further specification have been made under the general principle outlined above. The sociologist is interested in the comparative study of urban economic functions because it may be possible to derive some social consequences from a classification of economic functions in the city. However, the potential utility of such an index is limited almost from the start because many cities cannot be classified unequivocally. In addition, the classification is often quite arbitrary. Two of the best studies are by Chauncy D. Harris [3] and Grace M. Kneedler.[4] They used similar methods and differed mainly in their definitions of what was a "dominant economic activity." Each used employment figures and occupational distributions, the first taken from the census of manufactures, the second from the population census. Harris used 1930 information; Kneedler, data from 1940, but that difference is unimportant here.

Harris and Kneedler each began by specifying, arbitrarily, the minimum percentages needed in an economic sector in order to classify a city. Kneedler, for example, considered a manufacturing city as one with 50 per cent or more of the labor force employed in manufacturing, trade, or service activities. Harris, instead, distinguished two types of manufacturing cities: one in which manufacturing had at least 74 per cent of all those employed in manufacturing, retailing, and wholesaling and the second in which at least 60 per cent were so engaged. In another instance, Kneedler designated a wholesale trade city as one which had 25 per cent of the labor force in wholesale trade, but Harris settled for 20 per cent as the minimum.

Nothing is to be gained by further detailed comparisons. The examples should convey the general content and method used for classification. It might be informative, however, to present the classification of cities that each developed.

Harris	*Kneedler*
Manufacturing Cities (M' and M subtypes)	Manufacturing
Retail Centers	Industrial
Diversified Cities	Wholesale Trade
Transportation Centers	Retail Trade
Wholesale Centers	Diversified Cities
Mining Towns	Educational Centers
University Towns	Government Centers
Resort and Retirement Towns	Mining
	Transportation Centers
	Amusement or Health Resorts
	Dormitory Towns

The two classifications correspond fairly closely with one another even though Kneedler has more categories. Significantly, the category of "diversified cities" is used as catchall in both classifications to allow for those cities with no single dominating economic activity. In both classifications, therefore, Chicago and New York were classified as diversified because neither is primarily in any one economic field, as is true for a good many large cities. Yet, one would have wanted precisely those cities properly classified. Such omissions must be counted against the value of an economic index.

For sociological purposes a classification of cities by economic activity does not measure up well. The method of achieving a classification is too arbitrary. The discriminating proportion is apparently specified with some insight, but it is hard to justify the use of one figure rather than another. Hence, Kneedler calls a university town one with a college enrollment of 20 per cent or more of the city's permanent population, but Harris requires 25 per cent as the critical proportion. Perhaps five per cent is not worth the argument, but such differences do not inspire confidence in the index.

Another objection to an index of economic functions is that it comes out weakest where it is needed most and strongest where the classification is already quite obvious. Resort towns, educational centers, and government centers really are not much of a problem for classification. But the diversified cities are, and it is in these that the sociologist is most interested because they contain the most suggestive social complexity.

It is not at all clear that even with an acceptable index of economic functions we have learned much more about the social organization and social life of a city. Presumably, with the economic index other related urban features would emerge and some pattern of relationships would be the reward. Are there differences, say, in social cohesion between a manufacturing city and a wholesale trade center? What are the differences of social organization of a university town as compared with a resort center? Does the temporary residence of a large proportion of the population in both types make them alike or are there other factors, for example, money spent, that makes for significant differences? Perhaps the sociologist needs to take the matter up from here but he has not done so, I suspect, for good reasons that are related to the limitations of the index itself.

§ Occupational Distribution

The sociologist's dissatisfaction with an index of economic functions pointed toward an index that was, at once, more specific as regards economic activity and more directly sociological. An index of occupations seemed, therefore, inevitable. Occupations were reflections of economic functions and lent themselves more to the vocabulary of the sociologist. Everyone ought to know by now that occupations are correlated with such socially relevant facts as income, education, taste, and community participation.[5] It would seem to be a short step to construct an occupational index so as to distinguish cities sociologically. Cities populated mostly by professionals, managers, and white-collar workers ought to be different from cities that housed mainly skilled and unskilled workers.

Paul Gillen, in a study accurately entitled *The Distribution of Occupations As A City Yardstick*,[6] set for himself the task just described. From differences in occupational distributions he wanted to find differences that would indicate "the relative levels of various municipal functions such as education and health, for example." As Gillen stated the problem: "The device must be capable of uniform application to any city, regardless of size, location, type, age, or any other consideration. Simplicity of derivation and marked convenience of use must characterize the instrument. . . . The yardstick therefore, must be of such nature that it is basic to all that goes on in a city—in short, it must be involved in any important consideration respecting a city and its functioning." [7] The aim was admirable and worthwhile; the sophistication noteworthy.

Gillen surveyed 1,075 American cities which had 10,000 or more persons in 1940. He calculated the proportions of the employed labor force in each of nine occupational categories used by the census: professionals, semiprofessionals, proprietors and managers, clerical and sales, craftsmen and foremen, operatives, domestic services, other services, and finally, laborers. Next, he transformed these proportions into occupational scores, based upon a weighted income measure for each occupation and the overall distribution of occupations. In addition, Gillen also divided the cities he studied into four groups based on size in order to keep size constant.

Groups	Cities	Population
I	91	100,000 and over
II	107	50,000 to 99,999
III	213	25,000 to 49,999
IV	664	10,000 to 24,999

The first purpose of the occupational score was to index "fundamental" differences between cities, and Gillen set out to show how well the index worked in this regard. He did this by comparing occupational scores with other measures. Hence, the correlations between occupation and education ranged from .68 to .90 where 1.0 would be perfect. Occupations and infant mortality correlated from a negative .65 to a negative .70. Cities that contained more people in the "good" occupations tended to have lower infant mortality rates and higher educational achievements than did cities with people concentrated in the lower ranges of the occupational hierarchy. Similar relationships were found between occupational distributions and the proportion of white persons, as well as with the average rents paid.

Unfortunately, after this reasonable start, Gillen did not carry his discussion beyond suggestions for a classification. He suggested that a classification combining occupation, health, and education be devised. One wonders, why the bother with the calculation of occupational scores, since these three measures are fairly highly correlated anyway. But this may be quibbling.

In sum, it would seem that little new came from the exercise. It did not offer a broad pattern for classifying urban differences. The main result has not been much more productive than the indices of population size and economic functions. Since classification of cities is not the final goal, it is hard to see the point of having several classifications.

§ Moral Integration

Moral integration is another kind of index, a composite one slightly different from those already described. It seems to originate in a dissatisfaction with the city as a human environment, and its dominant tone is one of moral uplift, aimed at welfare planners and public health officials, to help them improve conditions. The earlier rural bias, in which we are never far from the view that the city is really unhealthy, immoral, and impersonal, and ought to be changed, shines through such studies. Angell, having remarked that "the city has long been regarded as a sinkhole of iniquity," recognized that this was not true of all cities. The purpose of his study, therefore, was to know why some cities have such severe "moral disorganization" while others have not.[8] Or, as he stated near the end of his report: "What are its [the study of moral integration's] practical implications for those who wish to improve our cities? What help can the pure scientist interested in a natural phenomenon called moral integration give to those who have a practical, meliorative goal?"[9]

Angell's study of moral integration was derived from an earlier effort in the same direction by Thorndike[10] on the "G" or "goodness" scores of American cities. Thorndike combined thirty-seven items to measure a city's goodness, including such features as health, educational opportunities, public recreational facilities, literacy, and others that "ran the gamut from the average wage through the degree of support of the YMCA to the value of city-owned property." [11] The items Thorndike selected to study were those that he believed all "reasonable persons would regard as significant for the goodness of life for good people in a city." [12]

Angell's interest was in measuring the goodness of cities, which term he has translated into "moral integration." By moral integration he meant "the degree to which there is a set of common ends and values toward which all are oriented and in terms of which the life of the group is organized." "Solidarity" and "morale" might be taken as synonyms.

The reason for including Angell's work here is not its practical goal of guiding welfare officials, but its utility for a theory of urban sociology. The inescapable judgment is that the index of moral integration holds little promise for a broader urban theory. At best, the index might tell us which cities are or are not integrated, but never why such is the case. It is very much the latter question that urban theorists are interested in, the former only being a possible means to that end.

The moral integration index, computed for forty-three cities of over 100,000 population, was based on a combination of "welfare effort index" and a "crime index." The first index was justified by this hypothesis: "The greater the moral integration, the more the citizens would sacrifice their private interests for the public interest." This hypothesis was translated into a statistical measure based upon the amount of money raised for community welfare funds, the number of people who pledged money, and the number of families in the area, all compared with the yearly retail sales.[13] In short, the welfare effort of a community was measured by how much it contributed to welfare funds, by how many contributed, and how this amount compared with the money spent for private consumption.

The reasoning behind the crime index was: "The more the people of a community are knit together in a real moral order, the less they will violate one another's persons or property."

The crime index was a composite of the measures of rates for murder, non-negligent manslaughter, robbery, and burglary.

From these two then, welfare effort and crime, the moral integration index was constructed. The first, Angell believed was a positive measure of moral integration in the sense of measuring positive actions toward improving integration; the second, a negative measure in that crime signified an absence of moral integration.

From this procedure he concluded that the best integrated cities in 1940 were Rochester, Syracuse, Worcester, Erie, Milwaukee, and Bridgeport. The worst cities from the bottom up were Atlanta, Miami, Tulsa, Memphis, Jacksonville, and Portland (Oregon).

Armed with this data on moral integration, Angell carried his analysis further. He interviewed persons in four cities concerning their attitudes toward moral integration: how satisfied were they with the community, with the participation in civic affairs, with the respect shown for law, and with the extent of social contact between the different income, racial, and nationality groups. The last was taken as an index of interpersonal integration and it was found not to correlate very highly with the moral integration index—on the average only .29 for all four cities taken together. Apparently, as Angell has noted, "People can be friendly with one another without taking much responsibility for their common life."

Angell then correlated the moral integration score with other measures. Absentee ownership of industry correlated negatively (—.46) with the moral integration index. The reason was that small businessmen have more civic enterprise than big businessmen. The number of married women working was negatively correlated with moral integration (—.54). The reason was that working women are away from home and from their primary responsibility and hence are detrimental to moral integration. The proportions belonging to some church showed no relationship with moral integration, nor did income as measured by per capita retail sales. Immigration and emigration were negatively correlated with moral integration (—.49). The reason was that population movement makes for disorder and instability.

These findings, the conclusion must be, do not hold much

promise for a theory of urban society which could explain the dynamics of social existence in the city.

§ Social Area Analysis

As the name implies, social area analysis is a technique for identifying sections within a city, or what its users perhaps more descriptively call "urban subcommunities." Although it deals with only one city at a time, social area analysis still resembles the other classifications that have been described in that it seeks some unit of analysis upon which systematically to classify urban phenomena. That it relies upon census tract data for one city at a time, rather than upon data for entire cities compared with one another, turns out to make not much diffence in the resulting classification.

The basic unit for analysis is the census tract, which is a group of contiguous blocks in a city, arbitrarily drawn to contain about 4,000 persons and intended to be as socially homogeneous as possible. The decennial census in the United States reports population and housing characteristics by census tracts for all cities. It is upon this information that social area analysis depends. Both the Bureau of the Census and the users of its reports generally are aware of the inherent problems in census tract analysis, problems to which there are no real solutions. Although it is possible to define census tracts at the outset in such a way that they are relatively homogeneous for a range of social characteristics, time and the movement of population soon destroy that homogeneity. Yet, the obvious alternative, to draw new boundaries when such change occurs, would mean that no comparisons could be made from one census to the next. The result is that for many American cities, older tract boundaries are maintained to allow for comparison over time even though there is usually no longer much homogeneity within those boundaries.

This inevitable condition does limit social area analysis. Even using a smaller unit of census data such as the block is no answer, inasmuch as the census returns by blocks are limited to housing characteristics, for the most part, and do not provide information on inhabitants.

Another kind of arbitrariness enters into this type of analysis in the measures that are chosen to make up the index. Social area analysis depends primarily upon an arbitrary grouping of several census measures into some kind of index. This brings us right back to the criticisms about arbitrariness made of other indices.

One of the clearest examples of social area analysis is a study by Bell, one of the main exponents of this technique.[14] He arranged census information into three groups of economic, family, and ethnic characteristics and from these derived a list of measures to construct area indices. The "index of economic status" averaged measures of rent, education, and occupation. The "index of family" depended upon fertility ratios, women not in the labor force, and a ratio of single-family dwellings. Finally, the "index of ethnic status" was taken from information on race, nativity, and Spanish surnames. The various steps taken to convert the raw measures into a standardized score and from there into a single index need not concern us.

Again, the arbitrary character of the indices is a bothersome point that even the final results do not clarify. Presumably, the analyst selects items of sociological relevance, but these are defined by fairly broad limits. The number of measures used for any one index can be large since they are combined into a single standarized score, anyway. The number of indices, however, is limited by the practical consideration of just how many things can be juggled at one time. Furthermore, since one would like ultimately to have contiguous census tracts with roughly similar scores, the number of indices perforce has to be limited. Even with three index scores, as in the example described, it becomes necessary to group them within broader categories of, say, 25 points, in order to go on with any further analysis. Hence, tracts with an index of family score from 1 to 25 would belong to one category, from 26 to 49 to another, and so on through 100.

There seems to be some rather severe criticism, not so much on the statistical measures used as on the utility of social area analysis for urban study. On the first point, the issue might be raised that the manner of selecting the measures is arbitrary, but then, any form of classification is likely to be so. The more significant criticism of social area analysis comes with an evaluation of the measures it uses. Bell has made these claims for the analysis: "(1). It is simple in statement. (2) It serves as an organizing principle. (3) It is theory-linked; it permits the derivation of testable propositions. (4) It is precise in its specification; it permits observer agreement. (5) It represents a continuity with similar formulations which it aims to replace." [15]

The enumeration of claims sounds fairly modest, but then the claims are not especially relevant or new. Take the first two claims above. Any classification must at least have an organizing principle, otherwise, why classify? Simplicity is a good thing, but it is not of highest priority in scientific analysis. The fourth claim for precision, is once again an inherent feature of scientific classification. The problem is not so much one of being precise, but more one of what one is to be precise about. The third claim, that the technique is theory-linked, does merit attention. If Bell means that social area analysis can suggest further research, then surely this advantage is not potentially unique to social area analysis.

The value of the technique for a theory of urban society, however, has yet to be proven. [16] Aside from the usual, and by now, familiar, correlations between the index and other measures, there are no bases for the suggestion of theory. The criticism has been voiced by Duncan in his review of Shevsky and Bell's book on social area analysis.

The discussion of theoretical reasons for choosing particular index variables does not lead to a unique selection of variables or even to a useful criterion for such selection. The matching of statistical manipulation with conceptual formulation remains on the level of operational nominalism; this is clearly shown by the fact that the authors do not even agree between themselves on what to call their "constructs." Moreover, little attempt is made to tie in the notion of "social area" . . . with any of the "underlying theory." *It is a purely classificatory concept.* [17] [Italics added.]

Bell's rejoinder does not deny the accuracy of the criticism made by Duncan. He has implied that classification is a form of theory but only by stretching the meaning of theory. Classification is necessary for the development of theory; it depends upon some implicit or explicit theoretical ideas; but it is not in itself scientific theory.

The last claim Bell has made, that social area analysis continues earlier formulations, is open to doubt because he gives no clear reference for what he has in mind. It does not, apparently, mean that social area analysis brings us closer to a systematic urban theory, as one would hope. Duncan's criticism is relevant once again.

The upshot of much of this research is that the point of diminishing returns is reached very soon in refining the technique of area delineation, unless one is working on specific hypotheses about area structure. Since the authors state no such hypotheses it can only be assumed that they intend their procedure to serve a variety of uses. With much less work one can establish a set of areas which will stratify a population well enough for most general purposes. Shevsky and Bell fail to show that their procedures have special advantages over others already in use.[18]

In summary, then, social area analysis is a somewhat different scheme for classification, but it is a classification nevertheless. It contains its own particular advantages and disadvantages, perhaps, but shares some of the more serious disadvantages with most other classification devices: the arbitrary manner of defining categories, and the lack of relevance for a broad theory. Like other systems of classification, it does have the advantage of some statistical precision and objective measurement as well as the ability to compress a great deal of data into a single composite score. However, these advantages lead us no closer to a theory of the city, valuable as they might be at a later point when hypotheses have been generated and proof becomes the next point at issue.

§ Conclusions

A balanced evaluation of the several attempts at urban classification must show that this entire line of study holds little promise, by itself, as a basis for a valid sociology of the city. The several indices discussed in this chapter represent, I believe, the best examples of urban classification and the most promising measures we have had to achieve it. It is not that the classifiers have lacked imagination or wisdom, but rather that the methodology of classification as used in these instances is too limited to be useful for the broader aims of an urban theory. The indices may prove useful later on, once a theory has been developed.

The major advantage that classification has offered, as it has been presented here, was its indices, which have been objective, measurable, and presumably reliable. The aim of any index, urban ones included, is to condense and simplify otherwise complex phenomena in a concise, objective, and reliable manner. This the indices have achieved reasonably well.

Arrayed against this single advantage are serious disadvantages. A major shortcoming of these classifications has been the failure to establish clearly the relevance of the index to the basic features of urban society. One could readily admit, for example, that the size of a city would appear to have direct consequences for the quality and character of the social environment; populous places are more impersonal, have a faster pace, and contain a greater variety of services than smaller cities. However, an index of size cannot firmly prove that generalization except at the extremes.

The advantages of simplicity were never realized in any of the measures here evaluated. It was as if the index itself became the object for statistical manipulation and all sense of its relevance as an index to something beyond itself was lost. There has been more involvement with technique than with the purpose of the index, more sharpening of knives than actual carving.

One conclusion that has emerged is that without a theory of the city, the concern with indices is premature. Perhaps when the structure of urban society becomes clearer, it may be possible to construct a type of index that works as it should, and to elucidate a relationship between the index and broader urban events. I am arguing basically for urban sociologists to recognize Whitehead's "fallacy of misplaced concreteness," to rise above what is empirically obvious and to consider abstract constructs as the way to bring understanding of urban society.

A second disadvantage, related to the first, is that none

of the indices devised for urban characteristics functioned properly as an index. One would expect that an index be able to chart the variations in the characteristics it measured in a regular manner. However, none of the indices really did. Although an index appeared to be regular and progressive, as in the case of population size, the regularity disappeared when the index was placed against the social phenomena it purported to chart. The correlation between size and phenomena it presumed to be related to it was always less than perfect and, therefore, erratic. Another example: Some cities did not seem to fit any categorization except when forced, as in the case of diversified cities according to the economic classification. In short, this failure detracted from the utility of the index.

A third disadvantage of these classifications was their unclear and uncertain purposes. Some of the indices, I would suspect, were derived from the knowledge that something was measurable rather than from any clearly formulated goal. The availability of statistics to measure the characteristics of cities is a consideration in the construction of an index, but it should not be the dominant one. The census in this manner has inadvertently become a drawback to sound analysis because the urban sociologist acts toward the census as a hungry man to a feast: something to be ingested quickly and without manners. Census information, however, is not always directly relevant and its promise of free statistics has to be approached cautiously. Perhaps the time has come for the urban sociologist to keep in mind the initial purposes of his study and, if necessary, to find his information in a way other than through the rich diet of the census volumes. By doing so he might even be in a position to suggest improvements in the handling of the census.

A final disadvantage of the indices is the lack of statistics over a reasonably long time period. Simple statistical measures such as size have, in 1960, eighteen censuses from which to draw in the United States. This is a mixed blessing because census definitions of urban have varied considerably over the period, in response to the changing pattern of urban settlement. In other measures, there has been little attempt to reapply the index in subsequent years. Time comparisons are vital to urban classification, if only to give some assurance that the relationships found today are somewhat lasting. It is possible to construct an index that appears to describe a set of data perfectly, only to find that it fails to take account of the inevitable changes that must come about.

Classification of cities, therefore, does not appear to be a useful line of inquiry in developing an urban theory. Working on the index before the theory is very much like putting the cart before the beast, with the added confusion of not knowing where the beast really is. The types of classification that have been described do provide information about the city in capsule form, but their limitations must be recognized.

v

THE ECOLOGISTS:
ANALYSTS OF
URBAN PATTERNS

HUMAN ECOLOGISTS, by the productivity of their research and by the caliber of their theoretical essays, have contributed much to our understanding of the city. In spite of its errors, ecology still is the closest we have come to a systematic theory of the city. So potent and so pervasive was the ecological point of view that it is fair to say that urban sociology in America really began with the ecologists, who combined theory with empirical research. In England, unlike America, the study of the city was closely tied to social welfare surveys, and in Germany, to theory and history.

Human ecology, as distinguished from plant and animal ecology, is concerned with the study of "typical constellations of persons and institutions" according to Robert E. Park, the innovator of this application of ecology and its most insistent advocate.[1] McKenzie, another early proponent of ecology, established as the aim of human ecology "to discover the principles

and factors involved in the changing patterns of spatial arrangement of population and institutions resulting from the interplay
of living beings in a continuously changing culture." [2] Neither
of these definitions by itself can mean much, nor can it convey
the scope of ecological study. The purpose of this chapter is to
describe the background out of which human ecology developed,
to analyze its application to the study of the city, and to evaluate
its success.

Let me admit at once that the ecologists do not fit com-
fortably into the empiricist category to which they have been
assigned in the typology of urban specialists. For one thing, they
possessed a theory that was broader and more sophisticated than
the attempted scientific rationales of other empiricists. Both the
early and the recent ecologists have not been addicted to measurement for its own sake. Instead, they developed a theory
within which the measurement of urban events became directed
and relevant. Yet, the ecologists should not be considered pure
theorists who aimed only to develop a set of abstract laws and
relationships. They observed, they counted, and they measured a
variety of urban phenomena to test their theory and to broaden
its range. More accurately stated, then, the ecologists bridge
the categories of empiricist and theoretician.

§ Intellectual Background

In 1916, soon after he came to the University of Chicago, Park
published an article in the *American Journal of Sociology* entitled, "The City: Suggestions For the Investigation of Human
Behavior in the Urban Environment." [3] This was the bench
mark for human ecology. The application of ecological theory
and methods to the study of the city was not accidental. It was
a straightforward projection of the ecological orientation which
directed one to look for natural patterns of spatial distribution.
Looking backwards, it is easy to see urban ecology implied in
plant and animal ecology and to see also how apparent was its
translation to human events. It is difficult, and possibly pointless,
to try to establish whether the interest in human ecology or in
the city as an ecological environment came first. Both were to

eventuate in the search for an urban pattern of social phenomena.
Certainly, the mixture of both motives was present in Park's
earliest comments. He wrote at one point: "I expect that I have
actually covered more ground tramping about in cities in different parts of the world, than any other living man. Out of all
this I gained, among other things, a conception of the city,
the community, and the region, not as geographical phenomenon
merely, but as a kind of social organism." [4]

Park was not alone in his view of society as a "kind of
social organism," although I do not mean that he fully accepted
an organismic view of society. Some sociologists during the first
decades of this century were attracted to the biological sciences, in which they saw a model for organizing their own
science. Some stretched the analogy to the extreme; society was
seen as a living organism that functioned according to the vital
processes of all organisms. For example, social pathology as
a concept and as a field of study derived from that era. Adaptation, social evolution, and function are concepts that still are
used and that originate from the same analogy. Other sociologists, including Park, turned to the biological sciences with
cautious enthusiasm. They entertained the analogy between
society and organism for the suggestions it might offer for
method and procedure, but they were never carried away completely by a view that social phenomena could be explained
by biological concepts. The sociologist's current excursions into
the vocabulary of communication theory probably is comparable. Ecology did not fail in this earliest period when it used
biological principles as a stimulus for methodological purposes,
however, but it failed later, for complex and uniquely sociological reasons.

The appeal of the biological model for social scientists is
understandable. Above all, there was the intellectual enticement
of applying Darwin's theory to social phenomena. Here was a
truly exciting explanation that seemed to account for so much
in the world of nature and that suggested dozens of counterparts in the social world. The impersonal, yet ultimately rational
forces that Darwin identified in nature seemed to find expression
in the social world with a tantalizing similarity. Certainly, social
forces were every bit as complex as the forces of nature. Cer-

tainly, it seemed they must operate according to some rationale and some pattern in the same impersonal way that Darwin had described. Analogies between society and biology were plentiful and each one seemed to make a *social* Darwinism that much more valid. The popular Darwinian concepts, the "struggle for existence," the "survival of the fittest," and a "biotic balance" apparently could be applied to society, and they seemed to fit so well. Unfortunately, some were carried away by this enthusiasm, and became slaves, taking dogmatically as invariable correspondence what was really no more than analogy, losing an understanding of the social material almost entirely. Although Park was not one of those, he came close to them at times in his ecological theory, and these instances were responsible for the final weakness of his theory.

The obvious fact that societies are composed of human beings, themselves "living organisms," probably also contributed to the appeal for sociologists of the biological model. Just as groups of cells combine and produce specialized organs, and as groups of organs combine to produce the human being, it seemed plausible, by another logical extension, that groups of people combined to produce society. By this reasoning, the study of society would become the final extrapolation of what was at root a biological datum.

Some impetus to accept biology must also have come from the sociologist's disillusionment with the trying metaphysics that had so occupied the field, a cumbersome explanation compared with the appealing simplicity of evolution. Psychologists had devised instincts to explain behavior, economists had their classical model, and, also following models from the sciences, sociologists in England, France, and Germany had begun to carve out some order in the complexity of social organization. So, too, Park and other American sociologists were trying to free sociology from philosophy and to align it with science. The biological model, for them at any rate, seemed to hold the best promise as a guide for sociology into the world of science.

When the smoke finally had cleared, it was evident that Park, his colleagues, and his students at Chicago had stimulated the most prolific, sustained, research effort that sociology had yet seen. They had enriched the literature on the city with theories of urban structure, urban process, and urban psychology, and with a series of descriptive monographs on the ghetto, the gold coast and slum, and the vice areas, as well as on such urban types as the hobo, the taxi-dance hall and burlesque show patron, and the hotel resident. The criticisms of the ecological school, and there were many, cannot detract from its immense productivity and the significance of the work it yielded.

The particular sector of the biological sciences to which Park and the human ecologists were attracted was that of plant and animal ecology, for these concretized Darwin's formulation about nature as an ecological process. This interest was consistent with the view that the natural world is a unity that moves according to regulated forces, which in turn are knowable because of the recurrent patterns that they create in nature.

According to this conception, the natural environment enforces an interdependence, now direct or now indirect, between all living things, each adapted to one another and to nature, as in terrain or climate. An environment is an organic unity, a "web of life." Although nature has no purpose, as we think of it, she does enforce consequences that give the impression of purpose. Any natural environment is impelled, so to speak, toward a "vital equilibrium" in which each living thing seems to move towards the most harmonious balance possible in relation to its environment. An analogy is a fish tank containing fish and snails. In a state of perfect equilibrium, which all devotees recognize as one in which the tank never seems to get dirty nor the water cloudy, there are only as many fish as the amount of water and its surface can supply with oxygen, and just enough snails to keep the sides of the tank and water clear. Add more fish, and the balance is upset, causing some fish to die. Add too many snails and they will outstrip their food supply. In the balanced fish tank, then, as in any natural environment, the interdependence of living organisms is as vital as it is delicate. The law of nature in this respect is an iron law from which there is no appeal; no species can exceed its food supply and all species must adapt themselves, to avoid extinction.

Ecological study of an environment thus includes a census of the species and organisms it contains, a tracing of the lines of interdependence, and a comparison over time of changes that have occurred.

The attraction of this line of study for human ecology lay in its simplicity. Questions of purpose, motivation or human will could, in a sense, be set aside so long as it could be shown that they yielded patterned consequences in spite of the diversity and supposed unpredictability of human volition. After all, the patterns in nature needed no reference to purpose, why should those of the social environment? In this way, the enormous complexity of individual psychology and social organization could be avoided. The social environment was to be studied in much the same manner as the natural environment, and the purpose was to discover regular patterns of social relationships. This did not deny that people were in fact motivated or that societies were organized according to other, more complex principles. Instead, the ecologist was to argue that motivation and social organization were not of first order priority for urban study. If necessary, they could be analyzed later, once the patterns they created had been analyzed. It was not to prove so simple, after all.

§ The Theory of Human Ecology

The debt of human ecology to plant and animal ecology is especially evident in the concepts that it used. In effect, human ecology had taken over ecological concepts and given them social equivalents.

Take the concept, "environment." In plant and animal ecology, the environment comprised an area that could be circumscribed, located, and within which natural processes were studied as part of a biological unity. The environment may have been a lake, a mountain range, a region, or any area that was relatively independent as a distinct natural locale. In human ecology, too, the environment had to be limited, so that there were reasonably clear social boundaries.

The city evidently met the boundary requirement exceptionally well, which was one reason, perhaps, why Park believed that an ecological study of the city held forth such promise for sociology. *Human* ecology thus became *urban* ecology. Although the city was tied to its surroundings and to the nation, as a community it was an independent entity and thereby an ecological environment. The city had a name; it had a fixed locale; and it had social meaning. Much more when Park wrote than today, the city was socially isolated. As Ernest Manheim has observed, "the city was an enclave." Farmers were not tied to the city by car, radio, or newspaper, and the boundaries between the city and the farm were as real as the Chinese Wall. So complete was the separation of the urban environment that, "the urban ecology which McKenzie and Park stimulated was designed to furnish an answer within the specific, restricted, urban frame of reference and without recourse to the American social system." [5] How logical, then, to designate the city as an ecological environment in the same manner as those designated by plant and animal ecologists!

Other environments that were so designated were the neighborhood and the region. For most ecological purposes these two were satisfactory, but they never possessed the sharp boundaries of the city, nor was the social unity in each so clear.

Hence, the human ecologist defined the city primarily as a natural environment. Within it he expected to study the effects of ecological forces and processes. Within it, he assumed, people and their social institutions would be interdependent. The city, in other words, was seen as an ecological unit in which patterns and processes could be discerned by the same techniques and from the same perspective as those in nature.

Another concept that human ecology borrowed from biological ecology was that of "natural processes." Competition was one such process, given substance in the natural world by the struggle for survival. Here an unceasing and inexorable ecological process by which each organism was pitted against the environment, other species, and even its own kind. Plants were in competition for nutrition, light, and space; animals, for food, water, and shelter.[6] Since the natural resources were limited, the competitive struggle continued, and the advantages gained by one necessarily were denied to the other. Similarly, the resources in the human environment also were limited, and the competitive struggle took place more at the social than at the biological level. Economic competition, in the lexicon of the ecologists, was the counterpart to biologic competition and had the same effects. In the city, as in nature, competition for limited resources meant that some group had to win.

Under the insistent pressure of competition, species evolved adaptations to improve their chances for survival. Each adaptation is subjected to test, for only those that enhance survival are successfully transmitted to subsequent generations. A similar consequence applies in society, as well. The division of labor, for example, can be considered as an adaptation for survival forced by economic competition. An occupational group (read: "species") establishes a monopoly over some activity by claiming its superiority. If the function is considered vital to the community's existence (healing the sick, teaching the young, administrating community affairs, investing money) and the group judged to be best equipped to do it, it is able to dictate demands, presumably for the general good, and at the same time to insure its own survival. Occupational organizations thus set standards for admission, for training, for practice, and for remuneration. The division of labor in society, like specialization in the natural world, can be considered as an adaptation for effective survival. For specialization is one way of insuring that the necessary work of a society is responsibly controlled and effectively completed.

Another ecological process that can be described is "dominance." In plant and animal ecology, the dominant "is an organism with such definite relations to climate and such significant reactions upon the habitat . . . as to control the community and assign to other species subordinate positions of varying rank." [7] The tallest trees, for example, are the dominants in a biotic community. In the urban community, industry and commerce are dominants in much the same way. The location of industry in the city inevitably colors and conditions the area which surrounds it, both in the use of land and in the classes of people who are attracted—or pushed—into the area. Before zoning restrictions, industrial location was very much a matter of economic demands alone. Once located, industry—its factories, its odors, and its wastes—set the character of the area and the people who lived within its shadow.

"Symbiosis" is another concept borrowed from plant and

animal ecology, to "denote a mutual dependence between unlike organisms," [8] nature's version of cooperation. A species that is the food for another reproduces itself in surplus to feed its predator, and still exist as a species. The predator, for its part, keeps the food species in balance by eating the surplus. In this way nature supports two different forms of life instead of one. In other instances, different species adjust to each other to such an extent that they come to evolve a harmonious and tightly interdependent relationship upon which they all depend for survival. "The dependence of herbivora upon bacteria to assist in breaking down the cells of plants taken into the stomach as food; the cooperation between certain plants and animals by which the animals are provided with fruit and the plants have their seeds scattered widely over the environment; the entrance of the little plover into the mouth of the crocodile to pick the blood-sucking leeches from the gums of that huge amphibian," these are all symbiotic relationships.[9]

Analogies are to be found in human communities among groups that are socially different. In the division of labor a symbiotic relationship exists between different occupations that contribute to each other's existence. Ethnic and racial groups within the city also can develop symbiotic relationships, less through conscious planning than through traditional cultural patterns. Although they differ in social position, more favorably placed ethnic and racial groups, under certain conditions, depend upon those lower in the hierarchy for their status superiority. After all, social superiority also means some one has to be considered as socially inferior.

Quite clearly, then, the concepts and orientation of plant and animal ecology were taken over into human ecology. However, what was needed and what Park supplied was the development of a suggestive analogy into a socially relevant theory. The human community, after all, is different from the natural community, no matter how numerous the analogies to be made. But, bearing this in mind, Park's purpose was to develop a rationale that would simplify the study of social organization and render it more amenable to analysis. To be sure, such is the aim of all theory. Park intended to construct an ecological theory and to claim ecology for effective sociological use.

Park went about this by dividing social organization into two levels: the biotic and the cultural. He recognized, of course, that these levels were interrelated, but stressed their analytical separation. At the biotic level, in the social as in the natural environment, competition was the guiding process. On the cultural level, communication and consensus between members of society were the distinctive processes. The guiding laws at the cultural level were those of tradition and the moral order; at the biotic, those of survival.

The cultural level, which Park called society, was in a sense a superstructure that depended on the biotic, or what Park called community. The two levels were connected so that what occurred at the lower had consequences for the higher. Furthermore, in human aggregates culture imposed restrictions upon the biotic level, which had to be met. "The cultural superstructure," wrote Park, "imposes itself as an instrument of direction and control upon the biotic substructure." [10] Ecological study, then, was to be at the biotic level, or community. The complexities of the cultural order, society, that is, were thereby avoided.

"A more practical reason [why sociological research begins with the community] is the fact that the community is a visible object. One can point it out, define its territorial limits, and plot its constituent elements, its population, and its institutions on maps. Its characteristics are more susceptible to statistical treatment than society." [11]

The attempt to cut out the complexity of society and to study what was the simpler entity would have been legitimate if one of two requirements had been satisfied: Either the biotic level had to be independent, or it had to reflect accurately what went on at the cultural level. Neither condition was true. Park's recognition of an interrelation between the biotic and the cultural was not enough. The relationship had to be specified, but that was really as difficult as studying the cultural level itself. "Human ecology is, fundamentally, an attempt to investigate the processes by which the biotic balance and the social equilibrium (1) are maintained once they are achieved and (2) the processes by which, when the biotic balance and the social equilibrium are disturbed, the transition is made from one relatively stable order to another." [12] Had the initial separation been supported by the facts, then the aim of human ecology might have been achieved.

Park's division of social organization into community and society needs to be detailed, because it is upon this division that the logic of his ecological theory finally depends.

Community, for Park, was a human aggregation living in a fixed, geographical locale and controlled by the subcultural processes of competition, cooperation, assimilation, and conflict. "Subcultural" means what it says: semi-natural laws. There is no need, at this level of analysis, to consider the thoughts, motivations, and values that bind people. Rather, aggregate actions, unencumbered by the effect of culture, are the only objects for study.

Population movement within the community is a good example. It can be measured and charted as an activity of the aggregate without giving any serious attention to the multiple forces that caused people to move. For the ecologist, it would be sufficient to describe the direction of movement and the characteristics of the migrants, such as their ages, sex, and the like. Or consider economic competition. The high price of land at the center of the city dictated the use to which land was put. Building of skyscrapers for offices was a direct consequence of land values in the business district; skyscrapers were a rational economic answer to high land costs. Similarly, the area around the central business district was in economic transition, dominated by rooming houses, cheap bars, and rundown hotels. Owners of land in this area, presumably, were waiting for the expansion of the business district to increase the value of their land holdings. In the meantime, they had no interest in improvements. Land values also directed residential movements. The middle and upper classes moved to the periphery of the city, while the lower class was caught in the slums.

Unlike the subtler features of culture, these aggregate features of the city, Park maintained, were accessible to study. Ecology need have but a minimal concern with the person, no more than the animal ecologist had with a single animal. What Park had attempted was a justification of this simplified approach to urban study, one separated from the usual psychological and sociological variables and modeled after plant and animal ecology.

This orientation is exemplified in the concept of the "natural area," defined as a geographic area the characteristics of which are determined by unplanned, impersonal, subcultural forces. "They are," Park wrote of natural areas, "the products of forces which are constantly at work to effect an orderly distribution of populations and functions within the urban complex." The slum, the ghetto, the industrial complex, and the central business district, all natural areas, were unplanned. They were consequences not of human design but of ecological processes such as competition. Furthermore, the unity of the natural area became further reinforced as the institutions and the individuals drawn into the area adapted to each other and to what finally became the dominant character of the area. The ghetto, produced by a constellation of ecological forces, was maintained by attracting precisely those inhabitants best fitted to live in it. "It is assumed . . . partly as a result of selection and segregation, and partly in view of the contagious character of cultural patterns, that people living in natural areas of the same general type and subject to the same social conditions will display, on the whole, the same characteristics." [13]

One aim of urban ecology, then, was to identify the natural areas of the city. With that inventory would come a picture of a city's social topography, all accomplished by dealing only with unplanned, aggregate effects of underlying cultural processes.

Society, on the other hand, was for Park a moral order based upon consensus. It comprised the cultural half of social organization. Society depended upon social solidarity, upon a common purpose as expressed in accepted cultural beliefs, and upon individuals acting collectively. The study of society required the analysis of the more complex features of behavior and organization. Society was a human characteristic, not found elsewhere in nature. It represented the uniquely human contribution to the ecological condition of nature. Social analysis, of course, was the eventual goal of the sociologist, but, Park maintained, that goal was best reached through ecological analysis.

Sociology . . . is primarily concerned with . . . the processes by which institutions develop and eventually evolve the specific and stable forms in which we know them. But customary cultural and moral relations are notoriously dependent on, and responsive to, political, economic, and, ultimately, those more elementary associations brought about by the sheer struggle for existence.[14]

The ecological study of the city, then, followed these paths of analysis: (1) the description of the characteristics of urban areas based on land use; (2) the description of the characteristics of the inhabitants of an area, by such variables as age, occupation, ethnic and religious backgrounds; and (3) the charting of changes both in population composition and in land use. Pursuit of these aims initiated the justly classic series of ecological studies of Chicago and its natural areas: the slums, the gold coast, the ghetto, hobohemia, the central business district, and many others.

§ The Ecology of the City

Probably the best known product of human ecological theory was its description of the city: particularly, the hypothesis of concentric circles which was developed by Burgess as an ecological map of Chicago, but was meant to apply to other American cities as well. This graphic description by Burgess was a high point of the ecological argument. The city, with all of its diversity, was reduced to a simple and suggestive pattern. With it, the urban sociologist could gain a toehold for any subsequent cultural analysis.

Visualize five circles, each larger than the one before it, and all with a common center. The smallest of these, Zone I, was defined as the "central business district" or, in the case of Chicago, the Loop. In this area where land values were highest were concentrated department stores, office buildings, banks, and any economic activity where profits were great enough to pay high rents. This area also contained amusement and service facilities, such as the better hotels, restaurants, and theaters. Zone I had the greatest number of people moving into and out of it each day, and it was the point of origin for most public transport. The central business district was the original area of settlement of the city, which explains its central position in the city's subsequent expansion.

Zone II, the "zone in transition," adjoined the central business district. Early in the city's history, it was a rural fringe that attracted the economically privileged citizens to once fashionable homes. The desire to live near but not in the center of the city obviously has had a long history in urban development. In time, however, the area deteriorated and was not reclaimed. Housing decayed and the population changed. The residences that remained, often solidly constructed, were converted into furnished rooms and were surrounded by cheap bars, flophouses, pawnshops, and houses of prostitution. Within this area, the city sought to contain the unwanted denizens and the undesirable marks of urban existence. The policy was successful up to a point, and the zone in transition remained one of the few areas where law enforcement was more lax, where strict morality was not demanded. Many activities that would not be permitted in any other part of the city found a welcome and profitable niche in the transition area.

The zone in transition best exemplified the ecological argument, and in many ways was a high point for that theory. For here was a natural area that had developed as a direct consequence of economic speculation, patterned, yet unplanned. Property owners were interested only in the profit they expected from the expansion of the central business district. These speculators had no interest in improving the area. Why spend money when the larger gain was to come from the land itself, not from its present use? The zone in transition, then, represented a future value. It was allowed to deteriorate, and consequently attracted only those residents who had no choice but to live there; they were followed by the services that would cater to them. To the transition zone came the petty criminals, bums, alcoholics, and drifters; the marginal minority groups that were denied better housing. In Chicago, in the middle 1920s, the transitional area contained the Jewish ghetto, the Italian Little Sicily, part of the Negro community, and Chinatown. As individuals from these groups were able to achieve a measure of economic stability and adjustment to the American urban culture, they moved.

Zone III was called the "zone of the workingmen's homes." As the name implied, it contained the inexpensive, small, frame homes of the working class. The character of the area was determined, usually, by the factory, such as the meatpacking district in Chicago. The predominant residents in the area were employees of the factory, and their settlement in the area was determined as much by convenience as by price in an essentially undesirable area. For some groups, migrating into the area and buying a home meant a move up in status, in economic security, and in an assimilation to American values.

Zone IV was one of "better residences." This was a middle-class area of good apartments and substantial private dwellings. Burgess said of this area almost thirty years ago, "This is the home of the great middle class with ideals still akin to those of rural American society." [15] Rural, or not, the ecology of the zone was described as one containing white-collar employees and professionals; the educated and literate segment of the urban population. Remember, this was in a period where such groups were less numerous than today. The area was also marked by local business districts, "satellite Loops," that duplicated some of those services located in the central business district.

Zone V, "the commuter's zone," ringed the city. Then as now, it was the suburb, either contained within the city limits or established as a series of smaller towns around it. This area was marked by substantial single family dwellings and by the well-to-do. It also contained, in some parts, small villages that were run for crime and vice, drawing their clientele from the city as a whole.

This ecological map of five circles was hypothetical. No one, least of all Burgess, expected a city to conform strictly to the symmetry of the ideal pattern. Even Chicago itself did not do so because Lake Michigan cut through the center of the five circles giving the city an ecological pattern of five hemispheres. Additionally, topography distorted the pattern. High elevations tended to attract better residences regardless of their spatial location in the city. Rivers and lakes distorted the pattern either by creating desirable residential areas along the shore, as in Chicago, or by lowering the residential appeal because of docking and warehousing facilities, as in New Orleans. The ideal pattern was also distorted by railroad tracks, public transit routes, parks, and major streets.

A general modification of the ideal pattern of concentric circles was contained in the concept of an ecological "gradient." It could not reasonably be assumed that the characteristics of any natural areas were evenly dispersed throughout each zone, abruptly ending at the boundaries of the next area. It seemed more plausible that these ecological characteristics were graded from area to area. The notion of a gradient was established by Burgess and his students when they plotted the rates for home ownership, divorce, delinquency, and proportions of foreign born on a base map of Chicago. The pattern of gradual increase and decrease seemed to support the gradient concept, and the divisions between the five zones were less marked than the original hypothesis had maintained. As Alihan has noted: "The standard zonal boundaries do not serve as demarcations in respect of the ecological or social phenomena they circumscribe, but are arbitrary divisions. They can be treated only as convenient methodological devices for the classification of data." [16]

The need for modification and alteration did not entirely vitiate the admittedly hypothetical patterns that Burgess had drawn. There followed in the next decade or so studies of other cities in the United States which tested Burgess's hypothesis. There were studies of St. Paul and Seattle,[17] Long Beach, California,[18] New Haven,[19] and Cleveland.[20] Bartholomew and his associates studied sixteen other cities.[21] The findings were best summarized by Davie, who had studied the ecology of New Haven. After studying the land use maps of twenty cities of different sizes and types in both the United States and Canada, he concluded that these cities showed the following characteristics:

(1) a central business district, irregular in size but more square or rectangular than circular, (2) commercial land use extending out the radial streets and concentrating at certain points to form sub-centers, (3) industry located near the means of transportation by water or rail, wherever in the city this may be—and it may be anywhere, (4) low-grade housing near the industrial and transportation areas, and (5) second- and first-class housing anywhere else. These seem to be the general principles governing the distribution of utilities. *There is no universal pattern, not even of an "ideal" type.*[22] [Italics added.]

The desire to find a universal urban pattern continued anyway, leading to different designs. Homer Hoyt [23] analyzed the distributions of rent for all blocks in 142 American cities and advanced the idea that the pattern was one of sectors rather than of concentric circles. The distribution of rents paid in the city, Hoyt maintained, formed a pattern of wedges, semicircles, and other geometric shapes. Every city had several clusters of high rent areas which then graded in slopes of different angles of descent to the lowest rent areas. This pattern was no more universal or stable than the Burgess pattern even though it was more complicated geometrically. Harris and Ullman [24] suggested another variation with a pattern of "multiple nuclei" even more irregular in shape than that proposed by Hoyt. The land use pattern of a city, they contended, was not always developed from a single center as Burgess had assumed, but could develop from several centers (nuclei) for any of several ecological reasons: (1) "Certain activities require specialized facilities," such as shipping or manufacturing; (2) "certain like activities group together because they profit from cohesion," such as retailing and financial activities; (3) "certain unlike activities are detrimental to each other," such as a factory and an upper class residential area; and (4) "certain activities are unable to afford the high rents of the most desirable sites," such as wholesaling and storage. The graphic patterns they drew were idiosyncratic, fitted to each city; they had no one pattern common to many cities. In its own way, the argument for multiple nuclei meant that there really was no basic pattern.

Criticism of urban ecology increased and was finally directed against the assumptions of the broader theory of human ecology. Park's attempt to divide society from community and to direct ecological analysis toward the latter was impossible to defend. Cultural factors cannot be so easily avoided, and ecology was to suffer the same criticisms as had geographic and biological determinism. The analogy between the social and natural environment was made on the basis of several tempting similarities. On the whole, however, the facts of culture and human volition transformed man's relationship to his environment. The ecologists wanted to find a scientific excuse to avoid the obstacle of studying the complexity of culture. Park's contention that cultural forces find their way into the more primitive ecological level may be true, but the relationship was too muddy to be understood. Just how the relationship between the biotic and cultural operated was never made clear.

Still more specifically, Alihan pointed out that the assumptions used by the ecologists were more limiting than they had recognized.[25] For example, the Burgess hypothesis assumed that urban growth would continue along the same lines. This assumption lay behind the explanation of the zone in transition which was created by the presumed expansion of the central business district. Furthermore, Burgess had described a commercial and industrial city, with Chicago as the model. The description did not hold for other cities. The hypothesis was also dependent upon the existence of population differences of the large immigrant populations that were typical of cities in the 1920s, but much less typical since. Finally, it must be noted that the effects of zoning, urban renewal, and expressways altered the urban pattern. Man's intervention, so to speak, made the ecological assumption even weaker.

Not only did deliberate and calculated human action upset the ecologist's theory but, as Firey [26] proved, culture could not be separated from the ecologist's main concern. Urban space, Firey argued, was not just a physical, culturally neutral resource whose use was exclusively determined by economic competition. The ecologist's plan to study land use patterns as the consequences of subcultural and unplanned processes was, therefore, unreal. It distorted the effects of culture and noneconomic motivation. Urban land, Firey pointed out, was used according to cultural demands set by community sentiments and symbols. To prove it he analyzed Boston's Beacon Hill, Commons, King Chapel Burying Ground, and North End. He found that there was nothing intrinsic to the land itself that gave the south slope of Beacon Hill its upper class character. Rather, the area traditionally had been a prestige neighborhood and continued to be one as long as its inhabitants were able to maintain their status and to resist attempts to invade the area. The Boston Commons and the Burying Ground were located in areas of the highest land value; areas that by the ecologist's prediction should have only been put to their most profitable economic use. These areas were "sacred sites," Firey found, symbolizing the history of the city and the nation. For that reason they were defended by public-minded groups in Boston against invasion by purely economic interests. The spirit of the past proved to be superior to the economic motives that would have transformed the areas.

The North End was a slum area, almost wholly occupied by

Americans of Italian descent. To convey some idea of the extent of dilapidation, Firey reported that around 1945 a twenty-apartment building was sold for only $500. Apparently, the attachment of the Italian residents to the area was so strong that many remained even though they could afford to move elsewhere. The attachment was expressed in the strong ties within the Italian family and in the ethnic ties to a large number of voluntary groups and associations. Residence in the North End, therefore, was not the inevitable consequence of economic factors or of the steady pressure of ecological competition, but was by deliberate choice, reflecting cultural and ethnic values.

Firey effectively proved, then, that ecology could not simplify the problem by omitting admittedly complex cultural factors. To do so was to render the human environment meaningless. The Commons, Beacon Hill, the North End, and their counterparts in cities throughout the world were at least as much cultural as biotic and ecological products.

This criticism destroyed the principal basis for ecological theory as Park and others had developed it. Not all was lost, however. Even without the assumptions taken from the biological sciences, the theory still retained some valid features, notably, the idea of process. The ecological processes of competition, conflict, invasion, and the like could still be usefully applied to urban analysis. As such, ecology still has some residual ideas about social change. With the rejection of the main outlines of its urban theory, however, the last broad conception of the city was defeated.

§ The Position of Ecology Today

In the years following the critical attacks, human ecologists seemed to withdraw to defend a smaller area of human ecology. The broad, and therefore vulnerable theory that Park, MacKenzie, Burgess, and their students had advanced was deserted for a smaller, and therefore a more tenable theory.

Urban ecologists undertook narrower, more precise, and less theoretically imaginative studies than the earlier studies. The distributions of mental disorders, juvenile delinquency, crime,

and other indices of urban maladjustment were conscientiously
plotted for different cities. The several zones of the city were
identified in the course of those investigations. The "central
business district" and the "area in transition" remained as the
most popular designations, especially among city planners and
other related practitioners. Indeed, these concepts were among
the few that weathered the storm of adverse criticism. In 1950,
for example, Dewey could still note, and with much support,
that "none has denied that the terms 'transition zone' or 'conversion zone' denote valid structure and processes which are associated with rapidly growing American cities. These areas of
mixed land uses immediately adjacent to central and auxiliary
business and industrial districts characterize all such urban
areas." [27]

There were studies of migration and mobility in the city
that were ecological in character. The demographic characteristics of persons moving into the city from rural areas were
described and analyzed, as was movement within the city itself.
Here and there, studies of when and how persons moved between home and work were made, sometimes as adjuncts to
transportation planning research.

The shifts of population within American cities from one
section to another were also described. This form of description
became especially cogent for analysis of the suburban movement and prediction of the trends of urban redevelopment. Some
investigations attempted broader generalizations, vaguely reminiscent of the earlier ecological theory. Schmid, for example,
undertook a detailed analysis to show that "the ecological structure of the large American city conforms to a consistent and
regular pattern in which the socio-economic status of the population is a dominant feature." [28] He found in his analysis of
twenty cities a substantial correlation between twelve indices
(age, race, income, education, etc.) and selected areas of the
city; enough so, that he was willing to conclude that his hypothesis was proven. Others devised generally successful combination indices to identify ecological areas of the city. Most of
these studies, however, did not show the application of these
indices, once computed. Valid as they were for statistically
defining certain homogeneous areas of the city, it was not always

clear what the point was to such definition. As one such study honestly concluded: "In the evaluation of indices of socio-economic rank, there is the important question: are the time and labor spent in applying those indices which require highly complex computations always justified?" [29] For city planners, perhaps there was some utility in the results of these computations; for urban sociologists, the gain was less apparent.

In spite of the interesting relationships that some of this ecological research uncovered, the impetus provided by the earlier broad ecological theory was no longer present. The enthusiasm born of the exciting prospect of having a theory capable of condensing urban complexity to a wondrously simple and orderly set of laws had disappeared, to be replaced by the inevitable cynicism that follows disappointment. There was something tragic in Park's own denial, in a 1939 review of Alihan's critical book, *Social Ecology*, that he and the other ecologists were even attempting to construct a theory.[30]

Even Wirth, undoubtedly one of the best of Park's students, wrote in 1945 that the scope of human ecology was more restricted than had been generally assumed and that Park had always intended this more limited view for ecology. For Park, he contended, "human ecology . . . was not a branch of sociology but rather a perspective, a method, and a body of knowledge essential for the scientific study of social life, and hence, like social psychology, a general discipline basic to all the social sciences." [31] There is no doubt that Wirth correctly ascribed this view to Park. Yet, there is substantial evidence in the ecologists' writing that they were thinking in terms of a broad theory and one, they hoped, that could organize the complexity of the city as well as of other social phenomena generally.

Wirth, it must be noted, was more cautious than most in keeping ecology within bounds. Even in his classic essay on "Urbanism as a Way of Life," published in 1938, he did not argue from an ecological position alone.[32] He was, of course, ready to recognize the validity of ecological methods for describing the city, its population, and its dominance over the countryside. However, he did not entirely accept ecology as the final urban theory. "As long as we identify urbanism with the physical entity of the city, viewing it merely as rigidly delimited in space, and proceed as if urban attributes abruptly ceased to be manifested beyond an arbitrary boundary line, we are not likely to arrive at any adequate conception of urbanism as a mode of life." Urbanization, Wirth argued, meant much more than the attraction of people to live in the city. It had to mean, as well, the accentuation of the urban way of life and its influence upon people, "wherever they may be, who have come under the spell of the influences which the city exerts by virtue of the power of its institutions and personalities operating through the means of communication and transportation." [33] The ecological purists, perhaps, might argue that these sentiments express a proper ecological orientation, but it seems more likely that in this essay Wirth tried consciously to avoid so total an identification of urban theory with ecology.

The history of human ecology might well have ended at this point. It would have gone down as one of the more imaginative attempts to construct an urban theory, but one that failed because its assumptions were too weak to support it. What would have remained as useful and valid for urban sociology would have been relatively limited: the identification of some social processes, such as competition, ecological invasion, and cooperation; a set of procedures and techniques for studying the city and the changes it underwent, for example, by spot maps, changes in land use, and gradients of change in any of several indices; and above all, perhaps, a perspective that might be useful at some stage of the research procedure, as in determining the social characteristics of urban areas. Ecology would have remained a method for social research, not a theory of urban society. Again, Wirth's observation is relevant.

Human ecology is not a substitute for, but a supplement to, the other frames of reference and methods of social investigation. By introducing some of the spirit and much of the substance and methods appropriate to the natural sciences into the study of social phenomena, human ecology has called attention to the wide areas where social life can properly be studied as if the observer were not an integral part of the observed. This beneficent influence would be negated, however, if the human ecologists were to proceed . . . as if they, unaided by others using different approaches, alone could comprehend and explain the complicated and elusive realities in the realm of the social.[34]

There has been a renewal of interest in, and defense of ecology as a theory. This neo-ecology, as I would call it, is intended to fill a more active role than I have implied in the decline of the earlier ecological theory.

Neo-ecology dates from 1950, specifically from Hawley's book, *Human Ecology*.[35] Like the earlier ecologists, Hawley saw human ecology as analogous to plant and animal ecology, and like them too, he emphasized the study of the community as the environment in which human ecological processes were seen to operate. However, he was quite unwilling to restrict ecology to the study of spatial patterns, for that would have been to admit that cultural processes were not amenable to ecological analysis. The earlier ecologists, it will be recalled, forced the separation of cultural from biotic phenomena and constructed their theory around the study of the latter. Hawley, principally concerned with developing a vigorous rationale for ecological theory, has contended that ecology did not need to make that separation. Ecology, as any other sociological theory, must cover the full range of social phenomena. He has sought to achieve the broad coverage by insisting that human behavior and culture are but complex extensions of man's organic or biotic character, different not in kind but only in degree.

Human behavior, in all its complexity, is but a further manifestation of the tremendous potential for adjustment inherent in organic life. Thus if we look upon culture as the totality of the habitual ways of acting that are general in a population and are transmitted from one generation to the next, there exist for human ecology no peculiar problems other than those involved in the fact of its complexity. . . . The elements of human culture are therefore identical in principle with the appetency of the bee for honey, the nest-building activities of birds, and the hunting habits of carnivora.[36]

By this view, then, human ecology studies population aggregates, however they may be delimited, and looks for the principles that keep the aggregate functioning, just as does plant or animal ecology. Culture is a complicating condition, but is nevertheless one that operates according to the same principles as those found in simpler ecological environments. According to Hawley, the task of the ecologist, then, is to describe the characteristics of the population aggregate; to analyze the community structure through which it functions and the tendencies within the structure leading toward differentiation and specialization; and, finally, to discern the effects of internal and external changes upon the organization of the human aggregate.

Hawley's ecological theory applied to the city does not reveal much that is substantially different from the earlier ecology, in spite of his insistence that the newer theory is more self-contained. For example, his conclusions on the growth of the city do not present anything radically new, nor what is more, anything greatly different from what Park or MacKenzie might have said. "The phenomenal rise of cities," he stated, "is a function of expansion," which means a growth by immigration to the city rather than by natural increase within the city itself. This is hardly unique. "The growth of the city is accompanied by extensions of its area and elaborations of its physical structure." Again, this is not a novel conclusion. "Specialized functions accumulate at the center of the city and drive out unspecialized and low intensity land uses. . . . Residences also abandon the central area for cheaper lands, their distance of removal varying directly with their rental value." These generalizations were expressed by Park and Burgess several decades before, in quite similar terms. "The central business district shifts its location from time to time partly to maintain a central location relative to population distribution and partly in response to traffic congestion." [37]

Although these quotations admittedly are taken from only two pages of Hawley's book and are his summary remarks, I believe they accurately represent the tone, the intent, and the content of his general conclusions. It is difficult to see, then, precisely what is the new dimension in ecological study or in the ecological theory of the city. For all of the broad coverage that Hawley wished to attribute to neo-ecology, not much that is different has materialized.

An even more explicit defense for neo-ecology has been undertaken by Duncan and by Schnore.[38] They have praised Hawley's work although they have admitted he stopped short of a full development of ecological theory. Ecology, Duncan has argued, has been unjustly condemned by its critics as a "biologistic theory of human behavior that ignores or discounts the importance of culture." Rather, he held, the ecologist has found the concept of culture a global and synthetic one and therefore ill-suited for "an analysis of the system of interdependent factors with which ecology must deal. . . . In short, the functional and analytical approach of human ecology involves a concern not with culture as an undifferentiated totality but with aspects of culture as they play into the process of adaptation." [39]

The line of argument of Duncan and Schnore which ascribes to ecology a major place in theory is more than vaguely reminiscent of Park's first arguments in the same behalf. The analysis of social organization, Duncan and Schnore argued, is the proper focus for the ecologist; an orientation, they contended, which avoids the reductionism of the behavioral approach and the "etherealism" of the cultural approach. Neither the "individual" nor "culture" are satisfactory objects for scientific social study. Both are needlessly abstract and their payoff in scientific gain is much less than the payoff from the ecological emphasis on social organization.[40]

But why "organization," it might be asked? Duncan phrased his argument as a syllogism. Society, and therefore culture, can exist only because of the organization of the population. "Organization represents an adaptation to the unavoidable circumstance that individuals are interdependent and that the collectivity of individuals must cope with concrete environmental conditions. . . . The 'social bond,' in its most basic aspect, is precisely this interdependence of units in a more or less elaborated division of labor, aptly described as a 'functional integration.' " [41]

Next: "Organization is assumed to be a property of the population that has evolved and is sustained in the process of adaption of the population to its environment, which may include other populations. Insofar as it is amenable to ecological study, organization tends to be investigated as a *ramification of sustenance activities,* broadly conceived, which utilize whatever technological apparatus is at the population's disposal or is developed by it." [42] [Italics added.]

As implied by the last statement, Duncan has specified a framework, or a complex, within which "organization" is to be studied. Included here are the variables of "environment," "technology," and "population," all interdependent with "organization." These four variables are "functionally interdependent" and comprise the "ecological complex." The primary task of the ecologist, then, was to analyze the nature of this interdependence and its consequences. In this way, it was argued, the ecologist avoided the problems of complexity raised by such concepts as "culture" and "society," and, at the same time, avoided the weaknesses inherent in the study of human behavior.

According to this view, the ecologist would continue to study the spatial distribution of social phenomena in a manner that by now should be familiar. This would be only one part of ecological study, however. Duncan and Schnore have also attempted to include other things within their theoretical framework. Culture, because it finds its expression through human activity, would be included, presumably through its effects on "technology" and "environment." Bureaucracy and stratification were similarly included in ecology, for they represented environmental conditions that were meaningful for human activity. The study of urbanization would be one of detailing "the precise technological, demographic, and environmental conditions under which various urban forms of organizations may be expected to appear and—once established—to develop at given rates." [43] Social or political power, as an area of sociological concern, was also within the range of ecology in that it had a "striking similarity" to the ecological concept of "dominance" whereby one species exerts its influence over another. Finally, even the study of social change would be greatly enhanced through ecological analysis. Changes would be "conceived as the transformations of patterns of social organization occurring over time rather than as, say, shifts in value systems or modal character structure." [44]

If I read the theory of neo-ecology correctly, it has simply rephrased the earlier ecological argument of Park and others. In addition, it has rescrambled and regrouped existing fields of sociological interest under categories of an ecological vocabulary. In its fundamentals, neo-ecology is not discernibly different from the earlier ecology. Duncan, Schnore, and Hawley have proceeded from the same assumption as Park, that man's biological character is primary, in that he must first sustain himself physiologically before he can proceed to the development of cultural components. Culture, the ecologist then as now argues, can be considered simply as another element in man's adaptation to his environment. True, culture gives man greater control than plants and animals possess, but this difference is primarily one of degree rather than kind. Hence, culture, society, and personality take their places in ecological theory, as adaptations, much by the same principle that animals adapt to meet their environment.

Whatever the environment in which human populations are found—cities, regions, or neighborhoods—ecological theory is directed to the study of the social organization that has been devised to meet the environment. Social organization is by this view but a primary means of adaptation by human populations to the environment, aided by culture or technology.

Again, if I read the theory of neo-ecology correctly, it has more than a faint trace of biological determinism, although admittedly not as crude a determinism as in some of the earlier ecological writings. It is naïve to maintain that all sciences concerned with the study of man must begin with biology. It seems legitimate to accept as given that man exists biologically, and to go on from there. The implied claim of the ecologists that theirs is somehow a more basic approach because it begins with the facts of life itself simply does not carry much weight as a scientific rationale.

Nor is it easy to see how the ecologists can avoid the trap of biological determinism. So long as the ecologist insists upon viewing human society primarily as subject to the same principles that guide organization in plant and animal aggregates, he confronts the same choice he has always faced: either he must be content to use ecology as a method subsidiary to a more sociologically based theory, or he must revert to some form of biological determinism. The dilemma cannot be avoided, given the primary assumptions upon which ecology depends for its identity. Only by a radical redefinition of the concept of culture can the ecologist contend that culture is simply another form of adaptation of man to his environment. To be sure, culture does serve that very important function, but most important, it also effectively transforms the environment so far as man is concerned. Religion, for example, can be considered as an institutional way for man to quiet his insecurities when faced by the unknown. However, knowledge of this fact is hardly enough to analyze the role of the Catholic Church, to chart the ideological changes that have taken place in the world's religious dogmas, or to effectively analyze the changing role of religion in human societies generally. Similarly, the division of labor is, from the ecological point of view, a form of differentiation for more efficient adaptation to the environment. This reasoning, however, is inadequate to explain why some occupations come to gain greater power and prestige than others. "Functional relevance" might be the ecologist's answer, but then his definition of function is either dependent on a notion of biological survival or it must let culture intrude to a greater degree than he seems to want.

As far as an urban theory is concerned, ecology provides at best some important techniques and insights, but not a self-contained theory. The criticisms that were once made are still valid. Park's approach has contributed as much to urban study, I would predict, as will the studies undertaken as a result of the more recent ecological formulations. We probably will produce more sophisticated studies of the urban environment but they still will be in terms of land uses, population characteristics, and changes in both of these over time. Probably, there will be methodological refinements of the techniques and procedures and undoubtedly, new measures to describe some features of the city that still escape effective description. However, these do not make for a theory of the city. This information can be meaningful only if relevant to the concepts and categories that an urban theory—not ecology—must devise.

The ecological period in the history of urban sociology was as valuable as it was necessary. Its value derived from the quantity of information gained about the city. It was necessary because, as in the development of any science, the more apparent clues have to be investigated and evaluated before more complex abstractions are possible. A theory of the city, if it is at all possible, can be achieved only by recognition of the complexity of the urban environment and creation of concepts that are abstract and general enough to deal with it. Not because there is anything inherently desirable about such abstraction over more

concrete forms, but rather because science is a form of explanation that again and again has been shown to require concepts of
high order abstractions to be valid for explanations of complex
phenomena. Stated another way, reality is never quite as simple
as we would like to think it is for the purpose of our explanation.
The city is, without doubt, the most complex form of environment devised by man and to understand it and his place in it, he
must recognize the complexity of the relationship.

vi

THE THEORETICIANS:
DEVELOPERS OF
THE URBAN CONCEPT

THE TITLE of this chapter should not be misread to imply that
the work of the urban analysts that has been discussed has been
entirely without theory. Even a classification of cities assumes
some theoretical outlook which gives the classification a justifying logic and relevance. Otherwise, there would be no rationale
for selecting any one set of facts over any other.

Of course there is more to theory than a rationalization for
the collection of facts. Theory means an attempt to weave together, in systematic and logical fashion, a set of propositions
about relationships between facts. An urban theory should be
broad enough to account for the essential features of the urban
environment. Not that every facet of the urban environment has
to be included, for that would be impossible and probably undesirable. Ideally, the theory should point to consequences of
urban social organization that have bearing for even the practical
problems that were considered in an earlier chapter. Although it

is unlikely that theory could furnish a solution for the city's traffic problems, it should, ideally, point to the sources that produce and acerbate the problem insofar as these are basic elements of the urban milieu. In short, what we would like to have is an explanation of the city that relates many of the facts that we know and that can tell us as much as possible about their relationships that we do not yet know.

§ Theories of Contrast: Rural-Urban Comparisons

By far the most frequent attempts at an urban theory have been the so-called theories of contrast. The terms have been different, as have the dimensions of comparison, but the idea of contrasting the qualities of an urban with a nonurban society has been a common feature. Here are some of the better known ones.

Author	Rural or Nonurban category	Urban category
Becker	Sacred	Secular
Durkheim	Mechanical Solidarity	Organic Solidarity
Maine	Status	Contract
Redfield	Folk	Urban
Spencer	Military	Industrial
Tönnies	Gemeinschaft	Gesellschaft
Weber	Traditional	Rational

The analysis of urban society by comparing it with its opposite, whatever it might be called, has a long history in sociology.

Aside from the obvious variety of concepts used, the several sets of contrasts also differ in whether they are defined as constituting *dichotomies*, or *continua*. Redfield conceived of the variations between folk and urban as being continuous, increasing or decreasing between one extreme and the other. Durkheim implied a dichotomous model with a society characterized by mechanical solidarity, typically a primitive society on the one end and a heterogeneous society in which people were interdependent upon one another at the other.

Each kind of model has distinct methodological consequences. A dichotomy is less specific as a means of identifying

characteristics than a continuum because the identification requires only that some particular characteristic be present or not.
A continuum, though, demands a specification of amount or
degree. The difference is the same as that between judgments
of whether one object weighs more than another and specifica-
tions of just how much each does weigh. Accordingly, it would
be easier to determine whether or not a society is an urban one
than it would be to judge how much more urbanized one society is than another.

Actually, such methodological issues are not of immediate
concern, for no theory of contrast has ever reached the point
where measurement was possible. Each theory specifies what it
considers to be the crucial variables but such specification is not
enough for measurement. Hence, distinctions grouped according
to a dichotomy are far simpler and more likely to be achieved.
But it is disturbing that even among dichotomies there is no
unanimity about which characteristics are urban. Reiss [1] has
argued that the characteristics usually assigned to urban society
are not unique to it. They can be found in nonurban societies
as well. His examples are factually correct. A complex division
of labor, for example, has frequently been designated as an urban
feature; yet, Reiss has shown that among coal miners in small
mountain settlements, a rather high degree of occupational specialization exists. Again, size and density have very often been
used as criteria of what is urban; but, Reiss contended, measures
of size and density do not serve as indices of urbanization when
applied to communities in the United States. These difficulties
were discussed in Chapter Four. Reiss has also disagreed with the
view that impersonality and anonymity were typically urban
characteristics. He has maintained, and the point appears plausible, that urbanites engage in many intimate interpersonal contacts outside the family, and are not as impersonal as they are
typically characterized to be. Conversely, people living in
sparsely settled regions have few intimate social or physical
contacts aside from those with persons living in the same house,
and they live a rather impersonal, anonymous, and solitary life.
Obviously, such features have to be identified and located with
greater precision if they are to be of any use as indices. Reiss
has similarly disputed the exclusive association with the city of

such characteristics as heterogeneity, the toleration of social differences, the extent of mobility, and the dependence on formal controls.

Other criticisms have been directed against the theories of urban-rural contrast. Stewart [2] has made a point that some of these theories have overlooked the fact that "the folk-primitive culture and the urban-secular culture are qualitatively different; they are not extremes along a quantitative dimension, nor are they the only distinct species of society." He has remarked that feudal society, for example, contained features that were common to both types of societies, being itself neither clearly folk nor clearly urban by the usual definitions. Still, most theories of contrast strongly imply, if they do not specifically say, that all societies could be fitted into the framework they propose. Stewart also criticized the use of size and density as determining where a society belonged. "Demographic concepts of urban and rural fail because they apply the same rules of numbers to advanced and backward countries, to farmers and peasants, to villagers and townsmen." The criticism is fair up to the point of cautioning against sloppy definitions. Some of the theories of contrast do suffer from being loosely historical, implying that the categories can be applied in all times and all places. I would not interpret Stewart's criticism to mean, however, that urban-rural contrasts are impossible to make; only that they should be drawn cautiously.

Further criticism of the contrast approach to urban theory has been detailed by Dewey,[3] who has contended that such theorists were themselves unclear about which were urban characteristics and which were not. Dewey analyzed eighteen books and articles on this subject and he counted a total of forty elements mentioned in the definitions of urbanism, but by no means accepted by all. The lack of consensus, Dewey wryly noted, was remarkable. Only one characteristic, "heterogeneity," was mentioned by as many as eleven of the eighteen authors. The remaining characteristics had considerably less popularity: fifteen items were included by one author only, eight items by only two, and eleven items by three authors. Of the remainder, two items were included by four authors, one item each by five, six, and seven writers. In the light of these findings,

Dewey's conclusions appeared eminently justified: "The only thing that seems to be agreed upon generally by writers on rural or urban topics is that in some vague way the terms in question are related to city and country, to community variations in size and density of population." Earlier he had rightly noted: "It is clear that the terms 'rural' and 'urban,' as now used and apparently understood, fall short of the standards to which they must conform if they are to be of value in teaching and research. If objective referents for the terms cannot be discovered, then it is reasonable to urge that they be abandoned."

It might also be worth mentioning that in most advanced societies, the former differences between rural and urban regions have disappeared to a great extent; a portent, perhaps, of what lies in the future for rural societies in change. In this connection, Swedner's [4] most detailed study of a Swedish town and rural area concluded that the differences between them are rapidly diminishing. The same has been true of practically all Western societies.

Against the backdrop of these general criticisms, I wish to look more closely at one example of a contrast theory.

§ Redfield: The Folk-Urban Continuum

Redfield's theory has been chosen for detailed analysis first, because he is more explicit than most other theorists; second, because the elements he has chosen to use are those most often used by others, as well; and third, because his theory is based upon field work.

The most complete report of his field work, together with a theoretical exposition of the folk-urban continuum, is contained in Redfield's book, *The Folk Culture of Yucatan.*[5] Field work in the Yucatan peninsula of Mexico was carried out by Redfield and his collaborators from about 1927 until 1936, with a different amount of time having been spent in each of the several communities. Four communities were studied, each meant to represent distinct points of development from a folk to an urban society. The significant contrasts between them are assumed to point to the major variables upon which the continuum depends. "The

chief objective of this investigation," Redfield wrote in the
opening chapter of his report, "is, then, to define differences in
the nature of isolated homogeneous society, on the one hand, and
mobile heterogeneous society, on the other, so far as these kinds
of societies are represented in Yucatan."

Merida was the largest city in Yucatan. It had a population
of about 100,000 at the time of the study and was the hub of
economic, social, and political life of the peninsula, as well as
the center for communication and transportation. In Merida
were located banks, department stores, hotels, most of the machine industry of Yucatan, and the seat of the state government.
It was a center for cultural activity, containing a university and
other schools, as well as a press and a theater for local and outside talent. Merida had a clear class structure, dominated by a
wealthy and educated elite that resided there, as seems to have
been typical for other cities in Latin America.[6] As in most cities,
almost no one was engaged in farming but people were, rather,
employed somewhere in the array of urban occupations. The
population was heterogeneous on other counts as well, containing immigrants from other places in Mexico as well as from
other countries. The population was also racially mixed, with a
majority from mixed white and Indian ancestry. Spanish was the
preferred language, although Maya remained as an important
secondary language, especially in the lower class. In sum, Merida
contained many characteristics that have come to be associated
with cities, including a class structure, a complex division of
labor, industry and commerce, and a socially heterogeneous
population.

Dzitas was a town one theoretical step removed from Merida
on the folk-urban continuum. It had a population of about 1,200.
Its major economic activity was as a production and shipping
center for maize, usually grown on large estates owned by
wealthy residents of Merida. Dzitas was connected by rail with
Merida and with other points on the peninsula, and, therefore,
was no more isolated than rural communities in the United
States. Although most persons were engaged in agriculture,
there were a few in specialized occupations, such as the district
judge, the school director, innkeepers, telegraph agents, butchers,
and industrial laborers. These occupations provided the basis for

a class system in Dzitas, ranging from the district judge at the top to the railroad freight handlers and track workers at the bottom. Although the lower class included natives of Dzitas, most of those in the upper class were not natives. In this as in other features, Dzitas demonstrated both urban and rural elements. As Redfield concluded, "Dzitas is typical of towns of Yucatan in that it is larger than most of the villages, in that it is a center of trade, in that it is an axis of important lines of communication, in that it contains organs of the national and state governments, and in that its population includes people of every degree of Indian and Spanish racial intermixture. It is further typical of the towns in that it lies on the frontier between the urban and rural ways of life." [7]

Chan Kom, a village, moved yet another step away from the urban pole. Its population was 250, smaller than the usual crossroads settlements that one would encounter driving through sections of the United States. Chan Kom, unlike Dzitas, was effectively isolated. Although Dzitas, the town, was within Merida's sphere of influence by railroad, Chan Kom was located in the deep bush, a day's walk from the railroad. The only source of livelihood in the village was the farming of maize, part of which was sold to buy necessities. There was no occupational specialization, nor indeed was there evidence of any other kind of social heterogeneity. All persons showed the same "relative purity" of Indian blood, and but for a single household, Maya was the only language spoken. Most of the men, Redfield reported, had traveled to Merida at one time or another, but no one had ever been outside of Yucatan. Whatever mail or communication there was with the outside was predominately government business. Towards the end of the study period, Redfield noted that Chan Kom was experiencing some important social changes, part of a movement by new leaders who were more sensitive to the outside world than the older leaders had been. In 1935, Chan Kom became the capital of the *municipio* and a civil registry and post office were opened there, as well as a municipal building, a small theater, and a school; and the buildings around a plaza had begun to give Chan Kom more of a town appearance than ever before. This was "the village that chose progress" Redfield later reported; for it was taking the first

small but significant steps toward urbanization. Chan Kom was
to leave behind the isolation and social homogeneity that had
dominated its past.

Tusik, the last of the four communities, was a tribal village.
It contained 106 persons, natives of one of the X-Cacal subtribes,
and was one of a chain of Mayan villages of central Quintana
Roo. Its inhabitants lived a three days' ride by horse or mule
from the village of Chan Kom, some indication of the isolation
of Tusik. They left the village very rarely. They were visited
by traveling merchants who came to buy chicle, the money
crop of the settlement. Maize was grown, but only for local consumption. These people were part of a highly homogeneous
tribe of Indians who had not recognized the Mexican government but who were still governed by local chieftains. They remained, as far as possible, completely independent of the town.

These four communities quite clearly were different. Redfield conveyed the impression of a *regular* variation between
them, from the city of Merida, at one extreme, to the isolated
tribal settlement of Tusik, at the other. It was Redfield's argument that these four communities represented a real and continuous process of social change; they were specimens of the stages
of urban development. Close comparison of their differences suggested to Redfield that the presence in varying degrees of particular variables distinguished them, and this was the theoretical
support for his theory of a folk-urban continuum. Much of the
value of Redfield's theory was precisely in locating the strategic
variables that separated folk from urban society. Redfield's own
summary of these ten variables deserves full quotation.

The most general conclusion is that the same relative order—an order
corresponding to their relative positions on the map: city, town,
peasant village, and tribal village—serves to range the four communities studied so as to represent the progressively increasing or decreasing extent to which several general social or cultural characters
are present . . . the peasant village as compared with the tribal village,
the town as compared with the peasant village, or the city as compared with the town is [1] less isolated; [2] more heterogeneous;
[3] characterized by a more complex division of labor; [4] has a more
completely developed money economy; [5] has professional specialists who are more secular and less sacred; [6] has kinship and
godparental institutions that are less well organized and less effective

cl. structure.

in social control; [7] is correspondingly more dependent on imper-
sonally acting institutions of control; [8] is less religious, with respect
both to beliefs and practices of Catholic origin as well as to those of
Indian origin; [9] exhibits less tendency to regard sickness as resulting
from a breach of moral or merely customary rule; [10] allows a
greater freedom of action and choice to the individual.[8]

These ten variables, then, described and measured the urbanization of folk society. Presumably, by the identification of
these variables other societies could be located on the continuum.

Redfield went on to refine the theory by combining these
characteristics into three major categories of urban change: the
increase in cultural disorganization, the increase in secularization,
and the increase in individualization.

Redfield saw cultural disorganization as a concomitant of
urbanization because, like other anthropologists, he believed that
the strong ties that integrated the individual into the folk or
peasant community were inevitably loosened or destroyed by the
growth of urban society. The tidy homogeneity of a folk society in which "the same kind of people are doing the same kind
of thing," created an unambiguous, monolithic social structure,
which was necessarily destroyed by the growth of the city. The
single social fabric of meanings, goals, and actions typical of
folk communities was torn and replaced by that of the numerous
social goals, actions, and meanings of urban society. The whole-
ness of folk culture in which all cultural elements were related,
became a cultural patchwork in urban society. As a result, conflict and disorganization were the inevitable marks of urban
culture.

Cities and towns, Redfield contended, also were more secular
in their values than were villages, a point with which most would
agree. Secularization lessened the importance of the church and
of religion in society and instead emphasized rational and practical judgments. Consequently, the individual was freed from
traditional controls, able to make his own decisions subject only
to secular controls, and less beholden to the will of a small community as expressed in its religious and traditional beliefs.

Urbanization also meant individualization. The person, not
the group, was now responsible for the decision taken and the
action that followed. This trend could be seen in various insti-

tutions. Collective functions disappeared, to be replaced by individual activity in the person's own behalf. Village residents frequently had given some of their time to civic enterprises, as a duty and without pay. Urban residents, however, do no such thing, except perhaps in philanthropy. The extended family, with its widespread network of obligations, was reduced to a small, nuclear, and self-contained unit. Religion declined both in practice and in its control, giving the individual still more freedom from the social ties that formerly had constrained his actions in the folk society.

Redfield's theory, then, is not only one of contrast, but also one of evolutionary change. The implication clearly is that the little community is giving way to the larger, urban, secular society. There is no doubt that Redfield was neither sanguine nor pleased about the changes. He preferred the small, primitive, isolated community which was the primary subject of the anthropologist. For the anthropologist had "the sole responsibility to report a remote and unfamiliar way of life," conversant with all the facets of a culture. "Where the student of civilized societies found himself studying some sliver of a great whole—a city slum, delinquency, settlement patterns, or a rural market—the anthropologist was giving us all of some very small whole." [9] The anthropologist, with the outlook given him by his training, sometimes translated this professional view into a personal ethos: The growth of cities was undesirable, it destroyed the peasant community, and with it, destroyed folk culture. In exchange for the tight security of life in a peasant society, urbanization gave the individual freedom, but at the same time, produced greater personal and social disorganization.

§ Criticisms of Redfield's Continuum

Tepoztlán is a village of about 3,500 people located sixty miles south of Mexico City. Although Redfield did not include it as one of the four places he studied, Tepoztlán was the source of his ideas about the folk-urban continuum. In 1926, he found in this village the characteristics that he later developed as the model for a folk society.[10] The significance of this event for the present discussion was to emerge seventeen years later. In 1943, Oscar Lewis, another anthropologist, returned to Tepoztlán to make a "broad ethnographic and historical study of the social, economic, political, and religious life of the community, with special emphasis upon an analysis of the changes which had occurred in the village since 1926." [11] This marked one of the rare occurrences of replication in anthropology: a second anthropologist returning to a community to compare his observations with those of the first.

This particular event had significance for an analysis of urban theory because (1) It was now possible to compare Lewis's observations with Redfield's in order to check the folk-urban theory; and (2) Lewis's own criticisms of Redfield's theory were supported by his findings.

On the first point, Lewis was coldly explicit. He did not find Tepoztlán to be the type of folk society Redfield had described and he pointed to Redfield's bias toward folk communities as the desired way of life.

The impression given by Redfield's study of Tepoztlán is that of a relatively homogeneous, isolated, smoothly functioning, and well-integrated society made up of a contented and well-adjusted people. His picture of the village has a Rousseauan quality which glosses lightly over evidence of violence, disruption, cruelty, disease, suffering, and maladjustment. We are told little of poverty, economic problems, or political schisms. Throughout his study we find an emphasis upon the cooperative and unifying factors in Tepoztlán society. Our findings, on the other hand, would emphasize the underlying individualism of Tepoztlán institutions and character, the lack of cooperation, the tensions between villages within the municipio, the schisms within the village, and the pervading quality of fear, envy, and distrust in interpersonal relations.[12]

According to Lewis, these differences were not simply the result of the seventeen years that had passed. Comparing Redfield's view to his own, he found differences that ranged "from discrepancies in factual details to differences in the over-all view of Tepoztecán society and its people." The Tepoztlán that Redfield saw and the Tepoztlán that Lewis saw seemed to be two different places.

For one thing, Lewis saw no basis for Redfield's emphasis

upon the role of community in the lives of folk peoples. Although there were communal lands in the village, Lewis found them to be individually cultivated, except for church lands, and the ideal of the Tepoztecán was someday to own his own private plot. For another thing, Redfield's emphasis upon collective labor, the *cuatequitl*, was mistaken; it was the first since the Revolution and there had been very few since that one.

A distinctive mark of the folk society for Redfield was the positive and integrative character of interpersonal relationships, giving folk society an appearance of contentment and peace. Lewis argued that Redfield had overlooked the negative and disruptive aspects of village life; for example, 175 crimes and misdemeanors were reported in Tepoztlán during the year that Redfield was there.

These several discrepancies between the two studies were typical of those reported by Lewis. It might be argued that they really make little difference so far as Redfield's theory is concerned. After all, Redfield's descriptive models of the folk village and the city need not depend on specific cases. It would be reassuring to have actual cases described, but for the purposes of the theory, not essential.

On logical grounds, the folk-urban continuum, as a theory, cannot be rejected no matter how many questions may arise about Redfield's field work. This error, if error it was, might affect the test of the theory, but would not affect its logical structure. Lewis obviously recognized that difference when he remarked, "Since the concept of the folk society as an ideal type is, after all, a matter of definition, there can be no quarrel with it as such, provided that it can be shown to have heuristic value." [13] But having trod the same ground as Redfield, Lewis was prepared to use his material as a basis for evaluating the theory, not only the facts. Lewis' assessment of Redfield's theory is worth considering in detail.[14]

1. As already remarked, the folk-urban idea contains a theory of change, by which, in Redfield's view, urbanization destroys the folk community. The fallacy, however, is to locate the source of change exclusively in urbanization. Even isolated folk cultures change because each new generation does things slightly differently, and because of the effects of natural changes in the

environment. Folk societies in Mexico, as Lewis noted, have been influencing each other for centuries, according to archeological records. Urban society, which is a more recent force, cannot then be considered as the only cause of change. The Agrarian Revolution in Mexico was no urban movement, yet it accounted for many widespread and significant changes in the folk villages of that country.

2. Although cultures change, this change is not always an evolutionary movement from folk toward urban society, as Redfield contended. In Tepoztlán particularly, Lewis pointed to the way Spanish rural elements were incorporated into the local culture. The plow, oxen, plants, and folk beliefs of the Spanish conquistadores did not move Tepoztlán towards urbanism but did create greater variations in folk culture than had previously existed.

3. Lewis found Redfield's model of the folk society difficult and inadequate because it did not distinguish some of the important differences between folk societies. It was quite possible, Lewis contended, for certain folk societies to resemble certain urban societies more than they did one another. Further, the "criteria used in the folk-urban classification are concerned with the purely formal aspects of society and are not the most crucial for cultural analysis." [15] This is probably true of Redfield's theory, but it might be argued that this is true of every theory where the deliberate intent is to simplify the actual phenomena in a scientific way. One cost of this procedure is to blur differences between folk societies. If the blurring of differences between folk societies is theoretically undesirable, then effective criticism would perhaps call for more clarification of Redfield's definitions.

4. A final criticism made by Lewis was less concerned with the theory and more with what he believed to be Redfield's motives. It seems substantially clear from Redfield's descriptions that he viewed the people of folk societies as noble, happy savages. Folk societies were good; urban societies were bad. This led Redfield, undoubtedly, to stress some characteristics rather than others; for example, that cities were a culturally disorganizing influence. To that extent, he weakened his theory, as many urban critics before him had weakened theirs.

Lewis also had something to say about Redfield's propositions that urbanization meant an increase in cultural disorganization, secularization, and individualization. Regarding the first,
Lewis disagreed that greater disorganization had occurred in
Tepoztlán during the seventeen years. The family was still
strong and cohesive in spite of urban influences. Parental
authority had not decreased. Some of the outward forms of
respect had altered, but respect for one's family, even in its
reduced size and scope of responsibilities, had not been seriously
modified.

Redfield had predicted a steady trend toward secularization
for Yucatán. Lewis found that the trend was equivocal, at least
for those features that could be compared. The attitude toward
corn continued to contain some religious elements, as in the
blessing of the corn on San Isidro's day and in the prayers
offered over the corn before planting. Regarding occupational
specialization, Lewis found that most of the older "folk specialists" still existed, and had even increased in number. Finally,
although secular marriages had been legalized, a church marriage
was still considered highly desirable.

Redfield argued that urbanization meant individualism. The
individual would become more self-centered and self-concerned
at the expense of his community ties and obligations. The point
was disputed by Lewis, who did not consider the folk society
to be as communally oriented as Redfield had contended. Private,
not communal land ownership, for example, was the ideal of
most Tepoztecáns. Yet, Lewis found relatively little movement
towards private ownership of communal resources. Eighty per
cent of the land was still in communal hands, which suggested
that individualism did not grow at the rapid rate that Redfield
had predicted. However, Redfield's fears concerning the break-
down of collective labor apparently have been fufilled. At the
time of Lewis's study increased difficulty was encountered in
getting members to help in the plowing and planting of the
barrio fields.

Taking all of these comparisons together, Lewis concluded
that "many of our findings for Tepoztlán might be interpreted
as confirming Redfield's more general findings for Yucatán, particularly in regard to the trend toward secularization and in-

dividualization, perhaps less so in regard to disorganization." [16]

Yet another critical evaluation of Redfield's important idea of a folk-urban continuum was made by Miner.[17] Miner's critique was based on his experience with two applications of Redfield's continuum outside of Mexico: field work in an isolated French-Canadian community as well as in a "densely populated, heterogeneous, non-isolated community," Timbuctoo, French West Africa. He was concerned with matters of methodology and definition, thus making his comments valuable for the discussion here.

Miner's first criticism concerned the difficulties in attempting to test Redfield's hypothesis. Miner argued that it was impossible, in effect, to handle all the variables by which Redfield defined the continuum. It was not only a problem of juggling everything at once. Rather, the complex and ill-defined interrelation between the variables made measurement virtually impossible. Much of the difficulty lay in the diffuse way the hypothesis was stated. Redfield had not specified the nature of the variables or the way they related to each other, thereby making scientific test quite impossible.

There was a related problem. It was likely that a society would contain some of the features that Redfield had specified, but it was very unlikely that it would have all of them. For Redfield's purpose it was not necessary that a society possess all of the features he designated as folk or urban. But he had to give some clue as to the relative importance of the several characteristics; otherwise, how is anyone to know where any society belongs on the continuum? The problem is compounded by the factor of change. Since societies undoubtedly change in different aspects at different rates, how is the scientist to assess the relative importance either of different characteristics or of different rates of change.

Miner's next criticism was of the definition of characteristics. To be scientifically useful, a typology must define the relevant elements with sufficient precision to permit them to be applied in a relatively standard fashion. Otherwise, different conclusions may be the result of imprecise definitions rather than of real differences in fact. It was Miner's opinion that the difference between what Redfield and Lewis saw in Tepoztlán was the consequence of using different standards of observation and judgment. For example, Lewis's finding that more than a hundred crimes were committed in Tepoztlán during the time Redfield was there may or may not be taken as an index of cultural disorganization. The number of crimes committed was beyond dispute, but the importance of the fact was blurred because Redfield failed to specify some index of disorganization. Lewis, therefore, was correct in using the crimes as a sign of disorganization in the folk society that was not due to urban influence. Yet, as a test of Redfield's hypothesis the datum is questionable because the hypothesis itself was too imprecise to allow such testing. "The weight of evidence seems to be that irrespective of the merits of the folk-urban continuum for theory building," Miner wrote, "the characteristics of the ideal type must be operationalized before relevant theory can be reliably tested cross-culturally." [18]

A final criticism of Miner's concerned the limited theoretical insights offered by the folk-urban continuum. This criticism must be considered as stemming from an anthropological bias, rather than from the sounder methodological reasoning which underlies Miner's earlier criticisms. The continuum, he observes, "deals with the form rather than with the content of culture traits." I do not agree. Despite the imprecision of Redfield's definitions and despite the difficulties in applying them, the great, if not the greatest, advantage of the theory was the order it introduced. It was not Redfield's purpose to consider the content of any particular culture, but instead to devise abstract categories by which cultures, or parts of them, might be analyzed comparatively. To criticize Redfield for his deliberate abstraction is to ignore one of the main purposes of his theory.

Recognizing the theoretical advantages of the folk-urban continuum, however, need not mean overlooking the considerable methodological and theoretical problems that have been described. Aside from the criticism already mentioned, Redfield's theory has the considerable shortcoming of not pointing out the main elements of urban society per se. It is not enough to use urban society as a contrast or as a foil for folk society.

Certainly, Redfield was properly concerned with folk society. Yet, even his own theory of the folk society has been weakened by his failure to consider urban society somewhat independently. Much of that failure stemmed from his deliberate insistence upon viewing urban society as simply the opposite of folk society, thereby giving little independence to typically urban elements. What may have appeared to be a significant contrast between the city and the village could still be quite unimportant for understanding urban society. Merida loomed large for the citizens of Chan Kom and Tusik, but how, did New York, Tokyo, or London look to the residents of Merida? An urban theory cannot consider the city only by way of contrast with the small town, but has to cope with the city as a phenomenon in its own right.

§ Theory by Deduction:
From the Physical to the Social

After theories of contrast, theories of deduction are the most frequently used to explain urban society. Theories of deduction begin with a few assumptions or propositions about the city and develop from these additional propositions. There are three principal weaknesses to any kind of deductive theory. First, the results, obviously, are only as good as the assumptions. If the assumptions are challenged, so, too, are the conclusions. Second, there is no adequate test of the deductions other than logical consistency, and no way of proving that the effects follow from the presumed causes. Further, alternative deductions are usually not considered, and if they were, and contradictory propositions appeared, there would be no standard by which to choose between them. Finally, several propositions may be logically related but may have no demonstrable cause and effect relationship.

These weaknesses, perhaps, are inherent in any deductive procedure. What is more to the point is that the application of this type of theory to urban sociology has produced no really new information, in spite of its popularity. At best, these theories have rearranged the available impressions and facts, but without really achieving a systematic model.

§ Wirth and Urbanism as a Way of Life

In 1938, Louis Wirth, one of Park's students at Chicago, wrote what was to become one of the classics in the literature on urbanism, "Urbanism as a Way of Life." [19] Wirth had a sense of prophecy that came from a deep understanding of the subjects that concerned him, including race relations, ecology, urban planning, and urban theory. The impetus for writing his essay on the city came from a recognition that there was no adequate urban theory nor even a clearly defined sociological orientation to the study of urban society. What he wrote in 1938 regarding the first point is as true today as it was then.

In the rich literature on the city we look in vain for a theory systematizing the available knowledge concerning the city as a social entity. We do indeed have excellent formulations of theories on . . . special problems . . . and we have a wealth of literature presenting insights of sociological relevance and empirical studies offering detailed information on a variety of particular aspects of urban life. But despite the multiplication of research and textbooks on the city, we do not as yet have a comprehensive body of competent hypotheses which may be derived from a set of postulates implicitly contained in a sociological definition of the city.[20]

Wirth made the indictment on the lack of sociological orientation after the voluminous work by the ecologists had been published. Even though he was careful to stress that Park's essay and Weber's work, "Die Stadt" (now translated as *The City*) were "penetrating," Wirth nevertheless concluded that "even these excellent contributions are far from constituting an ordered and coherent framework of theory upon which research might profitably proceed."

The core of Wirth's essay on urbanism contained three assumptions from which other propositions were then deduced:

size, density, and heterogeneity were seen as causes of urban characteristics. The first two were obviously ecological in character, the last, somewhat more sociological. Interestingly, however, heterogeneity does not really qualify as an assumption as do size and density, inasmuch as it can itself be deduced as a consequence of the latter two. Wirth himself indicated this.

Wirth's argument began with size as the principal ecological characteristic of the city, from which he next deduced propositions about urban society, in turn using these as a basis to deduce other propositions about the personality of urbanites.

It has long been recognized, Wirth argued, that large numbers permitted a wide range of individual variation and an increase in the potential differentiation within a population.[21] The larger the group or community, the greater the variations it contained. With that assumption, additional deductions were made: the greater the variation, the greater the increase in spatial segregation by color, ethnic heritage, and status. In its turn, spatial segregation weakened the bonds of kinship, neighborliness, and the "sentiments arising out of living together for generations under a common folk tradition." The weakening of these bonds then forced the substitution of competition and formal controls for the earlier informal bonds that held folk society together. By this logic, Wirth had moved from propositions about physical or ecological matters to propositions about urban society and personality.

Size can be used in a different way, to initiate another series of propositions. The increase in numbers, Wirth contended, limits "the possibility of each member of the community knowing all the others personally." Now, the limitation of personal interaction, in its turn, encourages the development of segmentalized social contacts, by which urbanites come to know fewer people and to know them less intimately than would be the case in a small community. Further, urbanites do not become involved with one another as total personalities, but in specialized segments, interaction being primarily for definite and instrumental reasons. This feature of urban society, in its turn, increased the superficiality, anonymity, and the transitory character of urban social relationships.

Our acquaintances tend to stand in a relationship of utility to us in the sense that the role which each one plays in our life is overwhelmingly regarded as a means for the achievement of our own ends. Whereas the individual gains, on the one hand, a certain degree of emancipation or freedom from the personal and emotional controls of intimate groups, he loses, on the other hand, the spontaneous self-expression, the morale, and the sense of participation that comes with living in an integrated society.[22]

The segmented life of urban society is more likely to expose the urban resident to feelings of anomie, to a sense of personal disorganization, and to a loss of spontaneity. In this series of deductions, size has been the single lever to raise a number of conclusions about urban social psychology.

Density was similarly handled by Wirth as a basic characteristic of urban society. In fact, it was assumed that density increased the social and psychological effects created by size. Density intensified the need for specialization and differentiation. Density also underlined the need for formal controls to "counteract irresponsibility and potential disorder" that were assumed to develop from the fact of large numbers in urban society. Finally, density increased the tendency toward spatial segregation, that is, toward social groups in the city separating themselves and forming relatively homogeneous neighborhoods.

Heterogeneity, as mentioned before, was itself a consequence of size and density. Heterogeneity developed principally as a social response to economic necessity, for example, the necessary division of labor, or simply as a consequence of the differences one would expect in any large group of people. Interaction of individuals from different backgrounds destroyed the rigid divisions of the smaller integrated society and introduced a more complex pattern of social stratification. The contact between those from different backgrounds, in turn, led to the sophistication and cosmopolitanism that were considered typical of the urbanite. Heterogeneity also led to greater mobility, both geographic and social, in that individuals moved more and changed groups more frequently because there were more alternatives open to them.

According to Wirth, heterogeneity also produced a counter-tendency by which a certain amount of social leveling occurred, in spite of the wide variation found in the city. The leveling was accomplished by means of the standardization of consumer goods and the standardization of beliefs. These forms of standardization, in turn, increased the impersonality of social intercourse in the city because urban residents came more or less to have common opinions and to react to one another in terms of stereo-typed conceptions.

When large numbers have to make common use of facilities and in-stitutions, those facilities and institutions must serve the needs of the average person rather than those of particular individuals. . . . If the individual would participate at all in the social, political, and economic life of the city, he must subordinate some of his individuality to the demands of the larger community and in that measure immerse him-self in mass movements.[23]

It should be remarked that the city has no monopoly on the forces of depersonalization; the folk society in its own way also forces depersonalization by making the person submerge his own needs and desires to the common good and welfare.

The deductive form of Wirth's argument should be clear from the above analysis. His arguments have been presented very much in the same sequence he followed in his essay, so no extensive reorganization was needed.

Two other examples of deductive theory can be mentioned. Simmel, in his essay "The Metropolis and Mental Life," [24] fol-lowed much the same deductive method. The major difference between him and Wirth was that Simmel used social rather than ecological characteristics as the basis from which to derive psychological consequences. Some of these, by the way, were incorporated by Wirth. For example, Simmel held that, com-pared with rural society, urban society demanded greater punc-tuality and exactness from urban residents in order for them to meet their obligations in the tightly interconnected web of urban functions. This requirement, in turn, forced the individual to be more rational and precise and less impulsive, if he was to survive in the city. Similarly, the money nexus of the city required that urbanites assume, as part of their own personalities, a sense of calculation, rationality, and intellectualism. Money and head, not spirit and heart were the qualities the urban resident needed for his survival. For each proposition, Simmel proceeded deductively from what might be accepted as typical for urban society to the psychological consequences that it produced. It might be noted that the social characteristics that Simmel had assumed might themselves, in turn, be deduced from assumptions about size and density, as Wirth had done.

In his book, *Human Society*, Davis [25] has followed very closely the argument of the deductive theory just detailed. From the assumption of an increase in size with urbanization, Davis deduced greater social heterogeneity, an increase in secondary rather than primary social relationships, and a rise in the number of voluntary associations. Greater density meant greater spatial segregation and greater individualization, which in turn led to the increase in secondary controls over behavior—law rather than conscience. From each of these Davis has drawn further consequences in the manner of Wirth and Simmel.

The deductive procedure, of course, is very much a part of the scientific process. The main objection raised here has not been against the use of deduction, per se, but rather that none of these deductive forays has added much to our information about the city or has significantly increased the probability of gaining new understanding. The deductive inferences sound plausible, principally because they point to the characteristics that have for so long been accepted as typically urban. Almost from the first, the city had been described by its impersonality, its emphasis upon formal and rational organization, and its spatial segregation of population and land use. To deduce these same characteristics from the facts of size and density does little to increase their usefulness for an urban theory.

Deductive theories give an impression of being systematic because their conclusions can be neatly grouped under a few categories, such as "size" or "density" or "heterogeneity," which presumably account for most urban phenomena. Such propositions are serially strung out from a common beginning and not systematically integrated because they are based on only one or two assumptions, and these, for the most part, are not sociological. For example, if size does "cause" the rise of segmentalized relationships between urban dwellers, precisely how does it affect the economy of the city or the accepted cultural values in urban society or the function of political institutions? Some of these suggested consequences might be deduced from the fact of size, but that places undue emphasis upon size as a causal factor. A great deal that occurs between the fact of size and any social or psychological fact must be explained, but deductive theory simply does not specify the interconnections. And it is precisely those interconnections that are the stuff out of which urban theory must be developed. The glaring fact that no theory has yet been developed as a consequence of these sets of deductive propositions suggests that it may not be worthwhile to pursue such procedures.

§ Speculative Generalizations about the City

The theories of contrast and the deductive theories do not exhaust all of the theoretical writing about the city. Although these two types have been most popular, there have been others. My purpose is not to inventory everything that has been written about urbanism, a pointless task. Rather, the standard of selection throughout this discussion has been the representativeness or generality of the point of view. Tönnies enthusiasts, for example, might object that his theory was not included here, but Tönnies' theory of *Gemeinschaft und Gesellschaft* was adequately represented in the analysis of Redfield's theory of the folk-urban continuum, as was Durkheim's theory of solidarity. Detailed analysis of these theorists here would not contribute anything significantly new to the points already discussed.

There are other writers who have not been mentioned, and I mention them here only to indicate that, although aware of them, I chose not to discuss their works. Cooley's location theory of cities has been omitted as have Spengler's views on the city and civilization. Adna Weber's classic survey on the growth of cities in the nineteenth century is covered in the next chapter, but is not discussed here because it is not a theory.

Deliberately limiting this book to the industrial city has made most of the historical analyses irrelevant. (I shall have more to say about this in the following chapter.) Therefore, Fustel de Coulanges' description, *The Ancient City*, or Pirenne's brilliant social and economic analysis, *Medieval Cities*, have not been mentioned. For one interested in the historical background preceding the rise of the industrial city, these books are indispensable, as is Mumford's *The City in History*. More recently, Sjoberg has written on the preindustrial city, tying together an extensive literature on the characteristics and features of the city during that period of history.

Also omitted is Max Weber's analysis of the city, recently translated by Martindale and Neuwirth as *The City*.[26] Informative and brilliant as was Weber's analysis, his purpose was more an attempt to set the groundwork for the development of a theory of urbanism than to formulate a theory. To that end, Weber surveyed the characteristics of what were considered as cities throughout the world, from antiquity through the medieval period. Weber primarily sought the characteristics of the urban community which would encompass the basic elements of the European city. These were his conclusions on the matter.

To constitute a full urban community, a settlement must display a relative predominance of trade-commercial relations with the settlement as a whole displaying the following features: 1. a fortification; 2. a market; 3. a court of its own and at least partially autonomous law; 4. a related form of association; and 5. at least partial autonomy and autocephaly, thus also an administration by authorities in the election of whom the burghers participated.[27]

Eisenstadt, in an excellent paper on cities in underdeveloped countries, has summarized Weber's principal contribution on the subject in a more felicitous style. "What distinguished the non-European city from the European is the fact that nowhere outside Europe did the cities develop as unified communities of their own, with a common *esprit de corps*, a common communal organization and some sort of political, or at least organizational autonomy." [28] Applicable as these characteristics might be to definitions of the occidental city historically, they are less important for the industrial city, which is the main interest here.

An interesting paper by Freeman and Winch,[29] which appeared in 1957, tried to specify empirically some of the historical dimensions behind urbanization. For some reason these suggestive ideas have not yet been picked up by those interested in the subject. The paper considered societal complexity and presented an intriguing idea for measuring the change towards greater complexity as a society urbanized.

Freeman and Winch's purpose was to define and measure the variables that were implied in folk-urban contrasts. The authors wanted to establish what those variables were and then determine the shifting priorities among them, as a society moved from traditionalism toward greater social complexity. They chose forty-eight societies about which information was available in the Cross-Cultural Survey and in the Human Relations Area Files, a compendium of ethnographic details taken from a vast literature in the social sciences. The societies were deliberately selected to yield cultural variability, hence, there were included societies from around the world and some societies from different historical periods. There is no need to list all forty-eight, but some impression can be gained by mentioned a few. From North America were selected the Creek, Crow, and Navaho. From Asia, the Koreans, Formosan aborigines, and Lakher. From Africa, the Azande, Hottentot, and Chagga. From the Middle East, the Iranians, Ancient Hebrews, and Siwans. From Oceania, the Balinese, and Andamanese. From Russia, the Ukrainians and Kazak. From South America, the Jivaro, and Yaruro. From Europe, the Czechs, Elizabethan English, Imperial Romans, and the Lapps. The societies were not meant to be representative of the continent from which they came, but they did cover a wide range of variability in terms of potential social complexity, which was, after all, the purpose of the study.

Eight variables were used to measure the stages of cultural complexity, each one dichotomized as follows:

Table 2—Variables for Measurement of Social Complexity

LEVEL OF SOCIAL COMPLEXITY

Variables	Complex Societies	Simple Societies
1. Exogamy	Incest taboos include only secondary relatives	Further extension of taboos
2. Punishment	Crimes against persons or property punished through government action	Crimes avenged by the person wronged, his kin group, or the gods
3. Government	Full-time bureaucrats unrelated to government head	Part-time bureaucrats, or bureaucrats related to government head
4. Education	Formal, with full-time specialized teacher	Informal, without full-time specialized teacher
5. Religion	Full-time specialized priest —not diviner or healer— present	No full-time specialized priest present
6. Economy	Symbolic medium of exchange—real money— present	Barter and exchange the sole economic mechanisms
7. Mate selection	Beauty stressed in desirability of a mate. Sometimes skill and fertility as well	Skill and fertility demanded to the exclusion of beauty
8. Written language	Written language present	Written language absent

Source: Linton C. Freeman and Robert F. Winch, "Societal Complexity: An Empirical Test of a Typology of Societies," American Journal of Sociology, 62 : 463, March, 1957.

Statistical analysis by means of a Guttman scale demonstrated that a scale did exist among six of the eight variables; i.e., that there was a regular progression from the simple to the complex societies in the order in which six variables appeared. Only exogamy and mate selection were excluded because they did not show the same social patterning as did the other variables.

Freeman and Winch concluded that "as a society of the least complex type became more complex, it would first adopt a money economy, then a formal legal system, full-time priests, educators, and government bureaucrats in that order, and, finally a written language." [30] Certainly, there is a ring of plausibility to this sequence and to the conclusions of Freeman and Winch, which were supported by the data they had collected. Although the authors did not intend their presentation to be a theory, their ideas are suggestive for one. They have detailed a plan that could lead to some clarification of variables in the theories of contrast.

§ Conclusions

The analysis of the theoreticians in this chapter completes the evaluation, begun in the second chapter, of the current state of knowledge about urbanism and urban society. It should be evident that the theoreticians, more than the other three types of urban specialists, have come closest to the central problem of this book: urban theory. This should be no surprise since they have been theory-oriented from the start.

The theoreticians have pointed up the need for thinking about urban society as a whole that includes social institutions, values, goals, and even personality characteristics encouraged by the urban milieu. A full understanding of the city cannot come from a consideration of only one or another facet of it. The city must be dealt with as a totality and with some awareness of its complex interrelationships. The segmentalized view of the classifiers, for example, cannot account for the core of urban society, for the city is more than an economic entity, more than a political entity, and more than just a psychological setting. The attempt to explain urban society by an index of only one or another of these dimensions, therefore, must fail because it is incomplete.

The efforts of the theoreticians have made us sensitive to the complexity of the numerous components that are involved. The deductive theories have given us a glimpse into some of the intricate connections between urban social structure and urban personality, even though they have not been able to specify and order them satisfactorily. Yet even these theories have been clear about the fact that the city is very much a social unity; that the consequences of economic institutions, say, pervade the attitudes of the urbanite, or that the proximity in which urbanites live can affect what they believe and what they do; in short, that no one facet of urban society can be considered independent of the others.

The theoreticians have also shown that urban society is the most recent stage in a process of change that probably began with simpler and smaller societies. This is not to say that the process is a unilinear one in some evolutionary way. Over time, social processes and social structure have assumed new forms. The social complexity of the city involves qualitative changes. Cities are not simply more populous and larger than were rural or folk communities. Rather, cities are unique social forms in which the fabric of social institutions achieves a special character. For example, the change to a money economy, which Freeman and Winch found to be important in the trend toward social complexity, carried with it a wide range of consequences for family organization, personality, politics, and education. For that reason, the city—and in this case the industrial city—must be considered as a special entity. Although it undoubtedly has ties to past history, the industrial city as we now find it must be studied in its own right.

Finally, the theoreticians have in a sense shown the effects of bias upon the theoretical product that each of them has produced. It is apparent that the consideration of urbanism has finally reached the point where the anti-urban bias is both recognizable and unwanted by those who are interested in an urban theory. The rural morality that pervaded so much of urban sociology about three decades ago can now be identified and perhaps discarded. It is evident from the recent literature on the city that anyone writing seriously on the subject can no longer take the view that the city is an unwanted product, a socially disorganized nightmare from which we ought to awaken. The steady increase in urban populations throughout the world should, at the very least, convince most people that urban society is here to stay, that it is the predominant social form of our time. We would do well to try to understand it since we must live with it or in it.

THE SCOPE OF
AN URBAN THEORY

IT IS IMPOSSIBLE to catalogue all the difficulties confronting the creation of a theory of the city; the one thing to keep in mind is that the city is a complex social phenomenon that so far has resisted any simple explanation. I do not mean to imply that an involved and tortuous theory is the only possible result, but rather that an adequate theory must reflect the urban complexity it seeks to explain. More specifically, this means reasonably establishing the boundaries of what is to be encompassed within the theory and what is not. An adequate urban theory is not likely to satisfy all students of the city, but it should, at the very least, make sense within its proscribed limits.

The ecologists and the theoreticians, to their credit, have recognized the social complexity of the city, unlike some of the other writers on urban life we have described. Their failure came more from the assumption they had to make than from anything else. For the ecologists, this false assumption was the separation of the "ecological" from the "cultural," while for the theoreticians it was the attempt to deal with the whole of urban history at once. It is quite impossible now to construct a theory that would apply to every city from Ur to Brazilia and also say very much, because of the complicated differences among different cultures at different times in history. Some would go to the other extreme and argue that each city is unique, but this point of view denies the possibility of having any theory at all.[1] Clearly, there must be a reasonable position between the two.

§ History and Urban Theory

The question of historical limits needs to be discussed in detail because of the common tendency to think of urbanization as a single, continuous, historical trend. The historical limits that are set here are those of the industrial city: the city that emerged in the West in the nineteenth century and that is emerging today in Africa, Asia, and most of Latin America. Industrial means more than simply containing factories. Some cities in the West contain no factories yet have unquestionably developed as a consequence of industrialization. The industrial city has to include not just factories but the whole social complex of attitudes, motives, ideologies, and structures that characterize Western civilization in the modern period.

The deliberate exclusion of all earlier cities—the medieval city, the city of antiquity, the Sumerian city—is justified in this discussion of the contemporary city and its development because the industrial city was a radical break from earlier urban history. With industrialization, indeed, began a true urban revolution, to borrow Gordon Childe's excellent phrase and to apply it to events 5,000 years later and a whole continent westward. Certainly cities existed before 1800. Certainly the roots of the industrial city reach into an earlier history. One does not have to either take into account all history or ignore it completely. The objective of urban theory is best served by examining only the recent history of the city. The preindustrial city, like preindustrial society, was different from its successor by almost every relevant criterion. There was the difference in size, for industrial technology increased the spread and density of the urban population. Changes in technology, education, and health had profound consequences that virtually recreated society into a new form and housed it in a new environment.

There are doubtless many who reject this historical demarcation and who insist upon the continuity of urban history. Gordon Childe and Lewis Mumford are among them. Both of these scholars prefer to examine the city in the perspective of the whole history of man. The city for them is essentially the same environment continuously modified through time. There are two arguments against that view, both of which concern the strategy of a scientific theory. Accepting the total historical spread as a basis necessarily means discounting a good many specific differences between cities. The broader the historical perspective, the fewer the common denominators between cities and the narrower the basis for theoretical analysis. This choice forces one back to population size as the one universally valid common denominator for all cities. Even so, one must not insist too rigorously upon this criterion. Occupational specialization, perhaps, is another general criterion that Childe, for one, used to characterize the city. The presence of some kind of urban attitude or urban spirit is a more questionable criterion, but one that has been suggested. It seems to be true enough of the city today, but how are we to know whether it was true for cities of the past? At best, this view of a continuous urban history produces rather gross criteria which cannot help much in further analysis. The inquiry becomes entirely directed toward piling all cities, dead or alive, into one category, or at most into very few categories. Consequently the conclusions of that inquiry can say little more than that cities are (relatively) large and have populations that are socially differentiated (but in different ways).

The second argument is that this evolutionary view of cities gets in the way not only of a comprehensive urban theory but also hampers a closer analysis of cities today, of the forces that have produced them, and of where they are likely to go in the future. Unfortunately either we must search for those elements in the present-day city that resemble elements in the ancient city, or we must direct attention to the character of the city before us; we cannot do both things at once. Making fugitive comparisons between cities, saying that ancient Rome, like modern New York and London, had its traffic problems, or that the commercial suburbs of the medieval city remind one of the suburbias of today, or that cities always seem to have slums, does not contribute much to a systematic theory. These are not systematic comparisons that can be shown to reveal a consistent pattern. At least no one has succeeded in revealing a pattern, although some have tried. The wiser strategy for inquiring into urban society would begin with the contemporary city. Once the social dynamics of the industrial city are better understood, it may be possible to turn backwards into history and perhaps to trace the origins of what has been established as critical in industrial urban society.

Let me be clear about my intentions and assumptions. The rise of the industrial city is sufficiently independent as an historical event to allow its separation from the general course of history. The evaluation of theories of urbanism in preceding chapters has shown that neither a narrow, unhistorical interest nor a total historical interest are productive. In the case of the latter we have become the slaves of the urban concept. The city is what we choose to make it for the purposes of analysis.

By considering only a limited period of urbanism, do we not thereby limit a theory to an historically unique event? I think not. For one thing, the time period of some 160 years is hardly a confined space of time, as far as sociology is concerned. For another, there is the opportunity to see the history of Western cities reiterated in the developing countries today. The event is no longer unique.

The urban process has begun in the rural and undeveloped countries of the world. From what is now known about it, that process of urbanization is strikingly close to the lines followed in the West a century and a half before. On scientific grounds, as upon humanitarian ones, there is a great urgency to understand the process as it unfolds in the underdeveloped countries. On the scientific side, there is the rare opportunity to study on a global scale cases of historical reiteration. The time seems especially opportune to sharpen our understanding of urban development and to test that understanding in reality. On the humanitarian side, there is also a great need to know. How wasteful it would be for the newly emerging cities to repeat the errors committed earlier in the West. As we now well know, slums, antiquated transport, blight, and inadequate planning are not inevitable features of the urban landscape. They are the heritage of ignorance, mediocrity, and the unbridled pursuit of self-interest of a minority at the expense of the majority. These errors might be avoided by a knowledge of the social forces that create them. I am not entirely sanguine about that prospect, even now, as cities in the underdeveloped countries have already created enormous problems.

§ Urbanization and Social Change

The phenomenon we are dealing with is not static; urbanization means rapid change. Today, the willingness to become urbanized is the impetus in society. The industrial city, especially, embracing the values of intellectualism, science, and technology, has quickened the pace of change.

Urbanization is social change on a vast scale. It means deep and irrevocable changes that alter all sectors of a society. In our own history the shift from an agricultural to an industrial society has altered every aspect of social life. The family shrank the boundaries of its allegiance and refashioned its relationships. The economy was drastically altered in style, purpose, and demands. Education was revised to fit urban and industrial needs. Politics occupied a different arena than before, with new participants, new rules, and new objectives. Although our action is long overdue, we in the United States seem to be on the verge of endowing the urban problem with as much political importance as we did the farm problem. The function and practice of religion was also revised to mesh with the secularism of urban life. In short, the whole institutional structure was affected as a consequence of our urban development. Apparently, the process is irreversible once begun. The impetus of urbanization upon society is such that society gives way to urban institutions, urban values, and urban demands.

Certainly the scope of this change makes the study of the city even more hazardous. The object of study is never really still, which requires that a theory of the city take these urban dynamics into account, or fail. The latest urban statistic, like the latest super highway, can quickly be put out of date. All the more reason exists, therefore, for grasping the elements of urban change.

Unfortunately, there exists at present no theory of social change which could be applied to an urban theory. The Marxian view of social change is not adequate even though it contains many incisive propositions about change in industrial society. More recent conflict theories of change are still incomplete. So too are the broad social psychological theories that depend on "achievement motives." Economists, especially those interested in economic development, are no further along than sociologists in this matter. Nor are the historians. Anthropologists have hardly fared any better, faced with the same problems as the urban sociologists. We do not understand the social dynamics that move a society from one form to another, and we do not fully comprehend the impact of change, except in the most general terms.

The visionaries, though they were architects of change, poorly understood the effects of their plans, and understood even less the means to realize them. Most of their pronouncements were naïve fantasies, impassioned arguments, or even rational dialogues, but were short on comprehension of just how society is to get from one level to another. The ecologists and theoreticians did not comprehend the problem of change either, although they were more aware of it than most. They recognized that social change was the real subject at hand, but neither group developed a systematic view of the change compatible with their theories about the city. Redfield, for example, knew that urbanization meant change but he was vague about the dynamics of the folk society as it moved into the urban orbit.

There is a need for a sense of history if one wishes to consider social change and urbanization. Within this work the historical limits remain those of the industrial city, which is our sole interest. Urbanization in this context means not only the transformation of rural, agricultural, or folk society, but also the continuous change within the industrial city itself. Urbanization does not stop but continues to change the city into ever different forms.

§ The Study of Underdeveloped Societies

The interest in urbanization leads inevitably to a study of development of underdeveloped societies, the best material we have on the subject of urban growth. In little more than a decade, social scientists from every discipline have come to the analysis of underdeveloped societies to illumine the study of industrial society and the urban process.

An underdeveloped country is often defined as one that has not yet made full use of its potentials, both economic and social. This definition is imperfect, as Shannon [2] has remarked, for countries that are relatively well along but capable of still further development would, strictly speaking, be classed as underdeveloped. Precise definitions are hard to come by, but those who use the term generally have in mind most of the countries of Africa, Asia, and Latin America, excepting South Africa, Japan, possibly Argentina, Uruguay, and Chile. The division is relative, and underdeveloped is an imperfect designation except in specific contexts. Generally, we refer to a country that is economically underdeveloped, and we include with that many associated consequences. Staley's definition can serve as well as any to give some ground for agreement: "A country characterized by mass poverty which is chronic and not the result of some temporary misfortune, and by obsolete methods of production and social organization, which means that the poverty is not entirely due to poor natural resources and hence could presumably be lessened by methods already proved in other countries." [3] I would add that the underdeveloped country is predominately rural. Even though there are cities in some underdeveloped countries, they are isolated oases in the midst of a society that is rural and agricultural.

For many social scientists, societies moving toward development provide the first significant perspective by which the main lines of industrial development of the West can be reconstructed, and they also provide invaluable comparisons on a mass scale. The United Nations, for example, has provided a rich supply of basic statistics of development, so that we can see more accurately what is occurring, at the time it happens, rather than through historical reconstruction alone. Indeed, for many countries it is the first time that any statistics on population and the economy have been collected.

These statements are especially applicable to the study of urbanization. The study of urbanization, as of economic development, technical assistance, or labor commitment inevitably turns to the study of developing societies. As was said before, here is the means to reconstruct industrial urban history in the West, and not for one, but for many countries. The time has come to stop concentrating upon Western countries alone as a source for urban theory because they cannot provide the contrast that is needed to develop a valid theory. The city in the West is already too complex and too differentiated in its organization for that purpose. Its origins are too well hidden by years of history. These conditions make it difficult, if not impossible, to pick out the social dynamics behind urbanization. The industrial city in Western societies is a proper subject for the study of advanced urbanization, but its mainsprings can perhaps be seen more clearly in the cities now emerging in the developing countries.

Underdeveloped societies today present an image that is reminiscent of Western society in the past. Although the two types began quite differently (I shall have more to say about that), the West, so deeply implicated in the development of such countries, is narrowing the differences between their points of origin. Although those countries began with a greater primitivism than did the West two centuries ago, the nations of the West have shortened the period of development for such countries by making available to them modern machine technology and modern aspirations. The Western standard has become the ideal toward which underdeveloped countries now strive. These facts are of critical importance in urban study.

To state meaningfully that history repeats itself requires an exposition of one's assumptions, for history repeats itself only within a set of categories that have been imposed upon it. The Preacher's insistence that there is nothing new under the sun is correct only when the Preacher's categories are used. It is our assumption that the history of the West from the nineteenth century onward is being reiterated in the underdeveloped countries today. This assumption needs to be clarified and justified. How, then, does the world today compare with what it was, and in what terms? The following sections consider the question as it applies to urbanization.

§ Differences in Urbanization

Let me specify the major differences in the urban situation between today's developing countries and that of the West around 1800.[4]

1. The process of industrial urbanization occurring today is more rapid than was the earlier urbanization of the West. Also, underdeveloped societies today have as a model an already established industrial urbanism, while the West, on the contrary, had to innovate.

Many of the problems encountered by developing societies spring from the speed of urbanization today. Painfully aware of the wide gap between where they are and where they want to be, those societies compress enormous changes into a brief time span. For the West there was no model to follow, no definite goal to achieve, and the pace of urban growth was slower and more tentative. The industrial city took more than a century to develop in the West and there was no single-minded push toward such a development. Not that this slower pace served to avoid urban problems, for ignorance and avarice created their own consequences. But for the newly industrializing and urbanizing societies, the pressures for social change are greater, and are further increased by the relatively greater instability of these societies during the transition period.

In the West we have come to accept urbanization so naturally that we often forget how gradual was our own urban development, compared with the urban explosions among the underdeveloped nations. We must remember that in the U.S. it was only in the census of 1950 that a majority of the population was classified as living in urban places.

Table 3—Population in Large Cities (100,000 and Over) By Major Continental Regions

Area	1800		1850		1900		1950	
	In Millions	Per Cent of Total Population	In Millions	Per Cent of Total Population	In Millions	Per Cent of Total Population	In Millions	Per Cent of Total Population
World	15.6	1.7	27.5	2.3	88.6	5.5	313.7	13.1
Asia	9.8	1.6	12.2	1.7	19.4	2.1	105.6	7.5
Europe [a]	5.4	2.9	13.2	4.9	48.0	11.9	118.2	19.9
Africa	.3	.3	.25	.2	1.4	1.1	10.2	5.2
America	.1	.4	1.8	3.0	18.6	12.8	74.6	22.6
Oceania					1.3	21.7	5.1	39.2

Source: United Nations, Report on the World Social Situation (New York: 1957), 114.

a. Including USSR.

During the nineteenth century Europe's urban population increased from five and one-half million to 48 million—a rise of 43.5 million. In Asia from 1900 to only 1950, the urban population increased from 19.5 million to over 105 million—an increase of 86 million in fifty years. In other words, Asia's population increased twice as much and twice as fast compared with the West. Perhaps, it can be argued, urbanization increases in an exponential manner; i.e., it starts slowly and then accelerates rapidly. Table 3 shows that Europe's urban population increased by almost 70 million during the period 1900 to 1950, when Asia's urban population was also expanding quickly. There certainly seems to be some support for this assumption. The central point, however, is that the growth in Europe beyond 1900 came after one hundred years of industrial urban growth that provided a base upon which to expand. In Asia, on the contrary, the urban explosion began from a more limited urban base. The urban increase in Africa after 1900 originated from even less of an urban base than Asia's, which already had major urban centers before 1900.

The main point of these comparisons is to emphasize the relative speed of urbanization in the underdeveloped countries, compared with the experience of the West. In Western history, the pace of rural displacement seemed almost leisurely by comparison.

Yet, the character of the urban transition and its social effects do not seem to be qualitatively different from the experience in the West. Although there is no easy way to prove this assumption, it is a distinct impression that one gains in reading the reports on urbanization today.[5] What is happening today in underdeveloped countries happens faster and even more catastrophically, but still is highly reminiscent of the process that occurred earlier in the West; for example, the alterations in social stratification, the leadership of the middle classes, the strident nationalism, the ecological patterns of cities, and the strong pull exerted by the newer cities. It is the comparability of these developments that makes the study of underdeveloped societies so valuable.

2. Urbanization today involves a greater number of people

than it did in the West. In addition, this urban movement generally precedes industrial development.

The greater numbers who migrate to the city make the problems of urbanization even more urgent. It seems likely that the growing cities of the West would have been in poorer shape today if by 1900 the rate of urban migration had been twice or three times greater than it actually was. Cities in underdeveloped societies are faced with a heavy, rapid, and apparently continuous migration from rural areas. It is not quite clear how this greater quantity affects the urban process, aside from the greater frictions, dislocations, and misery it has caused, which everyone is ready to acknowledge. For urban theory it might well mean only that a country is pushed more quickly into an urban position than it otherwise might be.

The point that urbanization precedes industrial development in some countries, on the other hand, does have relevance for theory as well as for practice. Concerning the practical problems raised, Albert Meister has remarked:

The new countries . . . present the serious danger of urbanization *preceding* industrialization. There as a consequence of too rapid demographic growth rather than of the attraction of the urban way of life, the inhabitants of rural districts are flooding into towns and cities which are little more than modern luxurious commercial centers. Around them the immigrant populations create wide belts of miserable slums while the host town or city lacks the resources to provide the newcomers with jobs, decent housing, minimum public services, with even the rudimentary protection for health and hygiene.[6]

The above description has been substantiated many times in many countries. The rural population in developing countries has been more willing to migrate to the city than was its counterpart in the West, but the reasons for migration today are a reiteration of what caused rural populations in the West to move to cities: rural poverty, urban attractions, money wages, a sense of greater freedom, and occupational aspirations.[7] For these and many other related reasons, rural populations have been and are being pulled to the city, as Table 3 so clearly documents. Yet the city in the underdeveloped country is unprepared for the influx. Where the West tended to force urban migration to fill the demand for industrial labor, as was the case in England, the United States, and the Soviet Union, the cities of under-developed nations are the embarrassed recipients of a labor force they cannot fully employ. Their inadequate urban facilities are overtaxed, their agricultural production suffers, and the eco-nomic situation becomes generally severe. Such was the conclu-sion of the World Population Conference in 1954.

Various observers of urban growth in Africa, Asia and Latin America have concluded that these regions are "over-urbanized" for their degree of economic development, particularly of industrialization—that the cities, as a whole, do not have the productive economic base that would be commensurate with their size and their proper func-tioning in the total economy. Frequently it will be found that one or two huge agglomerations—called "primate cities"—account for an inordinately high proportion of the total urban population. . . . These concentrations of people and resources in primate cities may serve to inhibit the growth of medium-sized cities more strategically placed for the development of various industries.[8]

3. In underdeveloped areas the bulk of the population is outside the area of impact of industrialization and the society that is thereby transformed.

Numerous though the urban migrants in underdeveloped countries are, they are still a minority of the total, which con-tinues to remain in rural areas, cut off from the transition to an industrial, urban society. In Egypt, for example, in 1947, 13 per cent of the labor force was employed in manufacturing, 22 per cent in service occupations, and 65 per cent still working in agriculture. In India in 1951, 10 per cent was engaged in manufacturing and 16 per cent in services, but over 70 per cent in agriculture. Similar proportional differences were seen in the countries of Latin America—Argentina, Uruguay, Chile, and a few Caribbean islands. To point up the contrast, in the U.S. in 1950, 37 per cent of the labor force was in manufactur-ing occupations, 50 per cent in services, and only 13 per cent in agriculture.[9]

The West, of course, in an earlier period of development was also predominately agricultural and rural. The shift to the cities was the *sine qua non* of urbanization, and remains so today. Yet the discrepancy between urban and rural in the West was not as decisive as it is in the developing countries today. These countries have much greater differences in development to overcome. The level of rural life is lower on every count than it was in Western countries, and the level of urban life can be higher, thus making the discrepancy even more marked.

The condition makes the situation of underdeveloped countries enormously difficult and threatens the success of development. But the impetus toward urbanization and the reiteration of the Western pattern are the critical features for an urban theory, and not necessarily the social dislocations that are created during the transition. It is the transition process which requires analysis.

4. The recent colonial status of most underdeveloped societies today differs from the experience in the West.

The experience with colonialism has unquestionably stamped a great many underdeveloped societies with a character quite different from that of the West in its period of heaviest urbanization. With the possible exception of the United States, the countries of the West entered the industrial century independently, rather than as actual or recently liberated colonies. This colonial relationship has meant both a push toward Western style urbanization and a delay in beginning such development.

For one thing, the only cities in some underdeveloped societies originated as administrative centers for the colonizing nation. It is from this base that future urban growth must begin, although the conversion of function for such cities may entail some difficulties. By itself, this is not a serious theoretical problem.

A more important problem consequent upon colonialism is that it generally restricted the development of an effective, indigenous leadership. There were differences, of course, between the colonial policies of different Western powers. But all of them had to limit and control the extent of native participation somewhere below the level where policy was decided. The indigenous leadership that did develop was principally revolutionary, organized around the banner of self-determination and independence, whether in the form of passive resistance or

Mau-Mau. To complicate the situation further, the skills for revolutionary leadership are not the same as those required for independence once it is attained, when order, not chaos, is the prime requisite.

Another complicating difference is that the leadership in underdeveloped countries, for the most part, is not trained on its own soil and in its own traditions but is Western educated and trained. It subscribes to the same values and the same slogans that are basic to Western beliefs, often to the latter's embarrassment. The socialization to Western ideals among the leaders of underdeveloped countries goes far to explain the similarity in development between them and the West.

5. Government involvement is more likely in urban development today than it was in the West.

The recency of colonial status means that underdeveloped countries have inherited an intentionally centralized administrative framework. Not only is it convenient, but it is necessary to success for the indigenous leadership to use this centralized political framework. It becomes almost automatic for a newly emerging native leadership to take over the elements of such centralized control and to bend it to its own needs.

Even more important, however, the condition of today's development is a matter between governments rather than between entrepreneurs. International organization and Western diplomacy require an interchange between heads of states. The programs of economic and technical assistance demand that the highest government levels be involved, both by the nations giving and those receiving it. Entrepreneurs may enter at a later stage of negotiation but this is unlikely in underdeveloped countries because of the severe shortage of economic entrepreneurs. The costs of assistance and the risks of politics are so high that Western governments must insure that they are dealing with legitimate and, if possible, constitutional representatives.

In the West, the entrepreneur was a major force for change and until his success was assured, government was more of an opponent than an ally to him. This phase of development is generally absent among the underdeveloped countries today. Governments, not individuals, have become the principals in development. Even when private corporations from Western countries become involved, they do so through their governments, for we are in a period of history when economic development is an extension and integral part of foreign policy. It is less likely today than ever before that such international economic interchange be in private hands. Moreover, as Adler has noted, the few wealthy persons in underdeveloped countries who might be able to assume an economic initiative insist on government subsidies and guarantees before they invest in their own country's economic development.[10]

Heavy governmental involvement demanded from both givers and receivers, means that industrial urban growth today is under greater central control than was true in the West in a comparable phase of its development. I do not mean that every step of the development process is planned or that the cities in developing nations therefore must reflect the best that logic and science have to offer. On the contrary, it is abundantly evident, even now, that such total planning is not practiced—perhaps it never can be. What is painfully clear is that many cities in underdeveloped countries are repeating the mistakes made earlier in Western cities. Some of this failure would seem to be due to the emphasis upon economic development, narrowly conceived, and the relatively little attention given to the social consequences of development.

Whatever the reasons may be, government involvement in the development process does not entirely alter the situation today as compared with the West. There is, of course, less talk about enlightened, private self-interest than there was in the West, but then the political rhetoric has changed in the last century. In other respects the process is similar, specifically in the growth of a middle class, in the development of cities and of an urban society, and in the impact of industrialization upon a traditional, essentially feudal society. These changes not even the most omnipotent or well-intentioned government can direct. Men in power can decide on political forms, on specific industrial programs, and on the priorities between several alternatives. But the broader, and from this perspective, the more significant social trends are outside the range of effective and continuous control by government.

6. Finally, the international economic scene today differs greatly from what it was in the past.

The generalization is obvious. Aside from features already

mentioned, as for example the role of government, I have in mind such features today as the structure of world trade, international economic controls as in cartels or patents, international economic organizations, and the economic dominance of the West over most of the world's markets. The underdeveloped countries must follow a different economic route in their industrial development than the West did, for they enter a world market that is beyond their ability to control effectively.

The process of economic development is complicated and I do not mean to imply otherwise by giving it such scant attention. However, economists differ a good deal among themselves on the matters involved and it is unlikely that a sociologist can be helpful on the plainly economic dimensions of development. This aspect will have to remain peripheral to the main concern here.

§ Similarities in Urbanization

Most underdeveloped countries today stand on the threshold of an industrial urban revolution. Predominately rural, primarily agricultural, and many of them recently independent from colonial domination, they are pursuing that revolution by their own choice and with a single-minded intensity. The policy is deliberate although its consequences can be only dimly seen. The "demonstration effect" of the West's standard of life has been a powerful magnet, attracting the underdeveloped countries. The answers to the very real problems in those countries have become phrased in terms of development: the creation of an industrial economy and an urban society and, willy-nilly, all of the social changes that must then follow as consequences. The solutions to political instability, to traditional poverty, to high rates of mortality, and to social and economic inequities in a country, for better or worse have been envisioned as tied up with economic development broadly conceived.

The enormity of this industrial urban revolution is overwhelming even to contemplate, so large is the number of people affected and so complex and radical is the social transition that has to be made. The 190 millions or so in North America and

Europe who were partners in the transition from an agricultural and rural existence to an industrial and urban existence are few, compared with today's numbers. The underdeveloped countries at present contain almost half of the world's population, or about 1.4 billion out of an estimated 2.4 billion. India or China alone contain more people than did North America and Europe combined in 1800, India having almost twice as many people, and China well above that number.[11]

The argument I wish to advance here is the remarkable similarity in development between the two periods and two types of societies. The resemblance between the West's experience and that of the underdeveloped countries seems to emanate from sources that we poorly understand as yet, not only from the deliberate intentions of policy makers and leaders today. There must be not an infinite, but a selected number of alternative ways whereby the transition from rural to an industrial urban society may be made; and once the goal of development is chosen, then a set of consequences must follow. I do not mean that a mystical, historical *geist* is involved, but rather that a set of necessary demands arises once the choice is made. Societies then shift and adjust themselves to meet those demands. For example, industry requires the development of cities because it must be located near resources and have access to a constant labor supply. Nowhere has industrialization, as we understand that process, occurred without urban development. Similarly, past history, as well as today's events, strongly supports the need of middle class leadership in the process of development. The reasons are complex; they are related to the challenges to pre-industrial power structures and to the alterations in the way power must be reallocated once development is initiated. Again, nationalism accompanies the change to an industrial urban society as the unifying ideology which mobilizes a society. These characteristics are as necessary for economic development as are machines, capital, and inanimate power supplies. Perhaps there are other paths by which industrial development can be achieved, but they have not yet appeared.

All of this is by way of introduction to a dominating theme of this book: that industrial urban development in the West and in the underdeveloped countries today is the same process although greatly separated in time and place. It is upon this basis that a theory of urbanization can be constructed, and thereby too, a theory of urban society, because both are parts of a single whole. The advantage of such a theory for the sociologist is its power to encompass a wide range of social phenomena under one rubric, as products of the industrial city, while cross-cultural and historical differences become less important. For it is signs of regularity and comparability that we seek, rather than the obvious dissimilarities. For the first time in the study of the city, there is the opportunity to consider the social elements that are implicated in urban growth and to cancel out, so to speak, the effects of unique cultural histories. If the advanced industrial cities of the West can be related to the urban developments taking place in Asia, Africa, and Latin America, then urbanization can be conceived of in universal rather than in regional terms. We gain, then, not only an understanding of how underdeveloped nations might move, but equally important, we can gain an understanding of the dynamics of growth for Western cities as well. These are the rewards of a theory of this universal scope, if it can be achieved and validated.

The first task is to specify the components of the theory, the basis used to compare the apparently great differences between urban societies. Four components are considered here as the elements of an urban theory: urban growth, industrialization, the emergence of a middle class into power, and the rise of nationalism as the dominating and unifying political ideology. Let me mention some limiting conditions so that the reader does not expect more than he should. First, these four components obviously are closely inter-related in the rise of the industrial city. The separation is analytically necessary. Secondly, the analysis is sociological, which means that we turn these four characteristics to show certain facets and not others. Industrialization, for example, is not the exclusive interest of the sociologist, but neither is it for the economist, anthropologist, or political scientist. These matters are too involved and many faceted to be handled comprehensively by any one academic discipline; a division of labor is both necessary and desirable for such study. Hence, just as the economist must consider industrialization as capital accumulation, labor recruitment, entrepreneurship, and technological innovation, similarly, the sociologist must occupy himself with the social relationships of industrial society. The same is true of the other components listed.

§ Urban Growth

Urbanization is considered here as a name for the whole process of social change, as well as one of the four components of that process. The difference in emphasis should cause no confusion because the context in which the term is used will make its meaning clear. Urbanization is not simply an automatic consequence of the other three components. Rather, there is a continuous interaction among all four so that urban expansion can affect, say, the rise of nationalism as well as the rise of nationalism contributing to urban expansion. Generally, to help keep these two aspects separate, the term "urban growth" is used when the component is meant and "urbanization" is used to denote the broader and total transformation of rural, agricultural societies to industrial urban ones.

The size of the urban revolution has already been specified in Table 3. Since 1900 the world has sustained not only a population explosion but also an explosion in the numbers of people who live in cities. The metropolitan growth of the world's great cities has accounted for a share of that increase, but an important increment has come from the growth of cities in underdeveloped countries, as well. Calcutta, for example, has grown from 848,000 at the beginning of this century to almost 3 million by 1955, with another 3 million in its metropolitan area.[12] Bombay, with some 776,000 in 1900, has increased to 3.5 million in 1955, and has another million in the metropolitan area. Nanking in 1900 had a population estimated to be 270,000; fifty years later this had grown to over a million. Buenos Aires multiplied from an estimated 821,000 in 1900 to 3.5 million in 1955, plus another 2 million in greater Buenos Aires. Cairo grew from 570,000 to 2.5 million in the same half century. This pace is not exceptional and can be documented for cities throughout the world.

The great cities, of course, in adding population during this period have spread this population over a greater land area. The Tokyo-Yokohama urban complex grew from over 2 million to over 11 million; metropolitan New York from over 3 to over 14 million; and greater London from about 5 to over 10 million people. The scale of urban growth has been immense and the figures are so overwhelming that it becomes hard to grasp the enormity of the change. This population movement and its attendant social consequences are without doubt the greatest social revolution in human history, and also the most continuous. Human societies everywhere have been transformed by the revolution, and at a speed that is astounding. Little wonder, then, that we seem to be overwhelmed by the problems that such changes have wrought.

Even the Western urbanite who has learned to take the city for granted has been confronted by effects of change that he has not yet learned to handle. How much more overwhelming must the change then be for the many millions for whom the city is a radically new environment, where very little is familiar, and where adjustment—even survival—can be a frightening and often impossible assignment. It is quite impossible to appreciate this fact in the West where the urban pattern has spread throughout an entire country, city and countryside alike. The rural "hick," the country bumpkin, is a character from history by now, and no longer an accurate characterization of the present migrant to the city.

What seems to be forgotten is that the West also had its time of urban shock. The number of people involved in the urban transition was smaller than it is today and the period of adjustment was considerably longer. Compared with the urban growth in underdeveloped countries in the last fifty or last twenty years, urban growth in the West during the whole of the last century seems to have been leisurely.

The feature of the industrial city innovated by the West that distinguished it from all earlier cities was the overwhelming dominance it exerted. It was an urban revolution by its power to change society. Preindustrial cities, no matter how large, did not impose their ways but remained relatively isolated. Although such cities were centers for administration, for intellectual and artistic progress, and for commerce, they were not emulated

Table 4—Urban Growth in Selected Western Countries During the Nineteenth Century

	CA. 1800		CA. 1850		CA. 1890	
	Per cent in Cities		Per cent in Cities		Per cent in Cities	
Country	100,000+	10,000+	100,000+	10,000+	100,000+	10,000+
England and Wales	9.7	21.3	22.6	39.5	31.8	61.7
Belgium		13.5	6.8	20.8	17.4	34.8
Prussia	1.8	7.3	3.1	10.6	12.9	30.0
United States		3.8	6.0	12.0	15.5	27.6
France	2.8	9.5	4.6	14.4	12.0	25.9
Denmark	10.9	10.9	9.6	9.6	17.3	23.6
Switzerland		4.3		7.3		16.5

Source: Adna F. Weber, *The Growth of Cities in the Nineteenth Century* (New York: The Macmillan Company, 1899), 144.

in the countryside. The preindustrial cities did not transform the societies that contained them. The majority of the population stayed rural, the source of wealth and power remained with the land, and the broader view of the world seen from the cities was not seen from the rural perspective. The industrial city, however, achieved undisputed dominance of the structure and shape of life. With the rise of the industrial city, the economic and political centers of gravity shifted to the city. The urban view infiltrated prevailing attitudes, sacred values, and real aspirations for most of the population. The industrial city, of course, had the means to do this, having better communication and faster transportation than had the earlier cities. These technical advantages only speeded the process along; they did not originate it.

There is no way of knowing just how the process began. Undoubtedly, as with most complex social phenomena, many factors were involved. Certainly the needs of industry determined the location of new cities, and even for established cities those needs became major reasons for transforming the environment. The industrial city, whether newly built or rebuilt, seems to have been very much the creature of economic demands, at least in the beginning. No other cause sounds as plausible as economic rationality and the economic motives of an industrial system. A factory requires a relatively large labor force that is permanent and that can provide the necessary skills. Preindustrial cities, by way of contrast, existed primarily as places of residence for aristocrats, the nobility, artisans, intellectuals, clerics, and merchants; there was no sustained economic pressure for expansion. With the rise of the factory, the city became necessary for economic reasons in a way that was not true before except for isolated examples, such as seaports or the glass ateliers of Venice. For perhaps the first time, there was the need for many people to be in the city and to remain there more or less permanently. Even those cities in the West that were great before industrialization had to be refashioned to fit the newer demands of an industrial society.

Once the economic rationale for the industrial city was established, then secondary factors began to operate. Large concentrations of people required increased services to maintain them: housing, sanitation, food, clothing, and amusements. In the West at the rise of the industrial city, these services were only minimally satisfied. The descriptions of the way the working classes lived in England and in the United States around 1800 leave no doubt that living standards were miserably and absolutely low, not low only in relation to our present high expectations. People lived in overcrowded, inadequate, and often overpriced houses. Working conditions were inhumane and dangerous, and working hours were overly long. Children and women were widely employed, much to the detriment of society, although only a few recognized that. Urban life was precarious. In the middle of the eighteenth century the death rate was approximately 40 per 1,000 population. By the beginning of the nineteenth century the rate had dropped to about 25 per 1,000. It is less than half that in industrial countries today.[13] The gains in life expectancy came from advances in medical knowledge, which, of course, had to be put into effect to do any good. Even by the latter half of the nineteenth century, when the knowledge was available, the death rate was highest in the large cities and always exceeded the rural death rate.[14] Generally, it was thought to be uneconomical to improve health conditions in the cities. Only later did values change enough to give human life a fairer share in the economic accounting.

In spite of these conditions the industrial city survived and flourished. High mortality rates were offset by high rates of immigration into the city as the rural population was alternately pushed off and pulled from the land. Through forcible ejection, as in the English Enclosure Acts from 1774 onwards, or because of rural poverty, or crop failures, large numbers were forced to leave the land. The early industrial city, inhumane and repellent as it may appear to us today, also exerted some attraction. For some, the city was possibly an improvement. For others, the move was simply an exchange of one set of miserable and inadequate living conditions for another. But for most, there was no alternative and no turning back. The choices seem no different than those faced by rural populations today in under-developed countries. In Egypt, in Colombia, and in Indonesia the choices resemble those that were faced by the rural inhabitants of England over a century ago.

In time, of course, the industrial city in the West developed its own style and raised itself from the mire. Medical knowledge put into practice lowered the death rate appreciably. A long overdue social consciousness erased the more glaring evils, which had been allowed to develop because of socially misguided and irresponsible economic motives. Child labor was eventually outlawed, safety was introduced into the factory and the mine, and working conditions were generally improved. Man began to achieve a status higher than the machines he operated. Gradually, through compulsory education, through the erosion of the principle of social Darwinism, and through the social tempering of self-interest, the conditions and aspirations of the urban population were raised. The industrial city then began to assume elements of the best rather than the worst face of civilization: enlightenment, recreation, the arts, and a higher material level of life. Once these advantages became characteristic, the city became ever more attractive to those living outside it, and the move to the city was no longer one so obviously born of desperation.

A social change of such proportions, even if only the number of people involved in it is taken as an index of its scope, clearly had to alter every social institution. No institution could ignore the new functions demanded of it by urbanization. Political forms and political styles were altered as the source of power shifted from land to factory. Family size and family relationships were limited to conform to the conditions of life in the industrial city. Education was transformed from an aristocratic privilege into a rationalized public system. Religious institutions had everywhere to style their appeals and their demands to fit the needs of an urban population; the mystical gave way to the rational. In short, urbanization created a massive social revolution that eventually transformed the whole of society.

The urban process in the developing countries today repeats many of the particulars just described for the West. There is abundant evidence of inadequate housing, high mortality, and social disorganization in developing cities. These problems occur not because of ignorance, or even because of a lack of desire to prevent the more inhumane aspects of the process of development today. Rather, these urban problems occur because social change is so great in scope that it cannot be controlled in a rational manner, no matter how earnestly one may try. High mortality rates, slum and worse than slum housing, subsistence and lower than subsistence standards, and generally inadequate conditions arise and persist because urbanization radically changes so many aspects of a society. The transition from a village society to an urban industrial society is not easy to achieve nor easy to direct. A United Nations report on underdeveloped countries has suggested that

many so-called consequences of industrialization [and of urbanization] turn out to be not the consequences of industrialization itself, but rather of the preservation—or attempted preservation—of preindustrial ways of life in an alien and inappropriate environment. Thus, child labour in factories may be regarded as a continuation of the much less harmful rural custom of child labour on the farm; and urban slums often reveal a carry-over to cities of rural methods of house construction, refuse disposal, use of water and so on. In fact, many—perhaps most—of the undesirable social consequences of industrialization are more properly regarded as results of failure to deal with the problems of social transition that inevitably arise from so basic a change in economic and social organization.[15]

The emergence of the industrial city, whenever it occurs, demands a severe alteration in existing social institutions, social beliefs, and existing patterns of order and authority. The re-appearance of the same undesirable urban conditions in the newer industrial cities as in the early Western ones suggests that some of the basic features of the West's urbanizing process are being reiterated today. In spite of the differences between the two time periods, the similarities would seem to indicate certain necessary features of industrial urbanization that cannot be avoided. The processes set in motion by the transition of a society to this later industrial stage seem to produce consequences of the type that has been described. If only in the manner just described, urbanization seems today to follow the Western experience of over a century ago.

The fact needs to be underlined that our greater wisdom and knowledge of these matters today cannot completely avoid the more far-reaching consequences of urbanization, although we might be able to shorten the time that the more undesirable aspects of the process persist. At the theoretical level, the re-appearance of urban characteristics in the newly industrializing cities strongly implies that the process of city growth has certain basic features that must emerge, features that are an integral part of the transition to an industrial urban society.

§ Industrialization

Industrialization is the second component of this urban theory and, like the first, is meant to draw the parallel between development in the West and in the developing countries today. It has strategic importance for theory because it has, in effect, created a type of city that is different from all earlier forms.

Industrialization is social change on a scale as massive as urban development, with which it is coupled. At the manifest level, it comprises the economic shift from agriculture to manufacturing, from the land to the factory. Obviously, this economic shift entails a host of accompanying alterations in the centers of economic power, in capital formation, in labor force composition, in the credit structure, and so on. At the latent level, a number of critical changes also occur in education, in family structure, in class structure, in political forms, and in dominant social values and beliefs. Nor do these exhaust the kinds of changes that come about. Diets are gradually altered, as is the whole set of spending and consuming patterns. Health and sanitary practices change. A whole array of subtle psychological changes also ensues and new standards are set for discipline, work, leisure, motivations, and aspirations. In short, a new way of life is forged. Industrialization makes it necessary, as Frankel has put it,

to repair and maintain; to think of tomorrow, not only of today; to educate and train one's children; to prepare oneself for new activities; to acquire new skills; to search out new contacts; to widen the horizon of one's experience; to invent, to improve, to question the "dead hand of custom" and the heritage of the past.[16]

Industrialization applies to the whole process of change and its accompanying consequences, as a society moves from an agricultural to an industrial economy; from a small, rural, homogeneous society to a large, metropolitan, heterogeneous massing. According to the standard by which social time is measured, the transition is radically swift and no facet of the institutional structure is immune.

With so complex a subject, the features that can be studied seem to be infinite, to cover every facet of social existence. Indeed, industrialization has been studied as economic growth,[17] economic and social history, technical change,[18] demographic change, acculturation, and labor force commitment,[19] and there has been a mass of studies of specific countries that have experienced this change. A large task force of specialists from each of the social sciences has been interested in the subject and in its ramifications. Clearly, some limit must be set for the purposes of the present exposition and analysis. Industrialization, after all, is but one feature, not the whole of an urban theory.

This scholarly division of labor should not be taken to imply that contradictions are engendered among academic specializations because the field has been narrowed for each. Fortunately, there is a close and consistent relationship among many facets of industrialization, so that in spite of different emphases, different conclusions are not likely to result, at least at the broader, theoretical level. Generally, most social scientists come to mean the same thing in their discussions of this phenomenon although different qualities are chosen for emphasis. For example, a United Nations analysis has shown a high statistical relationship between several economic and social indices of industrialization.[20]

Table 5—Coefficients of Rank Correlation Between Social and Economic Indices of Countries Grouped by Per Capita National Income

Variables Correlated	Rank Correlation
Per capita national income and:	
energy consumption [a]	.90
infant mortality [b]	—.84
school enrollment	.84
calorie consumption	.80
starch staples [c]	—.86
Energy consumption and:	
infant mortality	—.69
school enrollment	.76
Urbanization [d] and:	
infant mortality	—.69
school enrollment	.71
starch staples	—.66
calorie consumption	.69
Infant mortality and:	
school enrollment	—.67
inhabitants per physician	.43
calorie consumption	.81
Literacy and school enrollment	.78
Male labor force in agriculture and:	
infant mortality	.86
energy consumption	—.89
school enrollment	—.81

Source: United Nations, *Report on World Social Situation* (New York: 1961).
a. Per capita energy consumption in kilograms of coal equivalent, 1956-58 average.
b. Infant mortality rate, 1955-58 average.
c. Starch staples as percentage of total calories consumed.
d. Index calculated from proportions living in metropolitan areas of 100,000 and more.

All countries for which there were sufficient data were categorized into six groups based on the level of per capita national income. Group I included those countries with incomes of $1,000 and over; Group II, from $575 to $1,000, and so through Group VI which included countries with a per capita national income under $100. Averages for each of these groups were computed for eleven economic and social indicators, set once again by the data available, and rank correlations were computed.

The caveats about the statistics and their various methods of collection should be kept in mind, but there is little equivocation about the results of Table 5, many times supported by other statistics. Underdeveloped countries consistently show low rates of technological advance (which is self-evident), low standards of living, low levels of urban development, and low levels of education and literacy. They also show high rates of mortality, infirmity, and employment in agriculture. It is obvious that each of these factors supports the others.

There is a related matter not so unequivocally agreed to: the comparability between the underdeveloped countries of today and developments in the West at a similar stage. It is difficult to make valid quantitative comparisons to prove that hypothesis and, of course, a good deal depends on the categories one wishes to use for the comparison. The question of general comparability has been discussed. But as pertains to some of the specifics, the time difference has had some effect, though not necessarily a critical effect for the purposes of theory. For example, infant mortality rates were higher in the West than they are today in underdeveloped countries. Medical technology has so far improved and is available even to underdeveloped countries. Epidemics can be contained if not totally controlled today, and death from starvation is more likely than death from disease. Further, Kuznets has concluded that current per capita income levels in underdeveloped countries are well below those of the West before its industrialization.[21] Some evidence also suggests that literacy and school enrollments were considerably higher in the West around 1850 than they are today in the underdeveloped countries.

However, these specific, essentially quantitative differences are not really the main concern here. The outstanding feature of industrialization to be emphasized here is that as a form of social change it has produced social consequences resembling those in the West. The motives for industrial growth and its reverberations throughout a society appear today as they did in the West. As Firth and his colleagues have concluded:

Exogenously induced change [industrialization induced by the West into underdeveloped countries] seldom recapitulates the stages of development of the technology, economy, and society of the originating area. Although [this] is true, it is most true of the technological, least true of the social fields of life. *The technical contents of "industrial revolutions," etc., are never identical, but their social consequences are nearly always similar.*[22] [Italics added.]

In no small measure, the similarity arises because the West has helped to initiate, foster, and assist in the change among the underdeveloped countries. Perhaps there are alternative solutions to the social consequences of industrialization, either deliberately planned or not, but none has yet appeared. The technical requirements may be different and the economic strategy changed, yet the social impact seems to strike as it did in the West.

Another point is worth noting here. It is often implied that the technical or economic features of industrialization come first, then are followed by an array of echoing social consequences. Wilbert Moore has suggested that this tendency to put the economic first is a reflection of our cultural bias, which it most probably is. We are considering a complex of events; the causal sequence, the priority in which these events are seen to follow one another, is established by the perspective we take and by our sensitivity to particular facts. It is most likely that several events happened at the same time. There is no need here to establish a priority, and we need only assume that these events are on an equal level of importance. Technical innovations cannot be imposed upon a society and take root without a compensating shift in the social structure.[23] Neither, however, does the desire for technical change produce change if the technical means are absent. Nor can changes, even with the technical means available, occur without the human catalyst to put them into motion: the entrepreneur,[24] some types of social deviants, the intellectuals, the bourgeoisie, or any other members of a society that have a stake, as they see it, in pushing for the innovation.

§ The Emergence of a Middle Class

Much of the analysis of industrial and urban growth is taken up with an assessment of the obstacles to such growth and its consequences. For example, high population density and rapid population growth tend to limit industrial development. Large populations, understandably, are a drain on the limited resources of underdeveloped countries, and the margin left for industrial development is already a narrow one. The rise in standard of living is a long range effect that depends upon development and that standard is more likely to be lower at the beginning of the process. Family and kinship structures in most under-developed countries are also obstacles because they are fitted to a rural and agricultural society and are poorly prepared for the needs of an urban industrial society. At the economic level, a whole range of obstacles has been specified: [25] lack of capital; inadequate or no transportation facilities; lack of mechanical power, of market facilities, and of industrial skills. There are additional difficulties created by labor immobility, by a traditional unresponsiveness to monetary incentives, by customs and traditions that are irrational in an industrial setting, and by the lack of entrepreneurial skills.

As for urban growth, much attention is similarly turned towards the immediate hard problems: housing a rapidly expanding population, sanitation and health problems, problems of adjustment by recent rural migrants, and problems of maintaining order in what is a bewildering environment for many persons. The cutting of ties to the village, the family, and the clan that once enforced social stability creates traumata and many new problems, because in the transition period there are as yet no new ties of allegiance and loyalty.

The obstacles, problems, and difficulties of industrial urban development are serious. For many persons, these are the primary interests in the study of development. Not so here, where the interest goes beyond the practical questions to other matters. What is more germane is the question, Why does industrial urban development begin at all? Certainly the transition is not easy, for it creates immense social, economic, political, and psychological problems. Nor is such development a natural evolutionary, historical necessity. Somehow it is the consequence of human decisions which become realized. Sometimes it is conscious and deliberate, as in most developing countries today. Sometimes it is the effect of less explicit and less determinate reasons, as, for example, in the West. In any case, there are human beings behind the change, and explicit or not, the main outlines of the change seem to follow repetitive patterns.

The third component in this urban theory is the need to restructure power relationships within a society if it is to be moved toward industrial urban development. Both the West and the underdeveloped countries exhibited this feature in the industrial transition. It is not a simple case of power exchange from those who have it to those who want it, although that is what tends to occur. Power is never simple. Nor does the exchange of power always occur by a clear and deliberate policy in which the trends are unequivocal and expected. In the West, the process required several centuries to complete, and though the pace is faster today, it is still not a process to be completed quickly. For one thing, power is not surrendered willingly nor exchanged easily. For another, the participants cannot always foresee the next steps and cannot, therefore, move unequivocally toward their main objective.

The development and the emergence of a middle class and of middle class leadership provide an answer to the question of what drives a society to abandon its more primitive and agricultural condition to pursue the distant and unfamiliar goals of industrial urban development. The middle class supplies the agents of change who challenge the existing power structure, usually a feudal or colonial one.

Social restratification—the change in class relationships—accompanies the process of urbanization and is, therefore, a vital third component in this urban theory. We know that in the history of development in the West it was an accompanying feature, and it is evidently involved in the development process today as well. And class is a defining feature of industrial cities, important for social, economic, and political patterns as well as ecological ones.

Moreover, social restratification is considered here as an initiating force that moves a society toward development. Thereby, urbanization and industrialization become sociologically more meaningful. That is, cities can be considered as responses to the social demands of the middle class, not only to industry, as the narrow economic interpretation has it. The city is a *social* consequence; it takes more than rational, economic motives to stimulate and sustain the growth of the city.

A common error in earlier urban theories for example, those of urban location or economic functions, was to seek out simple economic interpretations for growth. For instance, applied to the present situation, the simplistic answer to the question of why underdeveloped countries start development is that they are moved to share in the evident material advantages of industrialization as demonstrated in Western countries. No doubt this demonstration effect is relevant here. All things considered, we can assume that indoor plumbing, a satisfying diet, and longer life are preferable to a contaminated and distant water supply, starvation, and early death. The error is to assume that these alternatives are somehow posed for all, that all or most individuals choose development. Populations do not behave unanimously in this way, particularly when the alternatives have no reality within their experiences.

The majority of the population cannot envision the meaning of industrialization, let alone its supposed benefits in a distant future. Generally illiterate and cut off from the broad communications media, they cannot accept the industrial image without careful preparation and some planning. The image has to be communicated to those who have little in their experience to enable them to assimilate the idea. In this respect, the situation today is not greatly different from what it was in the West at the beginning of industrial development. An illiterate and feudal peasantry, then as now, is not going to understand just what choices are involved, and it is nonsense to assume that it automatically will. The failures of some technical assistance programs have shown this all too well. Social changes of the kind that we are considering must begin from existing beliefs and traditions.[26]

On other grounds, too, the peasantry is not a force for

change. Like agriculturalists everywhere, it sees the situation in relatively narrow terms phrased by traditional values. The goal of a higher standard of living through industrial development can simply find no place among these conceptions. Change for the peasantry is predominately, if not entirely, seen in terms of agriculture and of local village relationships: land reform to correct injustices, land ownership, favorable alterations in personal credit and pricing procedures, and perhaps outside assistance in times of catastrophe. Even these views are relatively new, depending as they do upon a sophisticated concept of social relationships and social responsibilities. In the West, farmers and peasants accepted the consequences of industrial urban development reluctantly; they did not willingly take part in it, let alone help to force it. No wonder that land reform is often the most publicized feature of planning in underdeveloped countries; it is often the only way to win the support of the peasantry. Afterwards, the more sophisticated arguments can come.

The peasantry constitutes a serious barrier to industrial urban development in countries where it comprises the bulk of the population, which is to say in almost all underdeveloped countries. It is unwilling to leave the land, except where forced to do so by rural poverty or by administrative measures. Even then, migration may be only temporary, undertaken with the intention of returning to the land soon. On the land, the practice of subdivision according to familial principle creates a formidable barrier to mechanization, just as traditional farming methods make the introduction of scientific agronomy difficult. The methods and tools of past generations are tenaciously preserved. The fact that the peasantry is illiterate makes the job of preparing them for change a formidable one. In short, a complex social network has been spun within the agricultural society that makes it resistant to change, especially the pervasive social change brought by industrialization and urbanization. In the West, it was necessary to drive the peasantry from the land. The same is true today, although the styles have changed. Only in the long run do the advantages of development begin to show themselves to the majority of the population, and thereby motivate them toward change. By then, the peasantry has been transformed into an urban proletariat and a class of small farm entrepreneurs with values quite different from what they were before.

The resistance to change by the peasantry can be seen even among those who migrate to the cities, for whatever reason. Chinese emigrants maintain strong associations with the region from which they came and among themselves, within the cities to which they have moved. African migrants to the cities settle together according to their native tribe, and tribesmen maintain responsibility for one another in the cities.[27] Of course, this primary social relationship helps enormously in the adjustment of both peasants and primitives to the city and to its new and demanding discipline, just as it did during the decades of mass immigration to American cities. At the same time, however, such isolation of the rural primary group in the city lengthens the time for complete adjustment. The point I mean to reemphasize by these illustrations is that the peasant and the primitive are not the agents of social change; if anything, they are its enemies because of their reluctance to break with traditions.

Not only the peasantry, but all those who have favored status in things as they are, are opposed, for their own reasons, to change in the *status quo*. Landowners, the military, the clergy, administrative subalterns, artisans, and tradespeople have nothing immediate to gain and much immediately to lose by an alteration in the social structure. Change, as they correctly see it, means a worsening of their favored position. Unlike the peasantry, however, they have power.

As Kerr and his associates have indicated,[28] the elite in power in the preindustrial period may be forced to surrender or modify their control as the forces for industrial change grow. That group, called by Kerr the "dynastic elite," can respond in several ways. As "traditionalists" they may try to defend themselves and their position against any change by deflecting or stopping any move toward industrialization. In that effort they seek to keep the peasantry behind them by traditional appeals or by coercion. As "realists" they may try to live with the new changes and to take some part in them, at least to "avoid liquidation at worst or oblivion at best." Finally, as "decadents," the preindustrial elite may be oriented toward personal indulgence, which may be expressed in high living, corruption, attachment to a foreign culture or personal security through foreign investment, rather than toward national tradition or national progress.[29]

Perhaps a fourth alternative is possible, as Pareto suggested in his "circulation of elites," namely, the ruling elite coopting the leadership of the dissident factions and giving them positions in, and hence a commitment to, the elite itself.

In any case, industrialization is a dynamic process to which the elite must respond willingly or not, consciously or not. All historical instances, past and present, seem to indicate that the movement for change is too powerful to be stopped except where the traditional autocracy is too strong to be deposed. Wherever industrialization has begun, it has finally destroyed the preindustrial elite, or at least, forced it to assume a new guise and new functions.

The middle class has been the one social stratum most committed to the success of industrialization, and the group that provides the active agents for change. The middle class is at once the agent of industrial urban development and its principle beneficiary. For should the transition be achieved, it acceeds to the newly created positions of power and status.

In the West, the middle class was the bourgeoisie, the merchants, and the entrepreneurs. It was less conscious of itself as a class early in its development than it became later. It sought economic freedom and won political freedom at the same time. It is not at all clear that this class was indeed a revolutionary one, and some contend today that it did not want to actually destroy the older aristocratic order, but only wanted to ease its rigid hold, specifically in economic affairs. In any case the effect of the middle class's successful claim to power was a restratification and reshaping of society near the beginning of the industrial era. Today, the composition and the style of the middle class in underdeveloped countries is different from what it was in the West, although its social functions and consequences are the same in both periods. In the developing countries the active middle class is more likely to consist of teachers, clerks, and lawyers than it is of entrepreneurs in the Western sense. They are not as well educated or as economically secure as the designation "middle class" might imply for us today. But there is little doubt that they are the dominant leaders in today's developing nations and that they are distinguishable from the "imported European oligarchy and the representatives of the pre-colonial ruling class on the one hand, and the mass of peasants and the emergent wage-labouring class on the other." [30]

This movement by the emerging middle class appears more distinctive today than it did in the West, perhaps because we are now more sensitive to the trends, or perhaps because the forces involved are less complicated. For one thing, the middle class leadership in today's developing countries appears to move directly by means of political party organizations to gain control of government. In the West, on the contrary, the middle class sought freedom from government controls. Today's middle class leadership in underdeveloped countries sees the control of government as the quickest and most efficient means to achieve its ends. The fact that economic assistance from outside takes place through the government makes it even more necessary for the middle class to become legitimated, generally by Western political standards.

The aims of the emerging middle classes in the underdeveloped countries are clear. They must gain power, they must make their control legitimate and achieve recognition from outside powers, and they must make the industrial transition successfully in order to guarantee their own future.

These conclusions are supported by trends in a number of different countries. At its twenty-ninth session in 1955, the International Institute of Differing Civilizations reported its conclusions on the development of middle classes in tropical and subtropical countries.[31] They concluded that although this class was numerically small, it had played a major role in directing those countries toward economic and political advancement. Modern technology was given as one cause for the growth of the middle classes, thereby "interposing large numbers of small proprietors, administrators and technicians between the wealthy aristocracy and the impoverished masses of the old economy." A second source of growth came from the educational system, for in underdeveloped countries, "a higher education is often the passport that takes a man from the lower ranks of society into the middle classes."

The report further noted that the middle classes emerging today, as had been the case in the West, are sources of ferment and revolt; inevitably so because a society is in process of being altered at its most sensitive point: its system of allocating power, wealth, and prestige. For Indonesia,[32] Nigeria,[33] and Latin American countries,[34] the conclusions generally have been the same, and they undoubtedly are applicable to other areas of the world as well.

The middle class leadership today is frequently Western educated, which accounts in some measure for the political and economic direction it follows.[35] It is, in the nature of the case, a first-generation middle class that comes into the leadership. Therefore, because it is so at variance with the rest of the society, its position is all the more marginal. But, then, marginality is a prerequisite for leading a revolution of these proportions. The aims of this class are to break with tradition and with the older hierarchy in order to pursue the goals of urban industrialism. The fact that the leadership of this class may appeal to tradition in the service of the goals it seeks should not distract one from the revolutionary character of those goals. In countries still close to tribalism or colonialism the middle classes are often the sole agents for this change. In other countries, notably in Latin America where urbanism has developed and industrialization is proceeding, the middle classes have had to contend with several sectors of the population in addition to the wealthy and the landed aristocracy: the military, the clergy, and in some places, an organized urban proletariat. The first two, especially, may see their interests as different from those of the economic middle class, and they would not, therefore, be reliable partners in the movement toward change. The strategy of the middle class must take account of these power groups. The transition thus becomes one of shifting balances tenuously held, rather than unilateral change. Yet, the role of the middle class remains a pivotal one in the transition.

For these reasons, then, the emergence of a middle class is taken to be critical for an adequate urban theory. The members of the middle class, even in the early period of change, are urban residents, perhaps the only segment of the society that is truly urbanized. They are the models that presage the changes yet to be undergone by a majority of the population. The city is the home of this class and its arena for action.

§ The Rise of Nationalism

In the transition of societies to urban industrial status, nationalism has been an outstanding feature. That fact alone would be reason enough to consider it as a key element for a theory of urbanism. Like the other three elements already discussed— urban growth, industrialization, and the emergence of a middle class—nationalism is a pivotal element in the social transition that is being analyzed. Its social function, briefly, is to provide a social rationale that makes the transition possible. For nationalism supplies the ideology that can command loyalties, motivate action, and legitimate the changes to be effected.

According to Hans Kohn, one of the leading scholars of the subject, nationalism emerged as a political reality for the first time in the seventeenth century, with the development of industrialism and the rise of the middle class in Western societies. Again today in developing countries, the social functions of nationalism are being reiterated even though the styles and the forms taken by that ideology are somewhat different than they were in the West.

Only a minority desires social change. The bulk of the population, peasants and primitives at the bottom of the social hierarchy and the elite at the top, cling to things as they are. For the middle class, however, there is the motivation to change the social structure and to reach new positions of power and effectiveness. In order to mobilize a society behind that movement there must be an ideology: an explanation, a rationale, a body of plausible beliefs that justifies the change and that does so, presumably, for the good of society as a whole. The explanation should transcend the supposed interests of any one group. Nationalism fufills that exceedingly important requirement. Differences between tribes, groups, individuals, and localities can be submerged in favor of the nation as an entity, which

becomes the focal point for one's primary loyalty. This characteristic of the ideology makes it particularly fitting as a vehicle
for legitimate social change that aims to replace those traditions,
customs, and loyalties that are not adaptable. It is not that
nationalism necessarily destroys all former loyalties, but it
welds them into new functions serving the broader concept
of the nation.

Nationalism serves as a justifying rationale because it endows
the industrializing efforts of the middle class with honor and
purpose. This is not to say that nationalism is either good or
bad, a judgment that clearly would involve some independent
standard. Neither do I mean to imply that nationalism is a wav-
ing banner of idealism carried always by a Joan of Arc. There
can be, as there have been, fascistic and Machiavellian elements
in the uses of nationalism, and these doubtless may reappear in
history. But these judgments are extraneous to the present analysis, which is concerned only with the functions that nationalism
as an ideology and as a social value serves in the process of social
change. From the sociological perspective, the vital feature of
nationalism is its ability to mobilize a society and to convert
the energy and will of its inhabitants to the service of critical
changes in the social structure.

It is not accidental that nationalism in the West and in underdeveloped countries has been the ideology of the middle class
during the period of its emergence into power. As already indicated, it provides this class with a powerful and believable
social rationale for change. For that reason, nationalism can
supply cohesion and social solidarity during the transition period.
The middle class leads in that change, for not only is it politically vocal, but it is also committed most strongly to the goals
toward which nationalism is meant to lead. Industrialization,
therefore, is at one and the same time a means to establish the
nation, to develop its potential, and to improve the lot of the
nation's citizens. The identification of the middle class with
nationalism can often lead to what Silvert has called "arrested
nationalism," by which the ideology gets converted to a class
rather than to a supra-class cause.[36] "In the early years of European nations," Silvert noted, "nationalism was used to cohere
upper and middle groups; lower social elements were consistently

excluded from active participation in public affairs, from chances to ascend, and from wider economic horizons." Obviously, the same effects may emerge from today's nationalistic struggles as well.

A significant feature of nationalism is that it is an urban phenomenon. For one thing, as Emerson has noted, it is in the cities of colonial countries "that regular contact with the white man brings the vivid sense of contrast between his modes and standards of life and those of the native community." [37] For another, the city is the environment of the middle classes and it is here that their emergence into power begins. Most relevant, perhaps, nationalism is an urban phenomenon because only in the city can there be that broader social frame of reference that makes nationalism intelligible. To the peasant or the primitive who lives out his life in a small, relatively isolated region, the idea of the nation is meaningless. The village represents the boundaries of his social geography, and beyond it there is only the vast unknown.

Nationalism depends upon an abstract concept, often beyond the understanding of those who have lived out their lives within a small area. Although the nation does have territorial boundaries, these are not encountered with the same specificity or the same frequency as are those by which the villager knows his territory. It requires some imagination to conceive of the nation as a territory. It requires even more to translate this geographic conception into a social conception by which those who are within the boundaries are part of the nation and those who are outside them are outsiders. The urban citizen, from his broader social contacts and experience, from his awareness of the nation as a territory and as a social entity, has the basis upon which to develop and to sustain the idea of the nation.

Nationalism, thus, destroys the social geography by which the large mass of a preindustrial population organizes its world. It requires that one disregard the manifest differences between persons—differences in speech, manner, dress, language, and religion—and focus instead upon the latent and abstract commonalities that unite them into a nation. As Hodgkin has noted for African societies,[38] there are several factors that affect the development of this new social conception. The tempo of economic development and urbanization is important. So too are the levels of technological advance in communication, the extent of education and literacy, and the administrative policy of colonial governments, to the extent that they are permissive in allowing national identification to take root.

What, though, is the nation, the symbol around which nationalism organizes its loyalties? "The nation," according to Emerson, "is a community of people who feel they belong together in the double sense that they share deeply significant elements of a common heritage and that they have a common destiny for the future." [39] The criteria of a nation, according to the Royal Institute of International Affairs,[40] include a common language, a common origin (i.e., racial unity), a distinctive national character, a common religion, as well as a government, territory, and common interests. Or, as Silvert has defined it, "Nationalism is the social acceptance of the state as the impersonal and ultimate arbiter of human affairs." [41] These definitions emphasize a sense of community identification bolstered by evolving institutions and traditions which make nationalism not only a psychological quality but a social reality as well. Hence, the search for a common basis of unity such as language, ethnic origin, religion, custom, or race.

The concept of the nation begins with amorphous boundaries; only in time and by education does the nation become an effective social reality. These generally amorphous boundaries of the nation concept are a source both of strength and weakness. Strength comes from the fluidity of the concept by which the ideology of nationalism can be adapted to meet particular political needs. In the newly emerging nations of Africa, for example, the differences between tribes in language, dress, and heritage can be brushed aside as relatively unimportant against the larger, unifying concept of the nation. At least in principle this is the argument, although it is difficult to put into practice. Difficult though it may be because of the traditional diversity within the new nations, their success depends upon combining and unifying these manifest diversities into a new loyalty and a new sense of tradition organized around the ideology of the nation.

The amorphous boundaries of the nation concept are a

weakness coming from the lack of a traditional base upon which to build nationalism as a guiding ideology. It is difficult to dissuade individuals from their former loyalties in favor of nationalism. Where the manifest differences between people are great, the national concept is less persuasive and unifying. Where there are at least some common bases, such as language, religion, or cultural heritage, they can provide the means for enlarging the nation concept and giving it firmer boundaries.

Some tend to view today's nationalism as undesirable because it is tied so closely to aggressive and essentially negative social activities, as seen from the more mature nationalism of the West. After all, some have contended, nationalism in the West developed within each country, to achieve changes within a national territory. The participants were all citizens of an independent nation. Today's nationalism, on the contrary, depends heavily on anti-colonialism as its main feature; the principal adversary is the outsider who is made the scapegoat in order to help weld together the diverse social elements within a society. A political consequence of this situation is emphasis on the negative side of national development. Energies seem to be directed more to damning the outsider than to trying to build internal unity from the elements within the nation. As Emerson has insightfully remarked, in this type of situation the question of what nationalism positively stands for is postponed until a later time. "This negativism is most notably in evidence where the unity and coherence of the nation are most in doubt, and where the cultural background is least highly evolved." [42]

The negative road to national awakening can be most embarrassing and contradictory to the main goals of the newly emergent nations today. In many instances, these nations are dependent upon former colonial rulers and their allies for assistance. The nations of Africa, for example, depend upon England, France, Belgium, and the United States for economic assistance and technical aid. Or again, the Latin American nations are similarly tied into the U.S. orbit of influence for current economic reasons as well as past history. In both instances, the outsider is at once the target of a negative nationalism and its benefactor. The hand that feeds must also be bitten.

In the West nationalism was coupled with the emergence of

the positive values of Western culture: democracy, equality, and freedom. This was not accidental, for it was precisely those prerequisites that an emerging middle class needed to break the medieval mold of aristocracy and monarchy, prestige and absolutism. Nationalism in the history of the West did demand such freedoms in order to create the economic, political, and social conditions required for urban industrial growth. Those freedoms took time to filter down to the working class, of course. In England, for example, personal freedom was long reserved as the right only of those with property.[43] We are rightly concerned whether democratic institutions and democratic values will emerge from today's nationalistic movements. The whole question of the necessary linkage between nationalism and democracy is excellently put by Emerson, and deserves quotation here.

To reduce the question to its most basic terms, the argument linking democracy and nationalism would run something as follows. Nationalism is peculiarly a product of the distinctive forces which have gone into the shaping of the modern world. Those forces are inherently and inevitably "democratic" in the sense that they mobilize formerly submerged elements and classes of society into new social roles, eat away at traditional relationships, and work toward the building of a new great society into which, in principle, all men are actively drawn. Obviously what is involved here is by no means necessarily a democratic constitutional structure not even an immediate approximation of a society striving towards egalitarianism, although both of these are likely to be present at least as active aspirations. Far more, it is the general conception, derived from the changing social scene, that the people, the mass of ordinary human beings, are of consequence, that they are achieving a sense both of their own worth and of their right and ability to do something about it, and that the leaders must speak in their name. The national era comes to be an era of mass communications and mass production, inescapably headed toward mass politics.[44]

There are many instances today in which nationalism pursues a course that is plainly undemocratic; for instance, in the ruthless destruction of native opposition, in native dictatorships, and in shady political compromises that are seen as necessary in order to retain power. Even so, nationalism is the undisputed ideology behind political and social change today, and toward beneficent

change, at that. Under the aegis of nationalism, the first steps
toward urban industrial development are taken or forced, and
they are endowed with a sense of urgent purpose and with
the symbol of legitimacy. The rigid medieval or colonial social
hierarchy must be overwhelmed if industrial development is
to occur. The older, limiting sentiments and traditions of village
localism must be altered, and there must be substituted a new
and broader base for community identification. In this way,
the energies and resources of a society can be unified and
mobilized in one direction.

Born in the city, nationalism assumes control of a society's
destiny and in time spreads out to the countryside where it can
weld together the disparate social elements and social groups
into a unified community. As Silvert rightly concluded: "Nationalism as a social value has been the major cohesive force
to date within each separate modern society, and . . . its existence in underdeveloped areas is a natural part of the process of
development, very often anticipatory of the social class structure which is its only real justification and its only ultimately
legitimate social reason for being." [45]

viii

THE CITY
IN INDUSTRIAL
SOCIETY

THE PRECEDING chapters have been steps in a line of argument that began with critical appraisals of major conceptions about the city and that ended with a description of four components that are the core of an alternative view. The criticisms of earlier theories have emphasized three major faults that I believe do not appear in the analysis that follows, no matter what other faults it might contain.

One fault of the earlier views has been oversimplification. The city is not only an economic environment that has been developed out of economic needs or economic motives alone. Nor is it only a container for our architecture, however good or bad that might be. Nor is it only an administrative entity, confined within political boundaries that tradition or expediency have set for it. The city is all of these and more. A second fault has been to attempt to view the city only within the full sweep of history. By this view the city is a part of the continuous history

of mankind and as such is seen to have developed in an un-
broken line from antiquity to the present day. No doubt there
are some urban characteristics that have persisted from ancient
Athens to the cities of today. Many more characteristics, however, have not. To insist upon such historical continuity inevitably means that we lose the unique features that distinguish
the industrial city from all other urban forms. This is a high
price to pay if our interest is in the industrial city and its development. Finally, some of the earlier views of the city have
been unable to handle the social change that is so clearly the
mark of the industrial city. The city is a dynamic environment,
and this no urban theory can afford to overlook.

The description that follows is primarily concerned with
total societies and nations, rather than with cities as such. There
are several reasons for that emphasis. For one thing, the nation,
rather than the city, is the meaningful unit for the analysis of
urbanization and of the companion variables that have been
specified. With the advent of industrial society, change is no
longer confined within city boundaries. For another, the divisions between city and country that were characteristic of
earlier periods in history become blurred and eventually disap-
pear in the industrial urban phase. Not only is there the physical
spread of the city, but urban ideas and values also spread out
to dominate the whole of society. In the modern period, then,
cities are not isolated oases in the midst of an agricultural and
rural desert. Indeed, the mark of urban development today is its
social pervasiveness. Only in those societies that have not yet
reached a level of high urbanization do cities still remain rela-

tively isolated, even though they are portents of the prevalent form of society in the future. In the fully urbanized societies, however, such isolation of the city no longer exists. In every sense, the industrial city has become the dominating social feature of the society to which it belongs.

One merit of the approach taken here is to see the city through an analysis of industrial society. The four variables that have been designated—urban growth, industrialization, the growth of a middle class, and the rise of nationalism—are meaningful for societies, but are less so for cities alone. The city is heavily implicated in all of this, of course, for it is the initiator of such developments, as well as the recipient of the consequences. Yet, to understand the role of particular cities in that complex process, it is necessary first to establish the developments as they strike the totality of societies. Once we understand the dynamics of urban development through which a society moves, we might be better prepared to apply that knowledge to our understanding of the city itself.

The point that the sociological analysis of the city must begin with the analysis of society is not new. It was a characteristic point of view for the theoreticians discussed in Chapter Five, who consistently couched their urban analysis within the broader social framework and within an awareness of social change. Redfield, Tönnies, Weber, Durkheim, and Becker all agreed on that point.

Even so, we are never very far from the more restricted analysis of cities because they reflect and are implicated in the developmental stages through which societies pass. Every conclusion about *social* change has direct consequences for *urban* change. The scattered cities of underdeveloped and transitional societies reflect a particular stage of development, just as do the intensive cities of metropolitan societies. For example, in the underdeveloped countries, the shorter period that rural migrants usually spend in the cities is a consequence of the limited economic opportunities available to them and of the lack, as yet, of firm urban attachments. The more positive economic and psychological attractions exerted by metropolitan centers in advanced countries, on the other hand, are indicative of a fully urbanized and industrialized nation. In both cases the city is a direct reflection of the stage of development that the society has attained. Similar examples could be described for a whole range of urban phenomena, including the structuring of social institutions, the shape and rigidity of the class system, and the firmness of ecological segregation.

It is also clear that the sequence of development that a society follows will carry immediate consequences for the kinds of cities that it contains. Where the pace of urban growth outruns the rate of industrial expansion or the rate of middle class growth, the city will emerge as different on every count from cities where those several developments are more equal. A transitory population, unemployment, and slums are more likely under the first set of conditions than under the second. Therefore, appeals of demagogues and irrational mass movements are more likely to take hold under the first set of conditions than under the second, and the content of those appeals will be different.

In short, the path to urban analysis must run through a broader societal analysis, especially in the case of industrial urban development. The developed and the developing industrial cities are both creatures of societies at different stages of urbanization. Therefore, if we wish to learn about the city, we must first know something about the society to which it belongs. If we wish to understand the dynamics of change within the city, we must first understand the dynamics of broader social change as it pertains to urbanization.

§ Elements of a Typology

The description and analysis of the materials on urbanization are presented here in the form of a typology of urbanization. Societies have been classified on the basis of the four components that have been identified, and they have been arranged along a continuum meant to include the full spectrum of possible changes. Hence, at one extreme are to be found those societies that are underdeveloped, urbanized sparsely if at all, without a visible middle class, and without a foundation to support an ideology of nationalism. At the other extreme are those societies that are fully developed on each of these criteria. Between them is found an array of societies at different stages in their urban development.

Admittedly, a typology of this sort is a form of classification, not a theory. This has been discussed before and there is no need to repeat the distinction again. I wish only to emphasize that the creation of a typology must begin from a theory no matter how ill-defined, from a theoretical orientation from which the classifier makes his selection of relevant categories. In this sense, a typology is a device to translate theoretically relevant propositions into a systematic form which can then be tested and used to construct a more formal set of theoretical propositions and the relationships between them. Such is the intent of the present typology of urbanization. The four components of urbanization have been specified and they provide the basis for a typological construction. The utility of this procedure for understanding urban phenomena will be the justification for the typology. Although no effort has been made in this book to test the propositons on which the typology is based, such testing would be the next step as explained later. The utility of the typology, by contrast, can be evaluated now by whether it adds anything new to our knowledge.

Mention of a continuum of urbanization may seem hypocritical in view of the extended criticisms that were raised over Redfield's folk-urban continuum. There is a difference, however. The main point of the objection to the folk-urban continuum concerned the peculiar features of Redfield's orientation and the vagueness of some of the variables he used, not the technique itself. His intimation that there was a necessary evolutionary development, his generally anti-urban bias, his failure to specify variables in such a way that they could be identified, and his failure to limit the theory of urbanization to either an historical period or a geographic area were all subject to criticism that in no way commented upon the use of a continuum, but only upon his application of it. One might as well criticize the hammer and nails, rather than the carpenter.

The concept of a continuum does make sense for the study of urbanization. It provides a reasonably plausible characterization of what must happen as societies move along the path of urban development. Societies undergo continuous changes that seem properly represented by a continuum. In fact, they change in many more than the four aspects that have been specified. However, it is impossible to handle everything at once; therefore one must concentrate on those variables that seem important, relevant, and causative.

Although real societies provide the basis for the typology, the fact that it is based on current statistics should not be misinterpreted as proof of its validity. It is not within the scope of this book to test the validity of this typological model, a task that requires more information than is now available and, at the very least, later statistics. Sociologists usefully distinguish between theoretical and empirical typologies. In the first, the basis for the typology depends upon theoretical propositions, whether a priori or derived logically from other theoretical propositions. In the second, the typology depends upon empirical information. The urbanization typology is of the second sort, in that the countries are ordered on the basis of empirical characteristics. Clearly, these same measures cannot then be offered as proof of the typology's validity.

Not only would this be circular reasoning, but one should also remember that the indices used are more in the nature of approximations of a given characteristic than they are reliable and unequivocal measures. Realistically, one is forced to accept the approximation or do without. For some measures, as, for example, the size of the middle class or the relative strength of a nationalistic ideology, we must accept social features that are still imperfectly understood, let alone fully and adequately measured. Moreover, we simply do not always have the information we would like. It is a fact, unfortunately, that the objective measurement of a society's activities is itself a characteristic of advanced development. Underdeveloped societies, apparently, have no need, inclination, or skill to take censuses and to chart carefully the progress of their social and economic growth. And sometimes when they do, the results are a good deal less than accurate. Because such reports can have political and economic consequences, they are sometimes altered to fit the wish rather than the fact. It was mainly through the efforts of the United Nations that in 1950 many nations undertook their first population census. Even so, there is a great margin for error in these reports; some of the error is deliberate, most of it unintentional. Even after decades of experience the census of the United States contains errors because of the' fallibility of people in reporting information about themselves. How probable, then, to expect errors in the first census of a developing country, in which the population has still to be sufficiently educated to see the taking of a census as an ordinary and legitimate governmental action. It is the rule, not the exception, for United Nations's publications of census materials to contain the warning that the figures shown are probably inaccurate and should not be too heavily relied upon.

With all of these imposed restrictions it would be foolhardy to present the following analysis as anything more than tentative and suggestive. Proof is impossible for the materials generally at hand; further study to assemble more reliable statistics is mandatory. Additionally, more than one reading of the measures is called for, and this data for 1950 should not be taken as the last word. Repeated analysis in subsequent decades can provide the very test that is needed to establish the validity of the conclusions reached through the use of the typology.

The countries used in this analysis, then, are meant to provide illustrations for the categories of the typology, and are illustrations of the different stages of development that comprise the urbanizing process. The particular convergence of characteristics that is represented, say, by Italy or Colombia, is indicative of a particular stage of development, even though those countries might no longer be so placed ten or twenty years hence. (In fact, Italy's progress since 1950 has been considerable.) Indeed, since the typology is necessarily one of change, it must be expected that no country stands still, but rather that it gradually changes over time. The classification at any particular time simply represents an inventory of where countries stand in their development. Subsequent analysis should produce a rearrangement as countries succeed or fail in their urbanization experiences. I would also stress that the main point of the typology is the categories it describes rather than the placement of any particular country.

A brief explanation follows of the indices that have been chosen for each of the four variables in the typology.

1. *Urban Status*   The index used to measure this variable of urbanism is the proportion of the population living in cities of 100,000 or more. Definitions of urban places vary widely from country to country so that it would not be valid to compare them. Instead, a constant size has been established. The figure of 100,000, though arbitrary, seems high enough to insure that urban phenomena do exist. I am mindful of the criticisms against population size when used as a sociological criterion, but it is used here in a broader context that should make those criticisms inapplicable. Size alone does not classify a country in the typology and undue stress is not placed upon size as it is in the classifications discussed in Chapter Four.

2. *Industrial Status*   Industrialization, as noted before, means more than manufacturing. The term must also convey the character of a society that is organized around industry as a major feature of its existence. This means the social institutions, the aspirations, the beliefs, and the attitudes that belong to industrialized societies are also to be included in the definition. The index that has been chosen in this case does, therefore, not measure up fully: it is the percentage of the net domestic product that is contributed by manufacturing. But then, no single measure, or combination of measures, could fully convey the subtlety and the nuance of industrialization in the sense meant. Again, the choice must be made between as good an approximation as we can now use, and no measure at all. As noted before, I believe we must choose the first, knowing its limitations in advance and accordingly aiming to further our understanding. The measure that is used serves the purpose as well as any other and is better than most because it is not ambiguous. For example, a common measure of industrial development has been the number of persons engaged in agriculture: the higher the proportion in agriculture, the lower the industrial level of a country. This seems to be an indirect measure of industrialization and one that does not exclude mining or other nonindustrial activities. Furthermore, the measure that has here been designated is more frequently reported than any other.

3. *Prevalence of a Middle Class*   The middle class index is

based on the per capita income measured in terms of United States dollars. Let me say at once that class measures are the subject of extended dispute and dissatisfaction in sociology because class is a term with several meanings.[1] This is even more true, perhaps, for developing nations in which the middle class is as yet poorly formed and in which the accepted symbols of class have not yet taken hold. Occupation, for example, which some believe is the best class index we have in developed countries, could not serve the same purpose in the underdeveloped countries where industrial classes as we understand them have not yet appeared. In the latter countries a definitive class is much less evident than is an emerging elite whose functions and aims as a class will become clarified at a later time. Furthermore, there is the added difficulty brought on by the fact that the function of the class must inevitably change during the course of development; what begins as a revolutionary elite later settles down to a stable, conservative, and legitimate class as its goals are attained. The class does not stay the same throughout development, nor could it, given the dynamic changes that are inherent in urbanization. More discriminating measures than we now have are required to capture the functional alterations in the middle class that occur during development. Per capita income, however, used as an approximation, shows the strength of the middle class in a country relative to other countries, in a manner that is useful for the purposes here. The economics of class, after all, are correlated with income measures to a satisfactory degree. Although this index might prove unsatisfactory for identifying the several classes within an advanced nation, that objection is not so evidently true in comparisons between nations.

4. *Prevalence of Nationalism* Nationalism, like class, depends more upon psychological dimensions, social functions, and abstract symbols than upon concrete, directly observable, and measured behavior. Nationalism is a potential force expressed in many ways; it is as much a state of mind as a concrete act. To measure it at all, one must assume that individuals hold attitudes that can and do effectively guide their behavior in response to nationalism. The index used is the percentage of literate persons in the population of those fifteen years old and older. This measure, admittedly, is indirect and needs some clarification.

Literacy is considered here as a necessary condition for the growth of nationalism. It is not that nationalism can only emerge from an educated population, but that nationalism is abstract to a degree that requires some intellectual ability in order to be comprehended. The nation exists as a concept, not simply as real estate. This abstract quality is even more apparent in the early stages of its appearance, when the nation does not exist except as a future image. If nationalism is to be an effective determinant for attitudes and behavior, it is necessary for those responding to it to be able to imagine unity in the face of manifest diversity between the peoples of a nation. Such abstraction does not come easily to illiterate persons who tend to equate reality only with sensed experience. A minimal skill in reading and writing, therefore, can justifiably be used to index the ability of populations to understand the concept that is nationalism. Furthermore, it is that same ability that makes persons accessible to specific nationalistic appeals; a fact that has led developing nations to emphasize education as a high priority goal. In other words, literacy and education are necessary preparations for national development—improvements that developing countries are stressing and tying to their nationalistic appeals.

There are no national statistics that would allow for a plainly psychological or attitudinal measure of nationalism. Neither do we have valid behaviorial measures. The proportion of adults in each country who vote, for example, has been suggested as a possible index of nationalism. Such statistics are notoriously misleading. Voting in some of the newly emergent nations has been enforced by severe penalties, in the mistaken belief that a large turnout is a sign of democratic maturity. What does a voter turnout of 99 per cent mean in a nation that is less than a decade old, that has only one political party, and that has voting by decree rather than by choice and tradition?

Having given some rationale for each of the indices and having pointed to the shortcomings, I still feel called upon to alert the reader again to the arbitrary character of the indices I have used. It would be completely wrong to read the statistics, in the context in which they are used, as final or accurate measures of a particular phenomenon. Instead, they should be interpreted as approximations to a complex social phenomenon that cannot as yet be measured in any other satisfactory way. Hence, the extent of literacy in a country should not be read as being exactly equal to the extent of nationalism in that country. The same caution must be shown toward the other three indices, as well. It is because of such an admittedly unsatisfactory state of affairs that I have stressed the need to read the typology as a suggestive, not a proven, model. The proof, as I have earlier stated, will come from testing the typology against other statistics and other measures. However, I wish also to make it clear that the indices have been useful as a suggestive basis upon which to group countries. The typology does make sense and it does not depart strikingly from similar rankings of countries according to other criteria of development.

Table 6—Characteristics of Selected Countries on Four Urbanization Variables: 1950

Country	Per cent in cities of 100,000 and over [1]	Per cent national domestic product from manufacturing [2]	Per capita income (U.S. dollars) [3]	Per cent literate (15 years and older) [4]
England	51.9	37	773	98.5
United States	29.5	31	1453	97.5
Netherlands	32.7	32	502	98.5
Israel	43.5	36	389	93.7
West Germany	27.1	42	320	98.5
Austria	32.9	42	216	98.5
Denmark	33.5	30	689	98.5
Argentina	37.2	27	346	86.4
Chile	28.5	23	188	80.1
Japan	25.6	25	100	97.5
New Zealand	32.8	20	856	98.5
Canada	23.3	31	870	97.5
France	16.8	40	482	96.4
Poland	16.1	47	300	92.5
Hungary	19.7	46	269	95.3
Italy	20.4	31	235	87.5
Ireland	17.6	25	420	98.5
Norway	19.8	30	587	98.5
Union of South Africa	24.0	23	264	27.6
Panama	15.9	13	183	69.9

Table 6 (cont.)

Country	Per cent in cities of 100,000 and over [1]	Per cent national domestic product from manufacturing [2]	Per capita income (U.S. dollars) [3]	Per liter (15 y and c
Colombia	17.8	16	132	52
Egypt	19.3	11	100	19
Finland	14.2	32	348	98
Portugal	12.7	38	250	55
Greece	12.7	21	128	74
Paraguay	15.2	21	84	65
Nicaragua	10.3	14	89	38
Brazil	13.2	18	112	49
Mexico	15.1	18	121	46
Guatemala	10.2	20	77	29
Peru	10.0	11	100	47
Southern Rhodesia	11.4	9	101	22
Korea	14.8	10	35	37
Bulgaria	8.0	24	150	75
Thailand	9.9	13	36	52
Dominican Republic	8.5	20	75	4
Northern Rhodesia	0	13	100	22
India	6.6	15	47	19
El Salvador	8.7	8	92	3
Turkey	8.2	12	125	3
Philippines	9.3	12	44	6
Indonesia	7.3	9	25	1
Congo	2.7	5	70	3
Kenya	2.2	11	100	2
British Honduras	0	9	83	3

Sources: 1. United Nations, *Demographic Yearbook*, 1960. Table 8.
2. United Nations, *Statistics of National Income*, Series H, No. 7, Table 3. Also United *Statistical Yearbook*, 1951. Table 158.
3. United Nations, *Statistical Papers*, 1951. Series E-1 and E-3, Table 1.
4. UNESCO, *World Illiteracy at Mid-Century*, 1957.

N.B. The figures for income and manufacturing, especially, reflect only the immediate situation for many countries.

Information for forty-five countries on each index is presented in Table 6. Those were the only countries with published data, but they are adequate for the purpose, inasmuch as they cover the likely spectrum of countries from the least to the most developed. Also, it is possible to extrapolate from the countries listed. Hence, Kenya and the Congo can be taken as representative for a good many other African nations that do not publish all of the necessary information.

The next step was to translate the statistics into quantities that would be amenable to classification into a typology. Small differences had to be discarded in favor of a broader grouping of countries, or else the typology would become more cumbersome than useful. This step had the added advantage of under-emphasizing small numerical differences. Given the problematic accuracy of the figures, it was wiser to deal with relatively gross categories than with a classification that depended too heavily upon differences of a few percentage points one way or the other. The probability of erroneous classification is thereby reduced in direct proportion to the sizes of the categories used in ordering each measure.

The answer was a classification based upon quartile ranks, by which countries were ranked from the lowest to the highest on each index, and each index was then divided into four equal segments. Hence, the eleven countries with the highest percentages living in large cities were each given a rank of 1 on that index, the next eleven a rank of 2, and so on for the third and fourth ranks. The same procedure was followed for each variable, resulting in the quartile ranks shown in Table 7.

Table 7—Quartile Ranks of Selected Countries on Four Urbanization Variables: 1950

Country	Urbanism [1]	Industrialism [2]	Middle Class [3]	Nationalism [4]
England	1	1	1	1
United States	1	1	1	1
Netherlands	1	1	1	1
Israel	1	1	1	2
West Germany	1	1	2	1
Austria	1	1	2	1
Denmark	1	2	1	1
Argentina	1	2	2	2
Chile	1	2	2	2
Japan *	1	2	3	1
New Zealand *	1	3	1	1

Table 7 (cont.)

Country	Urbanism [1]	Industrialism [2]	Middle Class [3]	Nationalism [4]
Canada	2	1	1	1
France	2	1	1	2
Poland	2	1	2	2
Hungary	2	1	2	2
Italy	2	1	2	2
Ireland	2	2	1	1
Norway	2	2	1	1
Union of South Africa *	2	2	2	4
Panama	2	3	2	2
Colombia	2	3	3	3
Egypt	2	4	3	4
Finland *	3	1	1	1
Portugal	3	1	2	3
Greece	3	2	3	2
Paraguay *	3	2	4	3
Nicaragua	3	3	3	3
Brazil	3	3	3	3
Mexico	3	3	3	3
Guatemala	3	3	4	4
Peru	3	4	3	3
Southern Rhodesia	3	4	3	4
Korea	3	4	4	4
Bulgaria *	4	2	2	2
Thailand	4	3	4	3
Dominican Republic	4	3	4	3
Northern Rhodesia	4	3	4	4
India	4	3	4	4
El Salvador	4	4	3	3
Turkey	4	4	3	4
Philippines	4	4	4	3
Indonesia	4	4	4	4
Congo	4	4	4	4
Kenya	4	4	4	4
British Honduras	4	4	4	4

1. Percentage of total population in cities 100,000 and over.
2. Per cent of national domestic product from manufacturing.
3. Per capita national income.
4. Per cent literate in population fifteen years and older.
* Not included in the following typological analysis in Table 8 because of special circumstances. See Section on *Residual Societies* below for explanation.

Even a cursory glance at Table 7 gives an impression of order because the four indices are related. Very few countries show wide fluctuations between ranks on those measures. A good many countries are ranked the same on all of the four measures. Most do not vary more than one rank. A few span more than one rank. Bulgaria, for example, is high on three and lowest on urbanism. Similarly, New Zealand ranks in the first quartile for three indices, but in the third quartile for industrialism. Clearly, a country's position on one index gives a fairly close prediction as to its position on the others. However, the correlation is not perfect and it is this relative imperfection that gives the four measures their utility for a typology. Either perfect correlation or no correlation would not have served the purposes here, in the first case, because the four indices simply would have measured the same phenomenon; in the second, because no grouping of countries would have been possible since the fluctuations would have been too great to permit it.

Among the alternative procedures possible for constructing a typology I have selected the one which makes the best use of the quartile ranks. In fact, the results from several turned out to be enough alike so that any one procedure would have been as valid as another for handling the data at hand. The objective in arranging the variables was not only to create a typology of countries at different stages of urban industrial development, but also to emphasize the sequence that countries followed in that development. Urbanization, the term that we can use to denote the social transformation of societies, was considered as exhibiting four stages of development. In other words, countries in the lowest quartiles on all four indices were at the beginning stage of the development. The second stage included those countries that ranked in the third quartile on all the indices, and so on for the third and fourth stages, the last representing full development and including those countries that placed in the highest quartile in all indices. This arrangement was slightly modified, as is indicated later.

Let me return for a moment to the matter of sequence, the order in which countries pursue urbanization. Societies do not move evenly and simultaneously forward in all sectors during the process, and variations among priorities have appeared. Some countries begin moving forward by first concentrating upon industrial growth; others have urbanized first. Even after countries have moved beyond the first stage in urbanization, they are still confronted with the question of what is to have priority in the next step. Hence, once equality among the several facets of development has been reached at a given stage, some countries move to expand industrially, while others may turn instead toward expansion of the middle class or improvement in educational facilities. The confrontation with a variety of possible alternatives is never fully avoided as a country advances; it must make choices again and again at its various stages of development.

The sequence that is followed makes a difference. It can be argued, for example, that those countries that begin the process by increasing their urban populations are those also most likely to engender the problems of unemployment, depressed living standards, and social unrest in the cities, problems that arise because there are more people than can be supported. In a similar manner, where nationalism or the middle classes grow before all else, the political demands upon a developing country created thereby can become disastrous.

In order to systematically explore the patterns of development, the forty-five countries were grouped according to the sequence of development they seemed to be following, as determined by their ranks on the four indices. For example, looking at the bottom segment of Table 7, it is seen that Turkey and El Salvador shared a higher ranking on the middle class index than on either urbanism or industrialism. At the other extreme, Argentina and Chile ranked highest in urbanism and lower on the three remaining indices. By inspection, then, the countries were arranged into groups or types as shown in Table 8. The method followed in grouping was to locate a country in one of the four stages on the basis of its lowest rank on any index. A further specification of a country's place within any one of the subgroups was achieved by a form of scaling of its relative quartile rank on the remaining indices as these were shown in Table 7.

Table 8—A Typology of Urbanization

STAGE OF DEVELOPMENT	COUNTRY
Stage I	
Underdeveloped Societies	British Honduras
	Congo
	Indonesia
Nationalizing Societies	Philippines
	Turkey
	El Salvador
Industrializing Societies	India
	Northern Rhodesia
	Dominican Republic
	Thailand
Urbanizing Societies	Korea
	Southern Rhodesia
	Peru
	Egypt
	Guatemala
Stage II	
Transitional Societies	Mexico
	Brazil
	Nicaragua
Industrializing Societies	Greece
	Portugal
Unbalanced Urban Societies	Colombia
	Panama
Stage III	
Urban Transitional Societies	No cases
Rural Balanced Societies	Norway
	Ireland
Urban Industrial Societies	Italy
	Hungary
	Poland
Industrial Balanced Societies	France
	Canada

Table 8 *(cont.)*

STAGE OF DEVELOPMENT	COUNTRY
Stage IV	
Unbalanced Metropolitan Societies	Chile
	Argentina
Metropolitan Societies	Denmark
	Austria
	West Germany
	Israel
	England
	United States
	Netherlands

§ Urbanization: A Typology of Change

Urbanization is not a determined revolutionary change by which an undeveloped society moves in a unilinear direction toward transformation into a fully urbanized society. Alternatives among which societies must choose are constantly open. Some societies, apparently, initiate the process with industrial development and move on from there. Others are dominated first by the growth of cities, tending to delay the creation of a broader middle class base or industrial development. Still others begin with the creation of nationalistic ideologies and then seek to move toward industrial and urban development. Each choice carries its own consequences and the developmental choices at any given time impart to a society a set of accompanying characteristics. It is within that context that cities can be viewed as "parasitic" or "generative," for example, in line with the distinction that Hoselitz has drawn between cities that have a favorable or unfavorable impact upon the economic growth of a country.[2]

Urbanization is not a process that requires a society to go through the full cycle of change and to become, say, massively metropolitan. For reasons which we poorly understand as yet, some societies stop short, are retarded so to speak, at one or another stage. Hence, some do not go on to full metropolitan expansion even though they have attained all the other features of an urban industrial society. Doubtless there are reasons in each case to explain why some countries stop where they do and others continue to the next stage in the development process, but there is as yet no general explanation of them. Let me now describe the several types in general terms, recognizing that there may be particular exceptions to some of those general comments.

Stage I
a. *Underdeveloped Societies*

The underdeveloped societies, of course, are those that have made no move toward, among other things, urban change. They are identified in Table 7 as those countries that rank in the lowest quartiles on all four indices. Generally, these are the newly independent countries of Africa and of Southeast Asia, countries that have recently gained their independence from colonial status and that for the first time in the modern era have a measure of control over their own development.

Societies in this stage are largely traditionalistic, agricultural, and rural. This is not to say they are homogeneous; they are far from it. They are often split by differences in tribal, religious, and linguistic origins that are an integral part of their complexion. The fight for political independence is at one and the same time a prerequisite for national development and an internal power struggle between competing elite factions within the society. The struggle frequently appears as a negative nationalism; that is, a search for internal unity through attack on the outside colonial power as everyone's villain. Independence, once achieved (and sometimes even before), can threaten such unity as may have been established by the strife from subsequent attempts to gain power by the several contending elite leaders and their supporting factions. Another burden is thereby added to the already heavy load that must be carried in the course of change.

The cities within these countries are usually former colonial

administrative and economic centers. They served principally as
centers for colonial authority, places from which the economic
and political affairs of the colony could be directed. Given
these purposes, such cities, for the most part, were segregated
from the surrounding region where the bulk of the native population lived, as well as segregated within, housing two societies:
the colonial, administrative elite and the native population. After
independence, these cities in underdeveloped countries become
the locales for native administration and control. They remain
socially isolated areas for the most part, and they are not part
of the social perceptions held by most of the population. They
do serve, however, as effective symbols of independence, material
reminders of victory over the colonizing elites, and foci for
the development of nationalistic appeals.

The majority, though, is still at a tribal or primitive level
of social organization. Mainly uneducated and illiterate, although
the extent varies from country to country depending upon
the policies of the colonizers, the native population is still far
outside the modern era. Its loyalties are local, centering around
kin, tribe, village, and language. The attitudes necessary for
modernization have yet to be developed; the newer loyalties to
the nation have yet to be forged. For the few who are educated
and politically wise, the city provides a center for future
aspirations. They are the members of the new elite who provide
the impetus for independence and change. It is in the city they
have been nurtured and through which their activities will be
funneled. For the next period, at any rate, their future is united
with their nation's future; their aspirations must become broadly
held national aspirations.

Stage I
b. *Nationalizing Societies*

One direction in which a country can move as a first step
in development is nationalism. This may be a negative nationalism, sharply focused on the outsider but serving the useful
purpose of unifying the opposing elements within, behind a common cause. The experiences of many societies that have at-

tained independence in the postwar decades bear out the generalization. However, the new nations are not the only ones that have pursued this line of development. As seen in Table 8, El Salvador and Turkey also symbolize this type. What is common to them is the early emergence of a middle class and an emphasis upon nationalism. Countries of this type have not made any especially significant gains in either urban or industrial growth. It is this condition that puts them in the category of Stage I nationalizing societies.

The development of nationalism in such societies is accompanied by the emergence of a middle class elite, which is small, educated, and likely to consist of professionals, usually lawyers, the military leadership, and small landholders. No economic basis exists as yet for a sizable white-collar group; this comes later, along with industrial growth. The nationalizing countries have yet to start a sustained industrial development, so they remain predominately rural. The middle class elite provides the only personnel available at the moment to champion the ideology of nationalism.

Fortunately, Lerner gives us an excellent portrait of this nationalizing role of the middle class in Turkey.[3] Although Turkey ranks highest in modernization of the six middle-eastern countries that Lerner and his colleagues studied, it is still very near the beginning of its development, compared with advanced nations. The creative minority that Lerner calls the "moderns" constitute about ten per cent of the population, by his criteria. They are the guiding middle class elite who shape Turkey's future. They are urban, educated, young, and fill the higher income and occupational categories. They are cosmopolitan, well-read, informed, and unlike the tradition-minded Turks, they see where they want development to move, and are committed to its success. Clearly, on the success of this nationalizing middle class elite will depend where Turkey and similar countries move next in the development process.

Cities play an important role for countries of this type. Although they contain a minority of the population, the cities are the residence of the elites, and it is from the city that the power of the elite will emanate. The city serves as the center, as the locale for elite contacts with one another and with the world. The elite is not isolated and it rightly recognizes its need to know about the world outside. In fact, it may be better attuned to the world outside than to the country of its origin. As one of the respondents in Lerner's study of Turkey explained "I want to know what is happening. I want to get different opinions on it, and get a clear and unbiased idea. I want to find out where the world is heading." [4]

Stage I
c. *Industrializing Societies*

Some societies begin their development with industrial growth rather than with the middle class or nationalistic moves of the preceding type. The last two features are not entirely absent, relative to other facets of development, but the major effort seems to be behind industrialization. In other words, change begins primarily in the economic sector, with a lesser emphasis upon change in class structure or political ideologies. These are relative differences, of course, because it must be assumed that a middle class elite of sufficient strength and a nationalistic ideology of some force already exists to move the country toward industrial development. Certainly, this seems to be an accurate characterization of India, which is one of the countries in this category. For all of the change in the last decade or so the caste system in India has not been seriously modified as far as the bulk of the population is concerned, and the Indian middle class is still in a minority. Yet, the pressure toward industrialization has been great during that same period.

The important single feature of this type, then, is the push toward industrial development. The major emphasis upon industrialism best characterizes the usual sequence of development as it is most often described: Industrial ventures are seen as the take-off point from which underdeveloped countries move into the urbanizing process. In some measure the character of an industrial take-off today probably is a function of the type of economic assistance that is received. Technical and economic assistance programs for the underdeveloped countries tend to be based on the assumption that the effort to expand an industrial potential is the quickest way to induce a viable economy, which is especially important where the country has strategic political significance internationally. Any other approach takes more time because it depends so much upon inculcating a new set of attitudes in a large part of the population, be they attitudes toward education, new farming techniques and implements, or work disciplines. Attitudes necessary for effective industrialization are also new, to be sure, but they require less subtlety and individual discretion than others; industrial work routines can be group-taught, they can be minutely specified and efficiently supervised. I suspect, too, that Western countries as contributors to development understand the priority of industrial development in the light of their own histories more easily than they do other facets of the process. The West sees its own development as having been primarily due to industrialization and only followed by the other features we have come to link to the process.

One advantage of beginning with industrial development is its minimizing of some of the problems attending change, especially those associated with urban imbalance. Not that industrialization is an easy social transformation under any circumstances. But in relative terms, keeping the bulk of the population out of the cities until industrial development has reached the point where it can employ a significantly large labor force undoubtedly can ease several urban problems, including housing, unemployment, and living standards. The large cities in India, for example, suffer from the characteristic problems of cities in underdeveloped countries, but this affects only some six per cent of the total population. One is properly impressed by the several massive urban concentrations in India, by the million-plus cities of Bombay, Calcutta, Delhi, and Madras. Yet these are relatively small proportions of a population that is estimated to exceed 400 million persons. Any significant increase in that urban population before sufficient industrial growth to provide it with employment could only exacerbate the misery, perhaps bringing disaster. The countries that emphasize industrialization first have the likely advantage of inducting relatively small proportions of the population into the vortex of urban change at any one time. The other features of change can come soon enough, as history has shown. If the goal is industrial urbanization, the priority of industrial growth seems soundest, if it can be achieved.

Stage I
d. *Urbanizing Societies*

A final variation by which underdeveloped societies begin the process of change is the increasing of their urban centers. As noted before, the priority of urban growth is relative, for countries cannot urbanize without some alteration in the other indices of change. Of the five societies that fit in this type, Egypt, Guatemala, Peru, Southern Rhodesia, and Korea, only Korea indicated urban growth unaccompanied by similar changes in the other variables of development. This would suggest that at the initial stage of development, urban expansion depends upon some support from either a developing middle class or, less frequently, from industry. The validity of this conclusion is supported by Pye's analysis of the cities of Southeast Asia, where "the basis of the city has been commercial and administrative activities." [5]

The outstanding characteristic of this type is that urban growth takes place before a *comparable* industrial growth. It is worth quoting Pye again on Southeast Asia because his conclusions are so applicable to countries elsewhere.

It is extremely significant that the rapid growth of all the cities in the area occurred with almost no encouragement from industrial development. . . . In Southeast Asia people are being attracted to the cities with the expectation that they will be able to find a way of life and a standard of living that are dependent on industrial development. Also of course, people are being pushed toward the cities because of the bankruptcy of the peasant economy under the pressures of population growth and commercialization.[6]

Herein lies the tragedy. Urban growth under such conditions means that the economy is generally unable to support those who have come or have been pushed into the city. Whether they have been pushed by rural poverty or pulled to the city for positive reasons, the result is the overcrowding of these cities to the point that they cannot provide for the populations they contain. The cities are the unprepared recipients of a stream of population from the land which reaches the city without either the skills or the opportunities for employment.

The conditions of urban imbalance at the earliest stage of development make the process of change more severe, more destructive, and more painful than it would likely be at a later stage. Consider Egypt, with a population in 1947 of almost 19 million, of whom almost 20 per cent lived in the seven largest cities. At this time, 80 per cent of the population was illiterate and had a per capita income of about $100, and only 10 per cent of Egypt's national product came from manufacturing activities. Urban expansion under such conditions could only be the path to the greatest misery for the greatest number.

The countries that find themselves in this condition, where urban growth has progressed faster than industrial and middle class growth, are generally in a worse position than even the completely underdeveloped nations. In the latter case, at least, the great bulk of the population is still rural, and still rooted to the past and to tradition, for whatever security can be gained from that attachment. I do not mean to glorify tradition for its own sake or to romanticize the land; but, in this case, they are the lesser evils. Rural poverty is no more palatable than urban poverty, but the last can be worse because the individual has fewer community resources available to him in the city than he had in the village. The people in the cities of Stage I urbanizing societies, perhaps, do not have much choice between rural poverty and urban misery, but having chosen to migrate to the city they suffer most of the disadvantages of trying to exist in an alien environment.

Stage II
a. *Transitional Societies*

Societies at this level have moved ahead on all four of the development indices. They are still quite a way from urban industrial status, but they have already taken more than the first, faltering steps in the process toward it. Mexico, Brazil, and

Nicaragua typify the countries that belong in this category. There are, of course, differences between them, aside from those similarities here emphasized. Brazil is twice as populous as Mexico and, of course, their histories differ. Yet they compare on the measures used here. In both, about 15 per cent of the population resides in cities of 100,000 or more; about half of the population of each is literate; about 18 per cent of the net domestic product of each is contributed by manufacturing; and approximately the same per capita income, a little over $100, is characteristic of both countries.

The mark of these societies is the balance that exists between the several facets of development. Compared with other countries, their urban growth is more or less in line with industrial growth, with the size of the middle class, and with their nationalistic potential. Development could stop here, although the usual assumption is that it will continue. It is more likely that these Stage II societies are transitional and ready to change further, or, at least, such countries seem to be greatly and publicly concerned about not stopping at this point. This has been the case for Brazil, for example, which has not been able to pick up its development beyond this stage, as yet, and which seems to worry a good deal about its progress. The question that emerges is: Which direction is to be followed in the next step of development? As can be seen from those societies that have moved just beyond this stage, there are critical problems ahead, their nature depending upon the direction of change that is next taken. These are the same alternatives and reflections, once removed, that had to be faced by the underdeveloped societies at Stage I.

I do not wish to leave the impression that these are stable societies because they have attained a plateau of balance. The pressures toward succeeding changes are already formed within these transitional societies. It is to be expected, therefore, that internal tensions must accompany the complex decisions of where and how these societies are to move. The presence of a larger, more coherent, and politically oriented middle class than was found in the underdeveloped societies means that this class will engender a greater pressure toward development favorable to their aspirations. At the same time, the presence of a relatively stable urban population of some size means that other political voices aside from the middle class are heard, notably, that of an urban proletariat much less docile than the new urban migrants in the underdeveloped countries. For example, in Mexico, the professionals, managers, and white-collar workers comprise some 15 per cent of the total male labor force, and we can assume that most of them are urban and middle class. At the other end of the occupational hierarchy, however, are those employed in transportation, crafts, and services, comprising about 25 per cent of the labor force. They, too, are predominately urban but working class. The middle class, therefore, has no political monopoly but must contend with other classes. In Brazil, similar proportions obtain: about 12 per cent engaged in the professions, managerial, or white-collar occupations, and some 20 per cent engaged in the laboring occcupations.[7] It would seem to follow that class conflict is an inherent part of the urban political scene.

Cities within transitional societies are the locales in which future change is decided and begun. Here are concentrated the greater part of the educated middle class as well as the organized urban proletariat. From the political dynamics inherent in that confrontation, the decisions will most likely be forged. Though the middle class seeks a stable situation for future development, the population at large has not yet benefited from industrial gains. Urban slums are the most evident symbols of the failure of these societies to spread the benefits of whatever development has taken place. Though industrial production has increased beyond that of the Stage I societies, income disparities are a source of dissatisfaction. Compare for example, the per capita national product of Brazil ($230) and Mexico ($220) with such societies of Stage I as Guatemala ($160) and Egypt ($120).[8] With more wealth to distribute, the transitional countries have not solved the problems attendant to industrial urban development, as evidenced by the low living standards in the cities for those at the bottom of the economic scale—but then, neither have the more developed countries. The pressure for change, therefore, is relieved little, if at all, for these transitional societies.

Stage II
b. *Industrializing Societies*

One direction that can be followed by transitional societies, as was true for underdeveloped societies at an earlier stage, is to increase the tempo of industrial development over that of the other components. Today, of course, the origins of this movement are more complex than simply the wish or the desire to industrialize. The two societies in this category are both older—Greece and Portugal. The new nations are not yet at this stage, nor are the countries of Latin America. It is altogether likely that this type of Stage II industrialization is a more valid category for the past than for the future of developing societies. In the case of Greece and Portugal, we have countries that are more probably fixed at this stage of development than poised to move further ahead in that process. These are generally rural countries that have never caught up with the pace of urbanization set by England, Germany, or Italy. Nor does it seem likely that they will.

They are not highly industrialized countries, and by contemporary standards are decidedly rural and agricultural. Yet, if Greece and Portugal are disregarded for the moment and we consider instead the theoretical implications alone, this stage ideally represents one alternative in the development process. Industrialization has increased beyond the level of most transitional societies, and for developing societies this phase could represent an effective goal.

It is possible to consider this stage as one that was attained by Western countries in the course of their development. Urban development in the West followed industrial growth. Indeed the problem in Western cities was more often that of a shortage than of a surfeit of industrial labor. London in 1801, for example, was the only city in England and Wales with a population over 100,000, containing 11 per cent of the total population, approximately the same proportion as that for Greece and Portugal in 1950 (12.7 per cent). These societies, in other words, were not highly industrialized nor did they have large urban populations, but instead, were still moving toward that goal.

There is another parallel that can be drawn between Stage II industrializing societies today and Western countries a century and a half or so ago, if we assume that their levels of literacy and the size of the middle class were comparable to those of the countries that belong in this category today. From what we can tell, the power of nationalism was well developed in Great Britain and in the United States at the beginning of the last century, as was the cohesiveness of the emerging middle class, which lends credence to the similarity between past and present developments.

The main feature of this type is the emphasis on industrial growth rather than on urban growth. For whatever reason, rural areas still, and perhaps for almost the last time in this development process, remain able to hold their own, to dominate the scene. The agricultural village is still the residence for most of the population, apparently with sufficient vitality, either economically or by the force of tradition, to restrain a significant urban migration. More than half of the labor force in these countries, for example, is still engaged in agriculture. Urbanization under these circumstances appears more in balance with other facets of growth. On the basis of this type, it would seem that planning should maintain rural traditions and rural economies as a means of preventing the problems that could otherwise come from too rapid urban growth at this stage.

Stage II:
c. Unbalanced Urban Societies

Not all transitional societies are as fortunate. The societies in this category have moved from the point of balanced transition toward urban growth at a faster pace than economic growth. The two societies representative of this direction of development are Colombia and Panama. Panama has also evidenced advances in the middle class and nationalism indices; even so, for Panama the imbalance between urban and economic growth is the critical characteristic. Certainly for Panama, the involvement of the U.S. in the Canal Zone makes a difference.

The consequences of the imbalance between urban and industrial growth should be similar to those for Stage I urbanizing societies. The consequences are even more serious for a country like Colombia, where no comparable advance has taken place either in the expansion of the middle class or in nationalism. There is an explosive form of urban expansion with little or no support for change in other sectors of the process. The cities in this type of society are especially vulnerable to the stresses of change because they haven't an economic base sufficient to sustain them, nor do they have a significant middle class that might provide stability in this period. This would be more true for Colombia than Panama, as far as the information in Table 6 reveals. Of course, should industrial growth begin, as has been happening since 1950 in Cali, Colombia, then the imbalance and its effects might be alleviated. However, rapid industrial growth is not enough without the simultaneous growth of a more responsible middle class committed to the nation. The situation of imbalance engenders inadequate housing, minimal living standards, chronic unemployment, and urban discontent. In the case of Colombia, the effects of *la violencia* (marauding bands raiding and murdering) in the rural areas endanger the situation even more, by hampering the growth of a responsible middle class.

Societies of this type are still in their transitional period. In their development and in the accompanying stress, both political and economic, there prevail the effects of an urban population that is larger than it should be. City growth is more a symptom of weakness in the political and economic spheres of the nation than it is a positive indication of development. The relative absence of the middle class is further evidence of that weakness. It implies that urban migration occurs because of unsatisfactory conditions in the rural areas rather than as a consequence of urban attractiveness, as a growing middle class might suggest.

Stage III   TRANSITIONAL
a. *Urban Traditional Societies*

Societies at this stage have achieved a new level of balance in all four sectors of the industrial urban process. What is more, they are now urban societies, possibly on the way to the final stage of metropolitan growth. None of the countries that were studied fits this category, but the type is logically possible, and other countries might well be included here in the future.

Societies of this type would be similar to those described as Stage II transitional, but here would be distinguished by further development; urban growth, industrial growth, the emergence of the middle class, and the hold of nationalism would be well advanced. I would think that this urban transitional stage might represent a second plateau through which Western societies moved in the course of their development, around the middle of the last century in Britain and after the Civil War in the United States.

Insofar as reconstruction of the process is possible in terms of the dimensions considered here, there does seem to be a plausible basis for this interpretation. Around the middle of the nineteenth century, England had about a third of its population residing in cities of 50,000 or more and London had reached a population of about 2 million. These are high densities even by present standards, but relative to England's subsequent growth, that stage would resemble what is here defined as an urban transitional one. In the United States around 1870, about one third of the population was classified as urban, and the labor force was almost equally divided between farm and nonfarm workers.

Societies in the urban transitional phase are significantly urbanized and seem to be on the very edge of another chain of developments within a short time. These societies are still the kind, however, that can be described as Great Britain was in 1851 in its census of that year.

One of the moral effects of the increase of the people is an increase of their mental activity, as the aggregation in towns brings them oftener into combination and collision. The population of the towns is not so completely separated in England as it is in some other countries, from the population of the surrounding country: for the walls, gates, and castles which were destroyed in the civil wars, have never been rebuilt; and the population has outgrown the ancient limits; while stone lines of demarcation have never been drawn around the new centres of population. . . . The freemen in some of the towns enjoyed anciently exclusive privileges of trading; . . . and by the great measure of Municipal Reform (1835) every town has been thrown open to settlers from every quarter. At the same time, too, that the populations of the towns and of the country, have become so equally balanced in number . . . the union between them has become, by the circumstances that has led to the increase of the towns, more intimate than it was before; for they are now connected together by innumerable relationships, as well as by the associations of trade . . . a large proportion of the population in the market towns, the county-towns, the manufacturing towns, and the metropolis, was born in the country; and that, in England, town and country are bound together not only by the intercourse of commerce and the interchange of intelligence, but by a thousand ties of blood and affection.[9]

Cities in this phase grow, but they grow primarily as a result of immigration rather than of the natural increase of the urban population itself. This condition prevailed in American cities, for example, well into the twentieth century, and was the basis of a major complaint that rural romantics levied against urban society. In fact, the advantages of urban life described above for England in 1851 were not often encountered in other writings in England or the United States during the time. It must be recalled that it was this kind of urban existence that had driven Ebenezer Howard to expound plans for the garden city. This era in urban growth was not idyllic for most urban residents. For the wealthy, for the successful entrepreneurs, the city was a place to be enjoyably lived in; for others, the city manifested many of the evils that Howard and others usually ascribed to it.

In considering the future, it seems likely that developing societies will pass through an urban transitional stage more or less of this kind. However, given our knowledge of urban failures in the past, it is certainly not inevitable these newer societies reiterate the West's experience fully. Whether they will be able to avoid it is a question that will have to be answered in the future.

Stage III
b. *Rural Balanced Societies*

Rural societies at this stage are more influenced by urban developments than were the peasant and village societies at earlier stages. For all societies at this third stage are relatively advanced and heavily, though not predominately, urbanized. According to the information in Table 6, about 20 per cent of the population lives in large cities, which is a relatively high proportion. The characteristic urban feature of these societies is that there is a small population concentration in a few very large cities. Instead, there are more evenly dispersed, smaller, urban concentrations. Norway, for example, defines half of its population as urban but it is dispersed in some twelve relatively small cities. Ireland, too, has more than one quarter of its population living in eight cities of 20,000 persons or more, and only 18 per cent living in Dublin, the only city of more than 100,000 in Ireland.

Agriculture plays an important role in the economy of these rural, balanced societies, but it shares its economic importance with industrial facilities and is no longer entirely dominant. In terms of per capita income and of literacy these societies are on a level with the most developed metropolitan societies. They differ both in the relative absence of industry and in the lack of overly dense urban concentrations. These cities are more manageable than metropolitan concentrations because the countryside has remained viable and economically important. The pressures for urban migration are not as constant as they have become for the dense metropolitan societies.

Beginning with societies in this third stage of development, there is the possibility that urban development will stop instead of continuing on to an expanding metropolitan level. Such would seem to be true for Norway and Ireland. Once a certain urban level is reached, there are alternative directions that Stage III societies can pursue, such as the enlargement of the middle class and the stabilization of national ideology. This is accompanied by raising educational levels, as by raising the material standard of living for more persons in the society. These societies, however, remain essentially rural in character. Their cities are major industrial and commercial centers, separated but not isolated from the rural hinterland because urban attitudes and values are spread by means of the mass media and other socializing channels. We find in these rural balanced societies, then, a possible end point for development. Such societies can achieve a balance between agriculture and industry, between the rural and the urban.

Stage III
c. *Urban Industrial Societies*

Societies in this category, as typified by Italy, Hungary, and Poland, have continued their industrial expansion after having attained a reasonably high urban concentration. Urban concentration is below the high level attained by the fully metropolitan societies; about one quarter of the population lives in the large cities, which may number a dozen or more. Agriculture continues to play a significant role, but industrial growth has continued as well.

The striking feature of these societies is the fact that urban growth has reached a plateau and has not greatly increased, in spite of continued industrialization. Hungary, for example, had only increased from 30 per cent urban in 1900 to 34 per cent in 1949, a gain of five per cent during the fifty years.[10] In that respect the urban industrial societies are similar to the rural balanced ones just described. The major difference between them is that the former have continued their industrial expansion. In fact, the level of industrial development is equal to that attained by the most industrialized nations. Poland, for example, ranked first on the industrialization index with 47 per cent of the net domestic product contributed by manufacturing. Hungary followed next with 46 per cent. Yet, this advance apparently has been at the cost of other aspects of development. Middle class growth has been stabilized at a much lower level than industrialization. In spite of its relatively high industrial output, Poland in 1950 still had 5 to 10 per cent illiteracy and a per capita income of $300. Similar statistics have been obtained for Italy and Hungary as well. (Italy, of course, after 1950 would no longer belong in this category.)

What we find, in effect, are industrial societies that have as yet failed to distribute the advantages of development throughout the population as evenly as they might. Middle class standards are not widespread. Not that these standards are an unmixed blessing, but they do indicate a certain measure of material affluence, an advance in such things as health, nutrition, and education, that I presume is a desirable goal. Rural areas are more economically depressed here than in the societies of the preceding type. Urban problems are due less to an unmanageable density and much more to the failure of middle class growth to keep pace. Through maldistribution due to centralized control, or for other reasons, industrial expansion has exacerbated class differences within the city, as well as between the city and the countryside. Urban poverty, therefore, is more likely to be the dominant problem that cities have to contend with, rather than clogged transportation or similar problems characteristic of the more affluent metropolitan societies.

Stage III
d. *Industrial Balanced Societies*

The major difference between societies of this and the preceding type is that in these societies there has been commensurate development in living standards, nationalism, middle class growth, and industrial growth. Here, then, is found a more balanced variant of the urban industrial societies just described.

The countries that fit this category are France and Canada, both of which are urbanized, industrialized, and at the same time have a wider dispersal of middle class standards throughout the population than had the preceding type. France, for example, has more than half of its population classified as urban, but with only some 17 per cent living in twenty-four of its larger cities. Yet the rate of urban growth has not been startling, for France increased its urban population by only 10 per cent in the fifty years after 1900. In Canada, less than one-quarter of the population resided in its ten largest cities in 1950. At the same time, industrial development has been generally on a par with that of the most highly industrialized nations.

The cities in these societies are clearly cosmopolitan cities, but they are not as densely occupied as the cities in the fully metropolitan societies. A strong middle class exists, but the middle class is no longer the revolutionary elite seeking to change the power structure, as is the case in the developing nations. In these societies at the stage of industrial balance, middle class attitudes and values have been filtered down to other classes and become as dominant as urban values. Educational attainments are generally high, as are the levels of per capita income. By this point in development, if not earlier, the initiating middle class of an earlier phase has already won its battles and has succeeded in reaching its objectives of development.

Further urban growth is likely to take place as the population increases, although lower birth rates and lower death rates are characteristic demographic features of these societies because of the spread of urban and middle class values. What has tended to stabilize the urban growth potential in these societies is a widespread system of small landholding that has tended to be hereditary, thereby keeping a significant proportion of the population on the land. In France, for instance, a third of the population is engaged in agriculture, a proportion that is twice that found in the United States. As long as that tradition, which makes migration to the city unlikely, is maintained, and there is no reason for it to change sharply, and as long as urban natural increase is low, then *explosive* urban growth is not likely to occur. The circumstances of Algerian immigration into France during 1962 must be considered as exceptional. Cities will grow, but not overnight. They are also likely to spread out, as is already evident in both France and Canada, through suburbanization. That expansion has resulted from the raised living standards of a significant part of the population, coupled with the middle class aspirations for home ownership or, at the least, better housing than can be found in the older parts of the city. The French suburb, the *banlieue*, apparently has been increasing since the end of the war. Such movement outward from the city's center can be seen as a consequence of better living standards and the generally greater concern given to the appurtenances of status and prestige in an industrial urban society.

Stage IV
a. *Unbalanced Metropolitan Societies*

With this type we reach the first of two kinds of metro-politan societies. The distinguishing feature of this unbalanced form is a metropolitan growth that has outrun all the other facets of growth that we have been discussing. Chile and Argentina, the two countries that belong in this category, have urban concentrations that are comparable with anything found in other metropolitan countries. This is especially true for Argentina, where almost two-thirds of the population live in cities, with over one-third concentrated in the fifteen largest cities in the country. Moreover, the history of its urban de-velopment has matched that of the United States and, if anything, has been more rapid. For example, before 1900, Argentina's ur-ban population comprised 37 per cent of the total population, compared with 40 per cent in the United States. By 1914, Ar-gentina's urban population had reached 53 per cent, while in the United States for the closest comparable year it was only 46 per cent. By 1947, Argentina was 63 per cent urban while it took the United States until 1950 to reach a comparable proportion.[11]

Yet, with this rapid urban expansion, the unbalanced metropolitan societies have not been able to maintain comparable growth rates for other aspects of development. The middle class, for example, has not developed as rapidly as has metro-politan concentration. Illiteracy is still about 14 per cent in Argentina and almost 20 per cent in Chile. Per capita income in Argentina in 1950 was $346, and in Chile, a low $188, compared with the higher levels found in all other metropolitan coun-tries and even in some less urbanized countries, such as Norway. These figures symbolize an inadequate middle class base and consequently an inadequate dispersion of middle class views, which usually provide political and economic stability.

In large measure the failure to expand more evenly in these areas can be traced to inadequate industrial development. About one-third of the working population is still engaged in agri-

culture, which is a much higher proportion than in comparable
metropolitan countries.

The result of this unbalanced situation is burgeoning cities
with neither sufficient industrial support nor class stability.
Cities in this type of society are marked ecologically by the
segregation of those who are economically comfortable from
those who are economically deprived, which in turn contributes
to the presence of slums and similar urban inadequacies. Economic problems plague societies at this stage; there is a generally high and constant proportion of unemployment in the cities,
as well as a marked inequality of incomes. Such societies are
under chronic political stress created by the demands of a large
urban proletariat and the chronically unemployed, seeking to increase their benefits, clashing with the demands of a significant
middle class segment seeking to hold on to what it has.

Urban redevelopment is difficult under such circumstances,
first, because of the large populations that are involved, and
second, because of the chronic financial problems that leave
little room for supposedly unprofitable civic or welfare activities. The only hope for amelioration under such circumstances
would seem to be an industrial growth that is rapid enough
to exceed population growth, especially in the cities. Anything
less means that the imbalance continues for these societies and
they become unwilling heirs to all of the consequent difficulties
of metropolitanism.

Stage IV
b. *Metropolitan Societies*

This type includes the remaining societies of Table 7 that
are in or near the first quartile ranks on all four indices. In other
words, these are the developed, metropolitan societies that have
attained the final stage of industrial, urban development that
we have thus far experienced. A description of this type applies
to such countries as the United States and Great Britain.

I have also included in this type Denmark, Austria, West
Germany, and Israel, even though each of them ranks in the
second quartile on one index other than urban status. Denmark

is less industrialized than the other countries in this category; Austria and Germany have somewhat lower per capita income levels; and Israel has a somewhat lower level of literacy. But since these differences are not considered as crucial for societies at this point, these four countries have been grouped along with Great Britain, the United States, and the Netherlands.

There is little need to describe the urban characteristics of these societies since they have been the subject of all the preceding chapters. All that needs to be said here is that they represent the presently known limit of urbanization. The features of these metropolitan societies probably are less the consequences of an actual imbalance between urban and industrial development and more those of a failure to foresee the effects of continued urban expansion beyond the city to the metropolis. Generally, these countries have the economic means to redevelop and to maintain their metropolitan centers, but they have been late in acting and reluctant in changing traditional conceptions of political administration that no longer apply to the actual situation.

Hence, in both the United States and England a current metropolitan problem is to redefine the traditional limits of urban administration and responsibility in order to reflect the realities of metropolitan existence. The urban boundaries and their administrative units stemming from an earlier era have continued even though urban society no longer corresponds to those definitions. In both countries, steps have been taken, over much opposition, to bring metropolitan administration into being. Such administrative reorganization is not a solution for all metropolitan problems, but it would appear to be a step in the direction of placing those problems in a more relevant perspective for constructive discussion and action. Clearly, relying upon traditional *urban* solutions for what are essentially *metropolitan* problems is like using witchcraft to provide directions for building a space missile. The difficulties in realizing that a metropolitan approach is basically necessary indicate how far we must come, to plan for effective redevelopment. What good is any solution that cannot be put into effect at the metropolitan level? The power constellations that stand in the way of metropolitan reorganization are great, be it the opposition of the

Labour dominated London County Council or the powerful, conservative county and city officials in American metropolitan regions.

Residual Societies

Of the forty-five societies that were used to construct this typology, six have not been included in any category because each represents a special type: Finland, Bulgaria, Japan, New Zealand, the Union of South Africa, and Paraguay. It is not necessary to explain their exclusion in each instance, for Table 7 shows that each country has widely discrepant and idiosyncratic features.

For example, Japan ranked in the first quartile on urban status and on nationalism, but in the second quartile on industrial status and in the third quartile on the middle class index. This is undoubtedly a temporary classification for Japan, reflecting its status in 1950 and not at present. Industrialization was, of course, restricted by the postwar occupation and by the war itself. Japan's restricted middle class similarly was a consequence of the war, as well as of the generally depressed wages that prevailed in Japan around 1950. Indications at present are that wages since have increased significantly, as has Japan's industrial production. It seems likely, therefore, that Japan should be included among the Stage IV metropolitan societies, on the basis of current statistics.

Apartheid makes South Africa a unique case. The strict, repressive, legal segregation in South African cities creates, in reality, a dual urban society that appears nowhere else to a like extent. Comparisons of national statistics with other countries therefore are not really justified. Hence, the native population accounts for the low rank of South Africa on the nationalism index. Admittedly, this is an insensitive measure of nationalism in South Africa, where there are two opposing and bitterly militant nationalisms, the one a legacy of the Boers, the other an emerging nationalism among native Africans. (African nationalism, it should be noted, has made no headway, so that perhaps the index is not so insensitive.) Similarly, the relatively higher rank of South Africa on the middle class index as shown in Table 7, obviously has excluded most of the native population, and reflects only the minority white population. These difficulties stem from the biracial division of South African society that has been made rigid in the cities where Africans are housed within strictly segregated boundaries and kept under tight surveillance and control. Native Africans, for example, can live in the city only with the permission of the authorities, and even then under an enforced provision that requires them to be employed by the same employer for a period of time, in a kind of occupational immobility that harks back to feudalism.

Bulgaria was excluded because it had a unique pattern, ranking lowest on the urban index, but in the second quartile on the remaining three indices. This too, then, is a variant pattern that does not easily fit in with any other type. New Zealand is an urban society on all counts except for industrialism, and has not been included in the general discussion. It might be classed with Denmark, whose characteristics it generally shares on these four indices. Finland is under-urbanized relative to the other three indices. It is a special case that does not fit the typology easily. The same must be said for Paraguay, a country which strikes me as being the least understood of all Latin American countries.

§ Conclusions

This book began with the aim of finding a theory to explain the industrial city and its development. The aim cannot be said to have been completely achieved by this time. What has occupied us, however, was the preparatory task of rephrasing and reorienting our perspectives on urban society in such a way as to increase the probability of constructing a systematic and valid theory of the industrial city. It was to that end that the typological description of this chapter was directed.

The typology, for all of its inadequacies (largely due to lack of information on the dimensions specified) has, I believe, achieved a better comparative description of urbanization than any previous urban theory. It is clearly indebted to the mass of information that generations of scholars and experts on the city have accumulated, and that debt has been acknowledged throughout. The typology, I believe, is a significant advance toward the goal of systematically understanding the city, its elements, dynamics, and complexity.

The typology has shown too that the conception of cities in terms of size alone, or solely as social responses to industrial needs, is a tendency that has misled our best efforts in the past. Of course, both conceptions are somewhat valid, and to that extent they have been incorporated into the typology. However, size and industry are not inevitable concomitants of urbanization. Size, for one thing, must be shown to have sociological consequences, in the manner that was used here. Moreover, industrialization is not always the critical variable involved in development, as was illustrated in several types that moved in directions other than industrial growth. When urbanism and industrialism do occur simultaneously, and they frequently do, it is not enough to simply think of them as synonyms for one another, as is usually done. Each plays a special role in the process of development; each makes its own special contribution to the shape and content of the city.

It might be asked: Where do we go from here? The next step that is called for is detailed analysis of cities themselves, but one that is made within the framework of the typology. For this, there is already at hand a large and important literature, but the information available must be sifted for recognition of the fact that cities do not exist apart from the societies in which they are located. The statement is obvious but has too frequently been disregarded. We must now describe and compare cities drawn from the range of societies at different stages in their development. The aim of that analysis would be to compare institutional structures and the prevalence and content of a whole range of urban attitudes, major political and economic values, and distinctive ecological features. If there is any theoretical potential in the typology, and I am convinced that there is, it should appear in the differences between cities at different points in the development process and in the characteristics just mentioned. There is no doubt that such differences exist, but the need is to determine the framework within which those differences systematically appear.

Much would also be gained by analyzing the history of the metropolitan societies of the West. I have argued for the comparability, in a broader sense, between urban industrial developments in the West and those in currently developing countries. That contention needs yet to be substantiated, and some of the necessary information must be sought in the historical data available for Western countries. The logic behind the typology does not entirely depend upon that comparison, but if it could be validated, it would result in a more symmetrical and grander theory than would exist without it, and would also illuminate an important link between the past and the present, thereby greatly enhancing predictions for the future of developing as well as of metropolitan nations.

Relatively little mention has been made of what form the developed metropolitan societies and the massive cities they contain will take in the future. Since these societies are at the limit of our knowledge, prediction is more hazardous than for those societies that are further back in the sequence of industrial urban development. Every urban theory or near-theory thus far has stumbled on its prediction for future developments in metropolitan societies. This failure is a function of our ignorance and inadequacy to understand the process of urban change and especially the social dynamics that initiate and direct such change. Valid prediction, however, is not as difficult as it might seem at first glance. For example, the information needed to predict suburbanization was all there at least thirty years ago. What was missing was a valid framework within which to order that information. With such a framework, we would have been able to foresee, if not to avoid, many of the problems that have arisen directly from the geographic spread of the city: transportation, metropolitan government and planning, and urban service needs. Perhaps this is only hindsight, but I think not. The rise in the marriage rate, the decline in urban renewal, and the growing concern with social status were features of American society by the end of the war. Given an adequate theoretical orientation—one that recognized the existence and importance, for example, of class—suburbanization would have been at least one reasonable prediction that could have been made.

We are in a similar situation today. The elements of tomorrow's changes in metropolitan society are now forming but remain as yet unrecognized. Instead we choose to devote our resources on an ad hoc basis to trying to remedy mistakes of the past, as they cause present emergencies. The lag with which cities are providing temporary patchwork solutions to problems after the problems have become incontestable seems to be one constant and universal feature in urban history. For example, some are greatly exercised over the need for metropolitan government to replace outmoded city governments. The need is real. However, most solutions that have been suggested fail to recognize the obvious facts about the way political power is held and distributed within the metropolitan region. One might as soon hope for those who hold power under admittedly outmoded administrative units to give it up for the common good, as for a mad rush to begin tomorrow to the kind of city visualized for us by Frank Lloyd Wright. Both are idealistic and utopian views of the city's future and necessarily doomed to failure.

The quest for an urban theory is not an idle one. Nor are the steps suggested for subsequent urban research. Only from the systematic knowledge that such information can bring are we likely to discover the dynamics of the urban process. Only in that way is there any chance that we may learn enough to control our urban future, a future to which most of the world will very shortly be committed.

NOTES

§ Chapter I

1. Gordon Childe, *What Happened in History* (Baltimore: Penguin Books, 1942), 90-94.
2. William B. Munro, "City," *Encyclopedia of the Social Sciences* (New York: The Macmillan Co., 1930), 474.
3. *Ibid.*, 479.
4. Fustel de Coulanges, *The Ancient City* (New York: Doubleday & Company, 1956), 340.
5. Carl Bridenbaugh, *Cities in the Wilderness* (New York: Alfred A. Knopf, 1955), Ch. III.
6. *Ibid.*, 56.
7. *Ibid.*, 69-70.
8. *Ibid.*, 93.
9. Lewis Mumford, *The Culture of Cities* (New York: Harcourt, Brace & World, 1938), 77.
10. The two sources I have used for the description of the industrial city are Mumford, *ibid.*, especially 145 ff., and Gideon Sjoberg, "The Pre-industrial City," *American Journal of Sociology*, LX:438-45, March, 1955. The latter is in book form (New York: The Free Press of Glencoe, 1961).

§ Chapter II

1. C. McKim Norton, "Metropolitan Transportation," in *An Approach to Urban Planning*, G. Breeze and D. E. Whiteman, eds. (Princeton: Princeton University Press, 1953).
2. *Ibid.*, 87.
3. London: HMSO, October, 1960.
4. The following points have been taken from an excellent analysis by Victor Jones, "Local Government Organization in Metropolitan Areas: Its Relation to Urban Redevelopment," in *The Future of Cities and Urban Redevelopment*, Coleman Woodbury, ed. (Chicago: University of Chicago Press, 1953).
5. *Ibid.*, 587. A concrete example of the truth of Jones's dictum can be read in John C. Bollens, ed., *Exploring the Metropolitan Community* (Berkeley & Los Angeles: University of California Press, 1961). Here the failure of social scientists and the public to effect real changes in the St. Louis area is documented. Bollens and his colleagues learned that sincere and unselfish motives are not enough to make changes in the halls of power.

§ Chapter III

1. Lewis Mumford, *op. cit.*, 479.
2. Karl Mannheim, *Ideology and Utopia* (New York: Harcourt, Brace & World, 1946), 185.
3. Ebenezer Howard, *Garden Cities of Tomorrow* (London: Faber & Faber, 1946), 114.
4. F. J. Osborn in the preface to Howard, *op. cit.*, 9.
5. F. J. Osborn, quoted in Lloyd Rodwin, *The British New Towns Policy* (Cambridge: Harvard University Press, 1956), 11.
6. Howard, *op. cit.*, 42.
7. *Ibid.*, 44.
8. *Ibid.*, 146.
9. Quoted in Rodwin, *op. cit.*, 12.
10. The details of the history of Letchworth and Welwyn have been taken from Rodwin, *op. cit.*, 12-15.
11. *Ibid.*, 27-36.
12. *Ibid.*, 15.
13. *Ibid.*, 39.
14. Harold Orlans, *Utopia Ltd.* (New Haven: Yale University Press, 1953).
15. Quoted in Orlans, *op. cit.*, 67.
16. *Ibid.*, 82.
17. *Ibid.*, 87.
18. Note the remark made by Boumphrey, quoted in Orlans, *op. cit.*, 94. "The whole essence of Howard's idea was that by rehousing the working-class man in a garden city, he would be transported into a clean atmosphere and healthy surroundings . . . and instead of wasting his spare time in the gin palace, to the detriment of his health, pocket, and home life, he could spend it in the healthy and fascinating pursuit of gardening."
19. *Ibid.*, 95.
20. Quoted in Orlans, *op. cit.*, 96-7.
21. *Ibid.*, 99-100.
22. Quoted in Orlans, *op. cit.*, 100 f.n.
23. *Ibid.*, 282.
24. The analysis of Frank Lloyd Wright's plan is taken from his *When Democracy Builds* (Chicago: University of Chicago Press, 1945) and *The Living City* (New York: Horizon Press, 1958). The latter is a later edition of the first book. Wright quotes are reprinted by permission of the publisher, Horizon Press, Inc., from *The Living City* by Frank Lloyd Wright. Copyright 1938.
25. Wright, *Living City, op. cit.*, 20.
26. *Ibid.*, 25.
27. *Ibid.*, 46.
28. *Ibid.*, 33.
29. *Ibid.*, 33.
30. *Ibid.*, 34.
31. *Ibid.*, 193.
32. *Ibid.*, 193.

33. *Ibid.*, 221-2.
34. Lewis Mumford, *op. cit.* Mumford's recent book, *The City in History* (New York: Harcourt, Brace & World, 1961) appeared after this section was written. The last, however, is substantially the same as the earlier book, as far as this discussion is concerned. If anything, *The City in History* has become more mystical on the relevant points about the future of cities than was *The Culture of Cities.*
35. Arthur B. Gallion, *The Urban Pattern* (New York: D. Van Nostrand Co., 1950).
36. Percival and Paul Goodman, *Communitas: Means of Livelihood & Ways of Life* (Chicago: University of Chicago Press, 1947).
37. Mumford, *op. cit.*, 419.
38. *Ibid.*, 423.
39. *Ibid.*, 435-38.
40. *Ibid.*, 464.
41. *Ibid.*, 482.

§ Chapter IV

1. Otis D. Duncan and Albert J. Reiss, Jr., *Social Characteristics of Urban and Rural Communities, 1950* (New York: John Wiley and Sons, 1956), especially pp. 2-5 and Ch. 2.
2. P. Sargant Florence, "Economic Efficiency in the Metropolis," in *The Metropolis in Modern Life,* Robert M. Fisher, ed. (New York: Doubleday & Co., 1955), 116.
3. Chauncy D. Harris, "A Functional Classification of Cities in the United States," in *The Sociology of Urban Life,* T. Lynn Smith and C. A. McMahan, eds. (New York: The Dryden Press, 1951), 84-97.
4. Grace M. Kneedler, "Functional Types of Cities," *Public Management,* 27: 197-203, July, 1945.
5. Leonard Reissman, *Class in American Society* (New York: The Free Press of Glencoe, 1959), Ch. III.
6. Paul Bates Gillen, *The Distribution of Occupations As A City Yardstick* (New York: Kings Crown Press, 1951).
7. *Ibid.*, 2.
8. Robert C. Angell, "The Moral Integration of American Cities," *American Journal of Sociology,* 57: Part 2, July, 1951, p. 1.
9. *Ibid.*, 121.
10. Edward L. Thorndike, *Your City* (New York: Harcourt, Brace & World, 1939) and *144 Smaller Cities* (New York: Harcourt, Brace & World, 1940).
11. Angell, *op. cit.*, 3.
12. Quoted in Angell, *ibid.*, 3.
13. The formula reported on p. 124 of Angell was as follows:

$$\text{Welfare Effort Index} = \frac{\text{Amount Raised}}{\text{Quota}} + \frac{\text{Pledgers}}{\text{No. of families in the area}} + \frac{\text{Amount Raised}}{.0033 \text{ x yearly retail sales.}}$$

14. Wendell Bell, "Social Areas: Typology of Urban Neighborhoods," in *Community Structure and Analysis*, Marvin B. Sussman, ed. (New York: Thomas Y. Crowell, 1959), 61-92. This reference contains a bibliography of other studies that have been published. The three basic reports of the technique and its application are Eshref Shevsky and Bell, *Social Area Analysis* (Stanford: Stanford University Press, 1955); Shevsky and Marilyn Williams, *The Social Areas of Los Angeles and Typology* (Berkeley: University of California Press, 1949); Robert C. Tryon, *Identification of Social Areas By Cluster Analysis* (Berkeley: University of California Press, 1955).

15. *Op. cit.*, 89.

16. A recent book by James M. Beshars, *Urban Social Structure* (New York: The Free Press of Glencoe, 1962), does try to incorporate social area analysis into a theory, but without complete success. Beshars achieves his results primarily by simplifying "urban social structure" to a point where his type of analysis might seem to handle it.

17. Otis D. Duncan, review of Shevsky and Bell, *Social Area Analysis*, in *American Journal of Sociology*, 61: 84-85, July, 1955. See the exchange between Duncan and Bell in a later issue of the same *Journal*, November, 1955, pp. 260-2.

18. *Ibid.*, 262.

§ Chapter V

1. Robert E. Park, *Human Communities* (New York: The Free Press of Glencoe, 1952), 14.

2. R. D. McKenzie, "Human Ecology," *Encyclopedia of the Social Sciences* (New York: The Macmillan Co., 1931).

3. Robert E. Park, "The City: Suggestions For the Investigation of Human Behavior In the Urban Environment," *American Journal of Sociology*, 20:577-612, March, 1916. Reprinted in *Communities, op. cit.*, p. 5.

4. Quoted by Everett C. Hughes in his Preface to Park, *Communities, op. cit.*, 5.

5. Ernest Manheim, "Theoretical Prospects of Urban Sociology in an Urbanized Society," *American Journal of Sociology*, 6:226-30, Nov., 1960, 227.

6. Amos H. Hawley, *Human Ecology* (New York: The Ronald Press Company, 1950), 39-40.

7. Clements and Shelford, quoted in Hawley, *op. cit.*, 45.

8. *Ibid.*, 36.

9. *Ibid.*, 37-38.

10. Park, "Human Ecology," in *Communities, op. cit.*, 158.

11. *Ibid.*, 182.

12. *Ibid.*, 158.

13. *Ibid.*, 196.

14. "Symbiosis and Socialization," *Ibid.*, 244.

15. Ernest W. Burgess, "Residential Segregation," quoted in Milla Alihan, *Social Ecology* (New York: Columbia University Press, 1938), 218.

16. Alihan, *op. cit.*, pp. 224-5.

17. Calvin F. Schmid, *Social Saga of Two Cities* (Minneapolis: Minneapolis Council of Social Agencies, 1937); and *Social Trends in Seattle* (Seattle: University of Washington Press, 1944).
18. E. S. Longmoor and E. F. Young, "Ecological Interrelationships of Juvenile Delinquency, Dependency, and Population Mobility," *American Journal of Sociology*, quoted in Alihan, *op. cit.*, 213.
19. Maurice R. Davie, "The Pattern of Urban Growth," in P. K. Hatt and A. J. Reiss, Jr., eds., *Reader in Urban Sociology*, (New York: The Free Press of Glencoe, 1951).
20. H. W. Green, "Cultural Areas in the City of Cleveland," *American Journal of Sociology*, 38:356-67, 1932.
21. H. Bartholomew, *Urban Land Uses* (Cambridge: Harvard University Press, 1932).
22. Davie, *op. cit.*, 259.
23. Homer Hoyt, *The Structure and Growth of Residential Neighborhoods in American Cities* (Washington: Government Printing Office, 1939).
24. Chauncy S. Harris and Edward L. Ullman, "The Nature of Cities," in Hatt & Reiss, *op. cit.*
25. Alihan, *op. cit.*
26. Walter Firey, *Land Use in Central Boston* (Cambridge: Harvard University Press, 1946).
27. Richard Dewey, "The Neighborhood, Urban Ecology, and City Planners," *American Sociological Review*, 15:502-7, August, 1950, 503.
28. Calvin F. Schmid, "Generalizations Concerning the Ecology of the American City," *American Sociological Review*, 15:264-81, April, 1950, 266.
29. Bernard Farber and J. C. Osoinach, "An Index of Socio-Economic Rank of Census Tracts in Urban Areas," *American Sociological Review*, 24:630-40, Oct., 1959, 640. See also, E. Shevsky and W. Bell, *op. cit.*
30. In the *Annals of the American Academy of Political and Social Science*, 202:264-65, March, 1939.
31. Louis Wirth, "Human Ecology," in *Community Life and Social Policy* (Chicago: University of Chicago Press, 1956), 135.
32. Louis Wirth, "Urbanism as a Way of Life," reprinted in P. K. Hatt and A. J. Reiss, Jr., eds., *Cities and Society* (New York: The Free Press of Glencoe, 1957).
33. *Ibid.*, 48.
34. Wirth, "Ecology," *op. cit.*, 142.
35. Hawley, *Human Ecology*, *op. cit.*
36. *Ibid.*, 69.
37. *Ibid.*, 402-403.
38. Otis Dudley Duncan, "Human Ecology and Population Studies," in *The Study of Population*, P. M. Hauser and O. D. Duncan, eds., (Chicago: The University of Chicago Press, 1959); O. D. Duncan and Leo F. Schnore, "Cultural, Behavioral, and Ecological Perspectives in the Study of Social Organization," *American Journal of Sociology*, 65:132-53, September, 1959; O. D. Duncan, *et. al.*, *Metropolis and Region* (Baltimore: The Johns Hopkins Press, 1960); Leo F. Schnore, "Social Morphology and Human Ecology," *American Journal of Sociology*, 63:620-34, May, 1958.
39. Duncan, "Human Ecology *op. cit.*, 682.

40. I must also agree with Rossi's rejoinder to the Duncan and Schnore article, *American Journal of Sociology*, 65:146-9, September, 1959. Rossi correctly chastizes them for a "distressing tendency toward intellectual 'imperialism.' The ecological perspective is so loosely defined that it can be stretched to include what is regarded as praiseworthy . . . and contracted to avoid the apparently faulty." 148.
41. *Ibid.*, 683.
42. Duncan and Schnore, *op. cit.*, 136.
43. *Ibid.*, 138.
44. *Ibid.*, 142.

§ Chapter VI

1. Albert J. Reiss, Jr., "An Analysis of Urban Phenomena," in *The Metropolis in Modern Life*, Robert M. Fisher, ed. (New York: Doubleday & Company, 1955).
2. Charles T. Stewart, Jr., "The Urban-Rural Dichotomy: Concepts and Uses," *American Journal of Sociology*, 64:152-58, Sept., 1958.
3. Richard Dewey, "The Rural-Urban Continuum: Real But Relatively Unimportant," *American Journal of Sociology*, 66:60-66, July, 1960. There is a discrepancy between the text and Table I, and the latter was used to count the times a characteristic was used by writers.
4. Harald Swedner, *Ecological Differentiation of Habits and Attitudes* (Lund, Sweden: CWK Gleerup, 1960). Contains a detailed bibliography.
5. Robert Redfield, *The Folk Culture of Yucatan* (Chicago: University of Chicago Press, 1941).
6. Kingsley Davis and Ana Casis, "Urbanism in Latin America," *Milbank Memorial Fund Quarterly*, 24:186-207, April, 1946.
7. Redfield, *op. cit.*, 43.
8. *Op. cit.*, 338-39.
9. Robert Redfield, *Peasant Society and Culture* (Chicago: The University of Chicago Press, 1956), Phoenix Books edition, 8.
10. Robert Redfield, *Tepoztlán—A Mexican Village* (Chicago: University of Chicago Press, 1930).
11. Oscar Lewis, *Life In a Mexican Village: Tepoztlán Restudied* (Urbana: University of Illinois Press, 1951), xi.
12. *Op. cit.*, 428-29.
13. *Op. cit.*, 432.
14. *Op. cit.*, 432-40.
15. *Op. cit.*, 434.
16. *Op. cit.*, 440.
17. Horace Miner, "The Folk-Urban Continuum," *American Sociological Review*, 17:529-37, October, 1952.
18. *Ibid.*, 537.
19. Louis Wirth, "Urbanism As a Way of Life," *American Journal of Sociology*, 44:1-24, July, 1938. All page references here are taken from the posthumous collection of Wirth's papers, *Community Life and Social Policy* (Chicago: University of Chicago Press, 1956), 110-132.
20. *Op. cit.*, 116.
21. *Op. cit.*, 118-25.

22. *Op. cit.,* 120.
23. *Op. cit.,* 125.
24. Georg Simmel, "The Metropolis and Mental Life," reprinted in *Reader in Urban Sociology,* Paul K. Hatt & A. J. Reiss, Jr., eds. (New York: The Free Press of Glencoe, 1951), pp. 563-74.
25. Kingsley Davis, *Human Society* (New York: The Macmillan Co., 1948), 329-36.
26. Max Weber, *The City,* translated and edited by Don Martindale and Gertrude Neuwirth (New York: The Free Press of Glencoe, 1958).
27. *Op. cit.,* 80-81.
28. S. N. Eisenstadt, "Social Problems of Urban Organization and Planning In Underdeveloped Countries," in *Atti del congresso internazionale di studio sul problema delle aree arretrate* (Milan: D. A. Giuffree, 1955), II, 887-900.
29. Linton C. Freeman and Robert F. Winch, "Societal Complexity: An Empirical Test of a Typology of Societies," *American Journal of Sociology,* 62:461-66, March, 1957.
30. *Op. cit.,* 466.

§ Chapter VII

1. The point that each city is unique is raised by Émile Sicard, "Breve Ensayo Acerca del Lugar de la Sociológia Urbana en la Sociológia," in Instituto de Investigaciones Sociales de la Universidad Nacional Autónoma de Mexico, *Estudios Sociologicos (Sociológia Urbana)* (Mexico: Universidad de Nuevo León, 1956), 129-150. For a statement of the opposite view, that all cities have a set of common characteristics regardless of where they are located in history or in culture, see John Friedmann, "Cities in Social Transformation," *Comparative Studies in Society and History,* 4:86-103, November, 1961.
2. Lyle W. Shannon, *Underdeveloped Areas* (New York: Harper and Row, 1957), 1-12.
3. Quoted in Shannon, *ibid.,* 3.
4. United Nations, *Processes and Problems of Industrialization in Underdeveloped Countries* (New York: 1955), 18 ff. Some of the points mentioned in the discussion have been taken from this source.
5. I would mention specifically here the surveys of Jacques Denis, *Le phénomène urbain en Afrique centrale* (Brussels: 1958); UNESCO, *Social Implications of Industrialization and Urbanization in Africa South of the Sahara,* (Switzerland: 1956); UNESCO, *Urbanization in Asia and the Far East,* (Calcutta: Research Centre on the Social Implications of Industrialization in Southern Asia, 1957); UNESCO, *The Social Implications of Industrialization and Urbanization: Five Studies in Asia* (Calcutta: UNESCO Research Centre, 1956); UNESCO, *Urbanization in Latin America* (Belgium: 1961).
6. Albert Meister, "Introduction," *International Review of Community Development,* No. 7, 1961, p. 10. This issue is devoted to "Urbanization and Community Development."
7. For an analysis of these reasons see these excellent summaries: United Nations, *Report on the World Social Situation* (New York: 1957),

112-3; International Institute of Differing Civilizations, 27th Session (Florence: 1952), "The 'pull' exerted by urban and industrial centres in countries in the course of industrialization"; and Denis, *op. cit.*, Section II.

8. In *World Social Situation, op. cit.*, 124.

9. *Ibid.*, 125, Table 10.

10. J. H. Adler, *The Underdeveloped Areas and Their Industrialization* (New Haven: Yale University Press, 1949).

11. These figures are taken from W. S. and E. S. Woytinsky, *World Population and Production* (New York: The Twentieth Century Fund, 1953), 34, 46.

12. The 1900 figure is quoted in Woytinsky, *op. cit.*, 122. The 1955 estimate is quoted in International Urban Research, *The World's Metropolitan Areas* (Berkeley: University of California Press, 1959), 48. Figures for other comparisons are taken from these two sources respectively.

13. Woytinsky, *op. cit.*, 166.

14. Adna F. Weber, *The Growth of Cities in the Nineteenth Century* (New York: The Macmillan Company, 1899), 344-45.

15. United Nations, *Processes and Problems, op. cit.*, 119.

16. Herbert Frankel, *The Economic Impact on Under-developed Societies* (Oxford: Oxford University Press, 1953), 69. Quoted in United Nations, *Processes and Problems, op. cit.*, 23n.

17. From an extensive literature I would draw special attention to Bert F. Hoselitz, *Sociological Aspects of Economic Growth* (New York: The Free Press of Glencoe, 1960) for its relevance for sociologists.

18. A good, representative set of papers on technical change and its consequences can be found in *Changements techniques, economiques et sociaux* (Paris: Bureau International de Recherche sur les Implications Sociales du Progres Technique, UNESCO, 1958).

19. A suggestive anthology on this subject is Wilbert E. Moore and Arnold S. Feldman, eds., *Labor Commitment and Social Change* (New York: Social Science Research Council, 1960).

20. United Nations, *Report on the World Social Situation* (New York: 1961), Ch. III.

21. Simon Kuznets, "Quantitative Aspects of the Economic Growth of Nations," *Economic Development and Cultural Change*, 5, October, 1956. In *World Social Situation*, 1961, *op. cit.*

22. Raymond Firth, F. J. Fisher, and D. G. Macrae, "Social Implications of Technological Change as Regards Patterns and Models," in *Changements techniques, op. cit.*, 292.

23. This point is discussed with understanding by H. Th. Chabot, *et. al.*, "Social Change as Influenced by Technological Change," in *Changements techniques op. cit.*; also by Henri Lefebvre, "Les conditions sociales de l'industrialisation," in G. Gurvitch, ed., *Industrialisation et Technocratie* (Paris: Librairie A. Colin, 1949).

24. Yale Brozen, "Entrepreneurship and Technological Change," in *Economic Development*, Harold F. Williamson and J. A. Buttrick, eds. (New York: Prentice-Hall, 1954).

25. United Nations, *Processes and Problems, op. cit.*, Ch. 2.

26. See in this connection the papers by Spengler, Moore, Hoselitz, and

Herskovits in *Traditions, Values, and Socio-Economic Development*, R. Braibanti and J. J. Spengler, eds. (Durham: Duke University Press, 1961).

27. Philip Mayer, ed., *Townsmen and Tribesman* (London: Oxford University Press, 1961).

28. Clark Kerr, *et. al.*, *Industrialism and Industrial Man* (Cambridge: Harvard University Press, 1960), has a most insightful analysis of this and related matters concerning elites and elite control.

29. *Ibid.*, 52.

30. Thomas Hodgkin, *African Political Parties* (London: Penguin Books, 1961), p. 31. Hodgkin quotes the figures from two studies, one by J. H. Price and the other by J. L. Seurin, on the composition of the House of Assembly in Ghana and that of the Legislative Assembly in eight territories of former French West Africa, respectively. In the first, among 104 members there were the following: School teachers 30; Clerks, etc. 18; Liberal Professions 18; Entrepreneurs 18; Politicians 7; Farmers 4; Chiefs 3. In French West Africa the percentages ranged as follows: Teachers 22-33; Government officials 27; Doctors, etc. 15; Lawyers 5; Entrepreneurs and employees in industry 14-21; Farmers 3-11; Chiefs 7-25; Trade unionists 1.

31. *Development of a Middle Class in Tropical and Sub-tropical Countries*, International Institute of Differing Civilizations, 29th Session (Brussels: 1956). The quotations are taken from pp. 447-67.

32. *Cf.* Robert Van Niel, *The Emergence of the Modern Indonesian Elite*, 1956, and W. F. Wertheim, *Indonesian Society in Transition*, 1960 (The Hague: W. Van Howeve, Ltd.).

33. Hugh H. and Mabel M. Smythe, *The New Nigerian Elite* (Stanford: Stanford University Press, 1960).

34. Angel Palerm, "Observations on the Development of a Middle Class in Latin America," in *Development of a Middle Class op. cit.*, 67-87.

35. Rupert Emerson, *From Empire to Nation* (Cambridge: Harvard University Press, 1960), 197-99. The author concludes that "the revolution against imperialism has been carried on primarily under the leadership of Asians and Africans in whose formation the West itself had a very large share."

36. K. H. Silvert, ed., *Expectant Peoples: Nationalism and Development* (New York: Random House, 1964), 27 ff.

37. Emerson, *op. cit.*, 58.

38. Thomas Hodgkin, *Nationalism in Colonial Africa* (New York: New York University Press, 1960), 55 ff.

39. Emerson, *op. cit.*, 95.

40. Royal Institute of International Affairs, *Nationalism* (London: Oxford University Press, 1939), 254-59.

41. Silvert, *op. cit.*, 19.

42. Emerson, *op. cit.*, 153.

43. J. L. and Barbara Hammond, *The Town Labourer, 1760-1832* (London: Longmans, Green, & Co., 1949), Guild Books, 2 vols. "The normal Englishman was thought to be the Englishman with property, and a system that provided for him was equitable and just." Vol. I, p. 70. Again: "It is not too much to say, in the light of the Home Office Papers, that none of the personal rights attaching to Englishmen pos-

sessed any reality for the working classes." Vol. I, p. 80. See also Edward H. Carr, *Nationalism and After* (London: The Macmillan Company, 1945), 10 ff.

44. Emerson, *op. cit.*, 215.
45. Silvert, *op. cit.*, 26.

§ Chapter VIII

1. Leonard Reissman, *Class In American Society* (New York: The Free Press of Glencoe, 1959), Ch. III.
2. Bert F. Hoselitz, *Sociological Aspects of Economic Growth* (New York: The Free Press of Glencoe, 1960), Ch. 8.
3. Daniel Lerner, *The Passing of Traditional Society* (New York: The Free Press of Glencoe, 1958), especially Ch. V.
4. *Ibid.*, 157.
5. Lucian W. Pye, "The Politics of Southeast Asia," in G. A. Almond and J. S. Coleman, eds., *The Politics of the Developing Areas* (Princeton: Princeton University Press, 1960), 100.
6. *Ibid.*, 100.
7. The occupational distributions for Mexico and Brazil are taken from the United Nations, *Demographic Yearbook* (New York: 1956), Table 13. Figures are for 1950.
8. United Nations, *Statistical Papers*, E-4 (1956), Table 2.
9. *Census of England and Wales, 1851*, lxxxii-iv.
10. United Nations, *Demographic Yearbook* (New York, 1956), Table 13.
11. *Ibid.* Table 13.

INDEX

252

Index